INDISPENSABLE
ENEMIES

INDISPENSABLE ENEMIES

The Politics of Misrule in America

Walter Karp

NEW YORK

Copyright © 1993 Franklin Square Press

Published by Franklin Square Press, a division of Harper's Magazine, 666 Broadway, New York, N.Y. 10012.

First edition in paperback.

First printing in paperback 1993.

Library of Congress Cataloging-in-Publication Data
Karp, Walter.
Indispensable enemies : the politics of misrule in America / Walter Karp.
p. cm.
Includes index.
ISBN 1-879957-13-2 : $14.95
1. United States—Politics and government—20th century.
2. Political parties—United States. 3. Power (Social sciences)
I. Title.
JK271.K28   1993
324.273'09'04—dc20
93-31253
CIP

Indispensable Enemies: The Politics of Misrule in America by Walter Karp, edited by Ellen Rosenbush.

Designed by Deborah Thomas.

Manufactured in the United States of America.

This book has been produced on acid-free paper.

TABLE OF CONTENTS

PART I

THE ANATOMY OF THE PARTY SYSTEM

PART II

THE PARTIES v. REFORM

INDISPENSABLE ENEMIES

The Politics of Misrule in America

Walter Karp

NEW YORK

Published by Franklin Square Press, a division of Harper's Magazine,
666 Broadway, New York, N.Y. 10012.

First edition in paperback.

First printing in paperback 1993.

Library of Congress Cataloging-in-Publication Data
Karp, Walter.
Indispensable enemies : the politics of misrule in America / Walter Karp.
p. cm.
Includes index.
ISBN 1-879957-13-2 : $14.95
1. United States—Politics and government—20th century.
2. Political parties—United States. 3. Power (Social sciences)
I. Title.
JK271.K28   1993
324.273'09'04—dc20
93-31253
CIP

Indispensable Enemies: The Politics of Misrule in America by Walter Karp,
edited by Ellen Rosenbush.

Designed by Deborah Thomas.

Manufactured in the United States of America.

This book has been produced on acid-free paper.

TABLE OF CONTENTS

PART III

THE FRUITS OF OLIGARCHY

WALTER KARP
1934-1989

Walter Karp was the author of eight books, including *The Politics of War* (1973) and *Liberty Under Siege* (1988). He published more than two hundred articles and essays in *Harper's Magazine, Pageant, Horizon, American Heritage*, and many other magazines. In 1969, in collaboration with H. R. Shapiro, he wrote and published a journal about American politics called *The Public Life*. He was active on the Freedom to Write Committee of the PEN American Center, and wrote the foreword to a 1988 book sponsored by PEN, *Liberty Denied: the Current Rise of Censorship in America*. A collection of his essays on American politics, *Buried Alive: Essays on Our Endangered Republic*, was published in 1992 by Franklin Square Press. In 1993, *Liberty Under Siege*, his analysis of American party politics, was issued in paperback for the first time, also by Franklin Square Press. Born and reared in Brooklyn, New York, Karp graduated from Columbia College, where he was class valedictorian and was elected to Phi Beta Kappa. He died at the age of 55, after complications arising from surgery, leaving his wife, Regina, and two children, Roy and Jane.

Introduction

In all that concerns public matters we no longer understand why things happen as they do. There seems to be no rhyme or reason in our political affairs. A President promises not to send American troops to salvage a foreign regime; he then starts a major war to salvage that regime. Congress resolves to cut wasteful expenditures and spends fifty billion dollars putting men on the moon. A political party based on the cities controls national legislation for forty years, yet the nation's cities grow squalid with neglect. The country grows richer and public services decay. The nation undergoes a spasm of sharp discontent and nearly every incumbent Congressman wins reelection. Promised peace we get war, promised frugality we get waste, discontented we get the status quo and nobody understands quite why. The savage who consults his juju to explain a sudden cloudburst lives in no greater ignorance of nature than we live today in regard to our own politics.

There are political explanations, of course, but they are so shallow and contradictory, so indifferent to facts and to plain common sense, that they serve not to answer questions but to appease the questioner, like crumbs distributed to the hungry to get them from the door. We are constantly told, for example, that the neglect of the cities is due to "rural domination" of state legislatures and Congress. This is what passes for a political explanation—take it seriously for one minute and it falls to the ground. Every decade millions of farmers are forced to abandon farming, so apparently the rural population is powerful enough to harm city dwellers but not powerful enough to save its own farms. On the other hand, when Amtrak, the national railway corporation created in 1971, drastically curtailed rural passenger service,

Senate Majority Leader Mike Mansfield of Montana blamed the policy on the power of the cities. So apparently city dwellers are powerful
enough to hurt rural people but not powerful enough to get their own
streets cleaned. When a President fails to get his reforms passed in the
legislature, we are told of the great power of Congress and the "limits"
of Presidential power. When a President launches a war in utter disre-
gard of a submissive Congress, we are told of the inherent weakness of
the legislature in the face of the mighty office of the President. When
Congress votes down some measure for the general welfare, we are
told that powerful middle-class taxpayers dislike paying high taxes, yet
the power of the middle class never prevents Congress from spending
billions on moon flights. Poverty in America is often attributed to the
political impotence of the lower economic classes, yet racist politics in
the South and the cities is invariably attributed to the racism of the
poorer whites, who, like farmers and city dwellers, are just powerful
enough to harm others but not powerful enough to help themselves.
When a Democratic President fails to get his programs through a
Democratic Congress, the failure is often attributed to the power of
the South's legislative representatives, yet the South is the most misruled and benighted section of the country; so apparently Southerners, too, have enormous power to frustrate the will of others and
no power to improve their own lot. The alleged "money power" of
special interests also waxes and wanes in this inexplicable fashion.
When a corporate interest is detrimental to the common interest,
politicians appear in thrall to its power; when its interest happens to
coincide with the common interest—as in the case of Du Pont's failed
opposition to oil import quotas, which hurt it in overseas competition
with foreign petrochemical firms—it mysteriously loses its power.

All such current pseudo-explanations conform to a common pattern. A particular political act or policy is attributed to the presumed
power of a particular social group, class, bloc or branch of government—the rich, the poor, the middle class, the stingy taxpayer, the
corporate special interest, the city dweller, the countryman, the South,
Congress, the Presidency or what have you. By constantly shifting
from one of these alleged powers to another, political deeds are pre-

sumably explained. In fact, nothing whatever is explained. We are being given a runaround, like a man trying to get a straight answer from a bureaucracy. When Congress is profligate of the public wealth, we are referred to the power of the Pentagon; when Congress is niggardly, we are referred to the power of the middle-class taxpayer. When cities are neglected, we are referred to the countryside; when the countryside is neglected, we are referred to the cities. When tax loopholes are given to millionaires, we are referred to the power of the rich; when racist politics flourish, we are referred to the power of poor whites. It is certainly a curious picture of political power in America, one in which every group in the country has the power to harm others yet few have any power to help themselves, in which even those who can help themselves cannot get what they want when others would benefit simultaneously. This is not a picture of political reality. It is a picture of total confusion, a confusion which political commentators often describe as "pluralism" in America, as if the sum total of false explanations comprised one substantial truth. It is often described, too, as the "complexity" of American politics, as if putting a label to darkness shed light by which men could see.

The reason we no longer understand why things happen as they do has one and only one source. We no longer understand who really has power in America, how men have gained it and what they have done to keep it. The book which follows is an attempt to show as clearly as possible where power lies in twentieth-century America. It is not based on a "theory" of American politics or on any general theory of politics. It does not rest on question-begging assumptions about the "dominant economic interest" or any other axioms about "deeper" forces and processes presumed to underlie politics itself. What I have tried to do is carry out a political analysis of politics, an analysis, that is, which begins with the actual deeds of men and which takes as its primary data what men actually do in the public and political arena. It is an analysis based on a truth, indeed a truism, which is easily forgotten or ignored: that no institution exists in the public world and nothing happens in the public world apart from the deeds of men. A business enterprise, to take a simple example, is not an entity with a life and reality of its own. It exists by virtue of the fact that those who take part in the enterprise decide every morning to get up and go to work. If they all suddenly refused to do so, the business would cease to exist save as a legal entity in a bankruptcy proceeding and would cease to exist even as that if men ceased to obey the law. The fact that men sustain a social institution—or an entire system of government—by the constant iteration of certain actions does not transform that institution into a thing or substance apart from those repeated actions.

All this is obvious enough, yet in political matters today it is the obvious that most needs belaboring. Those who speak and write of public matters rarely recognize that political reality, first and foremost, is what men actually do. Commentators speak of institutions "growing" as if institutions were acorns, of "history" as if it were a person, of "social change" as if it were an independent substance. According to this sort of thinking, it is not enough to note, for example, that William McKinley, by his actions, launched America on overseas imperial adventures and to inquire why he did so. It is necessary to speak of America's "emergence as a world power" after 1896, as if that "emergence" were distinct from the political actions of McKinley and others and actually explained their actions. Again and again abstractions are accorded a reality which is denied to political deeds. To say, therefore, that political analysis begins with what men actually do is at once to state the obvious and to scuttle a great deal of ideological baggage now obscuring political reality.

There is no need, I think, to say more in these introductory remarks. How well the following political analysis of American politics illuminates our public life and explains why things happen as they do, the reader can judge for himself.

THE ANATOMY OF
THE PARTY SYSTEM

1.
The Foundations of
Party Power

Every election year some local party organization or other will try to defeat its own candidate. In 1970, for example, Vermont Democratic leaders campaigned openly for a Republican Senator against his Democratic rival, the former governor of the state. In 1969, the Jersey City Democrats openly repudiated the Democratic candidate for governor and delivered a large vote to his victorious rival. Often a party will ensure defeat by putting up for office men blatantly lacking in appeal, as the New York Republican party did in 1953 when it nominated a hotel manager for mayor of New York City, or as the New Mexico Republican party did in 1970 when it put up a slate of conservatives at a time when Republican reformers had won the party's only victories in living memory.

That such things happen is a matter of public record, but they are glossed over as minor aberrations, merely local exceptions to the fundamental rule of party politics, that the overriding motive of a political party, its very reason for being, is to win election victories. This is the central axiom of party politics, its Newtonian law of political motion. It has become the touchstone, implicit or explicit, of our political understanding, the spectacles, as it were, through which we see political reality. By the light of that axiom, the motives and interests of the parties give rise to no questions; their motives and their interests are self-explanatory: "to pick a winner," "to construct a victorious majority," "to find a man whom the majority of the voters will agree to support"—I quote randomly from established authorities. By the light of the parties' desire for victory, all the actions of parties, party caucuses, party leaders and party politicians are interpreted. When a party makes a certain public issue the theme of its election campaign, it is taken for granted that they expect it will bring victory; when a political issue, hotly debated all year, drops out of an election campaign, it is taken for granted that the voters have lost interest in it; should it appear that the voters have not lost interest, it is taken for granted that the parties misjudged the electorate. Due to their overriding concern for election victory, parties are not really held responsible for what happens, since the parties, essentially, do not act, but react— to circumstances, events and, above all, to public sentiment. They are commonly reproached, in fact, for reacting *too much,* for courting public favor *too* assiduously and for exerting *too little* leadership of their own.

The reasoning behind these views is familiar enough. Ruled by their need and desire for election victory, party leaders try their best to gauge public sentiment, to pick and groom the most appealing candidates, to raise the most popular issues and to voice the most common grievances. In this way, the political parties become, in the words of political scientist R. M. MacIver, "the agency by which public opinion is translated into political power." Nor can a party choose *not* to be the agent of public opinion. If it "translates" public sentiment poorly, it will sooner or later suffer defeat at the polls, because the other party, too, is ceaselessly trying to win. By competing for public favor, a competition that arises of necessity from each party's desire for victory, the American party system perpetually delivers over to the citizenry the ultimate power of decision. For this reason the parties are seen as the "instruments" of representative government and the "handmaidens of democracy," to quote the American historian Clinton Rossiter. As mere instruments, agents, servants and translators, the parties, in a profound sense, do not matter, for though they "operate at the center of the power struggle," they themselves have no real power.

Although this is essentially an apologist's view, it is far more widely accepted than some might imagine, for critics of the Left subscribe implicitly to much the same view of the political parties. They assume

that real power lies with "special interests," or "the dominant economic interest" or some other ruling force lying outside of party politics. It
would no more occur to a Marxist critic to locate real power in the
parties themselves than it would to the most shallow apologist for the
present party system. Both the apologist and the Marxist agree in this,
that the parties are political *servants;* of the people in the view of the
former, of "economic power" in the view of the latter.

Such, in brief, is the prevailing doctrine about the political parties,
minus the many qualifications called in to keep it plausible—the
effects of "public apathy," of "straight-ticket voting" and the like. That
doctrine whose essential principle is that parties are powerless rests
entirely on the axiom that parties have but one principle of action: to
win election victories at all costs. That has always been assumed in
advance. What happens, however, if we do not assume it in advance, if
we simply look at what political parties actually do? We will discover,
quickly enough, that the realities of party politics and the prevailing
doctrine about parties bear no resemblance whatever, that the reality
and the doctrine are exactly opposite.

The best place to begin is in the several states themselves, in part
because state parties are the basic constituents of the larger party syndicates known as the national parties, in part because state politics
confronts the prevailing doctrine of the parties with an immense and
inexplicable anomaly: in more than two-thirds of the states of the
Union, one party or the other has been predominant for thirty, fifty or
even a hundred years. Measured by control of the state assembly (and
why that measure is the important one will become clear later on),
most states can be described as permanently Democratic or permanently Republican. In these states the second party is a more or less
chronic legislative minority; on the occasions when it does gain a
majority, it usually loses it in the following election like water seeking
its own level. During this century the traditional Republican states
have included Maine, New Hampshire, Vermont, New York, New
Jersey, Pennsylvania, Delaware, Ohio, Indiana, Kansas, Nebraska,
Iowa, North Dakota, South Dakota, California, Oregon and, until the
1950s, Massachusetts, Wisconsin, Minnesota and Michigan. The

long-standing Democratic states include the eleven states of the Old Confederacy; the border states of Oklahoma, Kentucky and Missouri; Southwestern states such as Arizona, Nevada, Utah and New Mexico; Washington and Rhode Island.

Realignments have been remarkably few. Despite the great popularity of Franklin Roosevelt and the widespread disgust with Republicans during the 1930s, the legislative assemblies of only a few states moved decisively into the Democratic camp, New Mexico and Rhode Island among them. In 1958, the Massachusetts Democrats gained control of the state legislature for the first time in one hundred years. As V. O. Key, the best of all American political scientists, has put it: "Within a large proportion of the states only by the most generous characterization may it be said that political parties compete for power." For the most part, the relative status of the two parties in each state has remained little changed since the turn of the century, and it is worth stopping a moment to grasp what this implies. In the past seven decades, the United States has fought four major wars, undergone a profound economic collapse, seen the enormous growth of cities, the virtual disappearance of the small farmer, the rapid rise of giant trusts and corporations, the formation of huge trade unions, yet as far as state party politics is concerned next to nothing has happened.

This one-party predominance in many states has an even more revealing substratum. Within most states—including states where one party does not necessarily predominate in the legislature—each party is permanently predominant within a particular set of legislative districts. In these districts, the party is impregnable; its candidates for the legislature rarely lose. In many other districts of the state (if not all of them), its candidates rarely win. Each party, the minority as well as the majority one, has its own geographical strongholds, its own electoral bastions. The common characteristic of many of these states— Maine, New Hampshire, Vermont, Massachusetts, New York, New Jersey, Pennsylvania, Ohio, Indiana, Illinois, Missouri, Oklahoma, Montana and Washington among them—is the geographical division of virtually the entire state into more or less distinctive party satrapies, where effective competition for legislative seats can scarcely be said to exist. There are upstate New York districts which have not sent a Democrat to the Assembly since before the Civil War, and there are a great number of legislative districts with similar partisan records. Obviously the reason one party will predominate in a state is that its local strongholds send more lawmakers to the legislature than those of the other party. Insofar as the minority party is confined to its strongholds, it is usually the permanent minority. The confinement, so to speak, may border on political nonexistence. In South Dakota until the 1950s the Democrats at times had *no* seats at all in the legislature. For several decades they had no more than 20 percent of the seats in many Middle Western states. Were the second political party in those states a vegetarian party, it could hardly have done worse.

The patterns of confinement vary from state to state. In New York State, the minority Democrats are limited largely to one giant city, New York, which makes them a quite large, but still permanent legislative minority. In Maine, New Hampshire and Vermont, the Democrats are largely confined to ethnic voters in a few cities and towns. In Tennessee, the minority Republicans have been confined to one region: East Tennessee. Republicans in Democratic Missouri are restricted to the western part of the state, and in Democratic Oklahoma to the panhandle and the north-central section. The minority party may also be confined to geographically separate bastions, like the Democrats of Illinois, Ohio and Indiana, whose bastions include a few cities and some rural southerly districts. In Wisconsin the Democrats have been largely restricted to Milwaukee; in Washington, to Seattle; in Kansas, to Wichita, Kansas City and Topeka; in Montana, to the southwestern mining areas.

If the "basic purpose" of a party is to "find a man whom the majority of the voters will agree to support," to quote Pendleton Herring, author of *The Politics of Democracy in America,* it is plain that one party or the other permanently fails in a large majority of the more than five thousand legislative districts in the nation. According to the prevailing party doctrine, however, this cannot be for want of trying. How then explain such durable records of partisan failure, such endless frustration of a party's basic purpose? Assuming that parties *want* to win in the districts in which they rarely win, why is it that so many voters in so many districts evince such a fixed and enduring preference for one party and such an unswerving repugnance to the legislative candidates of the other, a repugnance, moreover, often aroused *only* by that party's legislative candidates, for even in states where one party comprises a tiny minority in the legislature, it will regularly poll 40 percent to 50 percent of the vote in statewide and Presidential elections.

Following the basic axiom that each party is trying its best to elect its candidates, two sorts of explanations have been offered. One is essentially sociological and rests on a presumed attraction between particular social categories of voters and a particular party label. The other is historical and rests on the presumed strength of local traditions of partisan voting. Each explains nothing while contradicting the other.

To explain why the Democrats' legislative bastions are so frequently confined to urban, ethnic, Catholic or industrial districts, political sociologists have suggested that the Democrats possess a strong magnetism for voters in these categories. The exact nature of this magnetism, be it noted, cannot be readily specified in political terms, since the Democrats do not necessarily serve the interests of these voters. For this reason, Rossiter, in *Parties and Politics in America*, speaks of "a natural, time-tested affinity between the restless Democratic party and the restless city." The term "natural affinity" is well advised, for so little do the Democrats serve the interests of city dwellers that, during their long hegemony over national affairs, most American cities have been deteriorating into islands of blight.

Leaving aside the cause of the "affinity" and assuming that it works like a magnet on iron filings, the sociological explanation falls apart anyway. The affinity between the Democratic (or Republican) party and given social categories of voters ought, by its nature, to be a nongeographical affinity, one that operates on members of the category wherever they happen to live. Alas, such is not the case: the affinities frequently cannot cross state lines; potent in one state, they will disappear in the state next door. The well-known affinity between the Democratic party and urban voters, for example, does not exist in Cincinnati, which is run by Republicans. It did not exist in St. Louis until the late 1930s. It was so absent among Philadelphia voters that the Philadelphia Democratic party existed only in name until 1951. The affinity is not even very strong in New York City, whose voters have elected Republican mayors about as often as the Republicans put up an attractive candidate—which is seldom. If city dwellers, as such, had an affinity for Democrats, the New York State Democratic party would be a permanent majority in the legislature instead of a permanent minority, for there are several thriving cities in the Republicans' upstate stronghold whose inhabitants have lost their urban affinity for Democratic legislative candidates and vote much like their rural neighbors.

The affinity of Catholics and Democrats is also altered by the geographical location of the Catholics. In Massachusetts, Irish Catholics heavily support the Democrats, while Italian Catholics much preferred the Republicans. Had they shown a proper Catholic "affinity" for Democrats, the Democratic party would have controlled the Massachusetts legislature for most of this century. In neighboring Vermont, on the other hand, Catholics in general tend to support the Democrats. Obviously whether a Catholic feels an affinity with the Democratic party's legislative candidates depends on which New England state he lives in. It even depends on which *district* of a state he lives in. Catholics in New York City were the backbone of the Democratic party, yet there is a larger percentage of Catholics living in the Republican strongholds outside of New York City. A fifty-mile move, and the affinity vanishes.

It is often said that ethnic voters, as such, have a strong affinity for the Democratic party, yet in Michigan, where 41 percent of the voters outside Detroit were of recent foreign extraction, the Michigan Democratic party scarcely existed until after the Second World War and even today its stronghold is Detroit. On the other hand, if Maine, New Hampshire and Vermont "ethnics" had the same disaffinities as the Michigan "ethnics," there would be no Democratic party in those states, since there the Democrats' appeal is mainly confined to ethnic voters. It all depends on where the ethnic vote lives.

Similarly with the affinity between Democrats and industrial workers. In Wisconsin, for example, Milwaukeeans regularly send Democrats to the legislature, but the industrial towns of the state are Republican strongholds, although they have a higher percentage of industrial workers than Milwaukee does. The Republican stronghold of upstate New York is also a heavily industrialized area where the affinity manages to vanish.

What then remains of these general affinities between social categories of voters and the Democratic party? All that can be said is that such affinities exist, except in Republican bastions, where they don't, an empty sort of explanation. Such as it is, the sociological explanation does not even begin to touch upon two main elements of one-party predominance in the nation's legislative districts. It does not explain, for one thing, why voters with a fixed affinity for a party's local legislative candidates should vote quite frequently for the other party's candidates for the Senate, the governorship or the Presidency. To account for this, the affinity would have to sprout new properties, such as the capacity to disappear not only from one state to the next but also from one line on a ballot to the next. Nor does the sociological explanation begin to explain why Democrats, say, should appeal chiefly to the urban, ethnic, Catholic or industrial worker vote in the states where they have it at all. The explanation for this would have to sprout yet more subordinate clauses to the effect that a party which appeals to these categories automatically *repels* nonurban, nonethnic, nonindustrial voters, which would require yet more subordinate clauses regarding a "natural" antipathy between these social categories and more subordinate clauses yet to account for cases when the antipathy disappears. In short, the sociological explanation explains nothing and raises a plethora of unanswered questions, which is surely reason enough to junk it.

Since a voter's "sociological" identity is so often less important than the location of his house, many political observers have fallen back on a second sort of explanation: the persistence of local traditions of partisan affiliation not only in the Deep South, but also throughout the country. As local historians have long observed, legislative districts settled at the time of the Civil War by Republicans have often remained

Republican to this day, while districts settled by migrating Southerners or Eastern Irish Catholics have remained Democratic to this day. This is often the case despite the fact that the long-standing Republican district and the long-standing Democratic district in a given state are today *alike* in every way and despite the fact that two long-standing Democratic (or Republican) districts are often *unalike* in every way. Such, allegedly, is the "force of local tradition." The explanation for this is, presumably, that in these districts one party originally was so prestigious and the other so scorned that these attitudes crystallized and kept the parties in their places down to the present day. This is no explanation at all. Even if the great majority of people in all these districts were actual descendants of the original hotly partisan settlers, we are still given no reason why they should vote as their great-grandparents did in state legislative contests. Consider, however, that in many of these legislative districts the majority of the inhabitants may not be the descendants of the original settlers, that the districts have undergone drastic changes of all sorts, that the farm population may have shrunk to a fraction of the voters, that the local sawmill has become a branch of an international corporation, that the villages have become towns, that Lincoln is not running for office, that the Union has been preserved, what is left of "local tradition" as an explanation? Simply this: that for some reason, still unexplained, a traditional Republican district persistently elects Republicans and a traditional Democratic district elects Democrats. Where does that leave us? Back at step one trying to explain why in so many legislative districts in so many different states, one party rarely loses and the other party rarely wins. Neither local tradition nor sociological affinities can explain this. On the self-evident axiom of party politics, that the parties' chief motive is to elect its candidates, it cannot be explained at all.

Consider, on the other hand, what state party leaders often do to ensure *defeat* outside their own local bastions and we come a little closer to an explanation. One common practice is simply to put up no candidate at all in the other party's strongholds, which helps considerably to make it the other party's stronghold. In Republican East

Tennessee, a great number of legislative seats go by default to Republican candidates. In the 1970 elections in the Knoxville area of East Tennessee, Republicans won nine of the ten legislative seats; in four there were no Democratic candidates, in the other five the opposition was described as "token" by the local press. The one Democrat who won also ran unopposed.

Such nonopposition is often explained away on the grounds that the party's chances were hopeless given the fixed affinity (traditional, sociological) of the voters for the other party's legislative candidates. This is, of course, a mere self-fulfilling prophecy. If a party does not put up any candidates, its chances of winning are truly hopeless—zero, in fact. And why should a major party's chances be hopeless? The majority of people in any state do not think they live in paradise. An opposition party can always find something or someone to oppose. Yet if hopelessness is a hollow alibi at best, what can be said of nonopposition when the minority party does not contest elections it will *win?* In Missouri, according to V. O. Key, Republicans and Democrats regularly put up no candidates in the other party's strongholds, "including districts in which the minority legislative candidates would poll quite respectable votes and even on occasion win." In such districts, the voters will show a fixed affinity for one party or the other only because they have no other choice.

In California, the minority Democrats' deliberate efforts to lose were disguised for years by the state's system of cross-filing wherein a candidate could win nomination in both parties' primaries. Democratic leaders worked so hard to nominate Republicans in their own primaries that as many as 73 percent of the seats were uncontested in the general election, and the Republicans controlled the legislature by wide margins until the mid-1950s, although Democratic voters had outnumbered Republican voters in the state since 1934. Similarly, in a dozen Middle Western Republican states, *not* trying to win legislative seats was the rigid policy of the minority Democrats all through the 1930s. As Key observed, the widespread repudiation of Republicans "certainly did not intensify efforts by the professionals to capture state governments." Given a unique opportunity to build up local party strength in the West and Middle West, the minority Democrats preferred to *remain* a minority party—a preference, as will be seen, which ran straight up to Roosevelt in the White House.

Another common way for parties to ensure defeat in the other party's stronghold is to provide their own candidates—usually nonentities, anyway—with little or no funds for campaigning. According to Alexander Heard, author of *The Costs of Democracy,* a study of political financing, state party leaders rarely spend money to elect legislators where the party, in Heard's words, is "a normal minority." Party leaders, says Heard, consider it a waste of precious campaign funds, but this is mere twaddle. If anything is wasteful, surely it is spending all the funds in districts where the party rarely loses, yet this is the common practice. The Massachusetts Democratic party, for example, disbursed in 1954 a derisory total of $15,000 for all candidates outside its Boston stronghold, which is one reason the Massachusetts Democrats did not gain control of the state legislature during one hundred years of allegedly trying.

Interestingly, state party leaders show very little interest in replacing local party leaders whose candidates never win. Quite the opposite is true. When patronage is given out by state party leaders, these permanently losing local leaders always get the share they need to remain local leaders. They are actually rewarded for losing. When a Democrat, Averell Harriman, was elected governor of New York in 1954, losing party leaders outside New York City received three-fourths of all the governor's patronage. According to Daniel P. Moynihan and James Q. Wilson, it was distributed with all the tact and diplomacy needed to enable these perennial losers to "keep the boys happy" and serve "organizational maintenance"—an oddly solicitous attitude toward leaders who permanently lead the party to defeat.

Nothing reveals the real electoral efforts of minority party leaders more than what happens when old-line leaders are overthrown: the minority party's candidates suddenly begin to win in districts where they had been a "normal" or even a "hopeless" minority for decades. Democratic support in California was not translated into legislative seats until after 1952 when grass-roots clubs sprang up and bypassed the old-line party leaders. Four years after the clubs emerged, the Democrats gained control of one house; two years later they gained control of both houses for the first time in many decades. The Oregon Democratic party, too, did not begin winning elections until the 1950s, when young reformers entered the party and weakened the power of the old-line regulars whose "basic purpose" was certainly not to find candidates "whom a majority of the voters would agree to support." Until reformers and activists entered the Wisconsin and Minnesota Democratic parties after the Second World War, these parties were no more than patronage cliques set up to lose—"receptacles for crumbs of Washington patronage," as Theodore White put it in his account of the 1960 Presidential election. The Philadelphia Democratic party was another losing patronage gang until a reformer, Joseph Clark, Jr., won the nomination for mayor and a strong election victory in 1951. What had the Philadelphia Democrats been doing all the years that the city was run by a corrupt Republican machine? What were the Democratic leaders of Oregon, Minnesota, Wisconsin and California doing for decades before the end of the Second World War? A great many things, but trying to win elections was not one of them.

The point, by now, should be clear. The reason the great majority of legislative districts are bastions of one party or the other is that both parties act to keep them that way. In a large majority of legislative districts, the abiding policy of one party or the other is to lose deliberately and perpetually. The desire to win elections is not the basic purpose of the political parties, it is not their overriding motive and interest. For the leaders of political parties, trying to win and trying to lose elections are equally useful means to a quite different political end.

It was a Republican state party boss, Senator Boies Penrose of Pennsylvania, who early this century stated with notable candor the basic principle and purpose of present-day party politics. In the face of a powerful state and national resurgence of reform and the sentiments of the majority of the Republican rank and file, Penrose put up a losing slate of stand-pat party hacks. When a fellow Republican accused him of ruining the party, Penrose replied, "Yes, but I'll preside over the ruins." Given a choice between winning elections with reform candidates and maintaining his and the regulars' control over the Pennsylvania party, Penrose chose to control the party. In 1918 when an insurgent group, known as the Nonpartisan League, beat the regular candidates in the Republican primaries of North Dakota and Idaho, Republican regulars in those states made the same choice. In the general election, they threw in with the opposition Democrats to defeat their fellow Republicans. In Iowa, four years later, Republican regulars worked strenuously to elect a Democrat when an insurgent Republican won the party's Senatorial nomination and for the same reason: the election of those Republican candidates threatened the regulars' control over the state party. To put the matter as concisely as possible: Insofar as a state party is controlled at all, the sole abiding purpose, the sole overriding interest of those who control it, is to maintain that control. This, not election victory, is the fundamental and unswerving principle of party politics in America, and the full implications of that principle of action, the extent to which it governs the deeds of party politicians from the most obscure to the most eminent, are the burden of all that follows in this book.

To begin to grasp what that principle of action means, it is essential to clear up an ambiguity regarding the term "party" itself, for party politics is largely hidden behind that ambiguity. Nominally a state party is a coalition of local party units—themselves smaller coalitions of politically active citizens from each legislative district of the state (the basic unit of a state party)—concerned with electing candidates of their choice to the state legislature and with voicing their views in the statewide party coalition. Insofar as each local party coalition is competing for election victory, it is independent, since the members are bound to concern themselves first and foremost with representing local sentiment, both in choosing local candidates to the legislature and in voicing their preferences in the statewide coalition's choice of statewide candidates. This is *one* meaning of the term "party," and the prevailing party doctrine describes to some extent the politics of such a party.

The term also refers to a statewide party organization, the local elements of which are not independent coalitions but subordinate units of an organization, one whose leaders are commonly and correctly known as "bosses" and whose members, significantly, are often called party "workers." In an organized party, and this is what defines it as such, a few party managers concentrate in their hands the means to satisfy or to thwart the varied ambitions of most party members. They can confer rich rewards for obedience—campaign funds, patronage, a favorable press, lucrative sinecures, nominations, uncontested primaries, gerrymandered districts and so on. They can also inflict harsh punishment—electoral defeat for one. I say rewards and punishments to underscore a fundamental point: a party organization is *not* held together by party loyalty—if it depended on party loyalty alone it would fall apart overnight—but precisely by the capacity of a few cooperating bosses to gather into their hands the means to hold the membership in line, "to keep the boys happy."

The first sort of party—and it has been approximated to some degree in several Western states—is one in which no cabal can gain durable ascendancy since the local coalitions, being formed around the determination to win local elections, are too subject to local sentiment to be permanently obedient to a state party oligarchy. The second sort of party is governed exclusively by its fundamental principle of action: the constant endeavor to prevent the organization from fragmenting into an unbossed coalition of independent local coalitions, into a party of the first sort. If it fragmented this way, the would-be party bosses would lose control of the party and with it control over nominations and political power itself. The prevailing doctrine of the parties thus describes what party organizations are perpetually striving to *avoid.*

Given control over the nominations—which itself requires control over most of the state party's members—organization leaders can ensure to a great extent that no man can run for office who has not proven himself amenable to the organization and willing to serve its interests, or, at the least, shown himself indifferent to reforms and issues that might weaken the party organization. By their control over nominations, organizations and their leaders hold the careers of elected officials in their hands, for they can deny them renomination, remove them from public life or bar their further political advance.

The hold which a cohesive party organization can exert over elected officials is very tight indeed. "It was not necessary to give orders," reported a contemporary about Boss Tom Platt's New York Republican organization at the turn of the century. "It was quite sufficient to have it understood by example that the man that stood by the organization benefited because the organization stood by him and that if he did not stand by the organization he got punished . . . he failed to make a record, he could not satisfy his constituents, his bills were not passed, or his work failed in other ways, and that he did not get renominated and he was eliminated." The description still holds.

When Lyndon Johnson was Majority Leader of the Senate (to cite one example out of thousands), he appeared to be a peculiarly powerful Senator, yet, according to Rowland Evans and Robert Novak's *Lyndon B. Johnson: The Exercise of Power*, he never once dared to act independently of the ruling clique of the Texas Democratic party. Since he depended absolutely on that clique to secure his renomination, he did everything in his power to strengthen their hold over the Texas party, which is to say, he served their interests. What was true of Johnson is true of thousands of lesser elected officials. When a party organization is in control, its leaders do not merely put up candidates for elective office, they *control* what a substantial number of these men do once elected. Such a party does not merely "manage the succession to power," it has power and wields power.

In saying this I do not mean that party bosses or ruling cliques have detailed "programs" of legislation for the officials under their command. Organization control is more general and constitutes a precise travesty of representative government. Under a representative system, the electors control those they elect, not by dictating their specific actions but by holding them accountable for those actions. They entrust an elected official with their power for a temporary period and remove him from power should he be found to have betrayed their trust. Party control works exactly the same way. The organization entrusts an elected official with *its* power, holds him accountable for his actions and removes him from power should he betray the organization—the tacit threat is usually sufficient. What is more, party leaders do not ignorantly repose their trust. They know their "man" very well. Before most politicians win a party organization's favor, they have been subject to the closest scrutiny. A local political club may look dark and grubby to outsiders, but within it the bright light of politics glares unmercifully. Called upon constantly to make small, revealing decisions, as small and revealing perhaps as a handshake, party politicians know each other better after acting together for three months than two co-workers in a factory or two executives in a corporation will know each other after five years. By the time a party politician has become a Senate prospect or "Presidential timber"—to go ahead for a moment—it is safe to say that party bosses know him inside and out. They have sometimes been mistaken in their man, but the occasions have been exceedingly rare.

Control of elected officials means real political power, and party organizations use that power, first and foremost, in order to serve themselves—party organizations are neither malevolent nor benevolent; they are self-interested. And the fundamental interest of those who head a party organization is, as I said, to maintain that party organization, which is the sole foundation of their power. In holding elected officials accountable to them, they will see to it that no laws are passed which might weaken the organization; that no public issues are raised which might strengthen the chances of insurgents and independents; that special privileges are not stripped away from special interests that have been paying the organization heavily for protecting those privileges. They use their power continually to maintain their control over patronage, over campaign funds, over nominations, over the avenues to public renown, over the whole arsenal of political rewards and punishments without which the organization would collapse in a trice. A party organization is not like a building which, once erected, requires no further human effort. Keeping a party organization intact requires constant and unremitting effort in the teeth of perpetual and unremitting peril. If a party organization can be likened to anything, it would be to an exceedingly complicated juggling act, in which the jugglers—the party managers—must endeavor at all times to keep innu-merable Indian clubs simultaneously flying in predictable arcs, for if a few were to get out of hand, the others would tumble to the ground. A party organization has no choice but to be self-serving. Should it lose control over elected officials, the power of those officials can only, in time, work against it. From the point of view of a party organization, every elected official is a potential menace.

Suppose, for example, that a party's candidate for governor wins the election. Nothing in principle prevents him from ignoring the party entirely, from using his patronage to build up a purely personal fol-lowing, from attempting to oust local party leaders, from bringing new men into the party ranks, from passing reforms that weaken the party organization, from winning public support so strong that the organization cannot deny him renomination. This was done by Robert La Follette of Wisconsin, Hiram Johnson of California and a half-dozen other insurgent Republican governors who overthrew Republican organizations in the Western states in the years before the First World War. So far from gaining power by the mere fact of win-ning an election, a party organization may see its power threatened and even destroyed. There are times, therefore, when losing an elec-tion becomes an absolute necessity.

Should the party organization fail for some reason to prevent an insurgent candidate from winning an important primary, its first recourse is to prevent him from winning the election. When Democratic insurgents in Connecticut—former supporters of Eugene McCarthy's insurgent bid for the Democratic Presidential nomination in 1968—succeeded in nominating one of their own, Reverend Joseph P. Duffey, in the 1970 Senate primary, John Bailey, the state boss of the Connecticut Democratic party, had former Senator Thomas Dodd run as an "independent" to split the Democratic vote and ensure the election of a Republican. In Vermont, in that same year, the Democratic bosses could not prevent the Senate nomination of former governor Philip Hoff, who had also supported McCarthy in 1968. Since his election would have strengthened the nonbossed frag-ment of the losing Vermont Democracy, the party bosses openly campaigned for his Republican Senate rival. This is nothing new. Throughout the years between 1918 and 1922, insurgent party candidates imperiled so many state party organizations in the West that dumping elections became a virtual routine. In Idaho, insurgents captured Democratic primaries and immediately the so-called straight Democrats helped to elect large Republican majorities in both houses of the state legislature. In Minnesota, the regular Democrats, too, threw in with the Republican opposition in order to defeat an insurgent Democrat. In Wisconsin in 1920 Republican regulars supported the Democratic candidate for governor against the insurgent Republican standard-bearer.

The simple truth is, a party organization will dump any election whenever its control over the party would be weakened by the victory of its own party's candidate.

Party organizations cannot afford to take chances. They will even try to defeat a party hack if his victory would prove inconvenient. In 1956, Richard Daley, Democratic boss of Cook County, was still consolidating his hold over the Illinois party, and he feared that *any* Democratic governor might stand in the way. Unfortunately for Daley, open scandal in the Republican administration made the election of a Democratic governor highly likely. To help ensure defeat, Daley gave the nomination to a machine hack with proven lack of statewide appeal, namely the former Cook County treasurer. By mid-September, however, when it became clear that the Democratic candidate was faring well, the newspapers were mysteriously provided with proof that the former Cook County treasurer had been fiddling with public funds. Having supplied the proof, Daley now indignantly demanded that the guilty man step out of the race. In his place Daley put up an even more obscure figure, who averted danger to the Democratic organization by narrowly losing. *Not* winning elections is not always easy.

Fear of the party's own elected officials is often a determining feature of party politics regardless of who holds the office. In Boston, according to Edward Banfield's *Big City Politics*, Democratic regulars always fear an independent mayor of Boston. Since the best way for an elected official to pursue an independent course is to carry out popular reforms, the constant practice of the Boston regulars is to see that Boston's mayors do not "make a record." They do this by ordering their minions in the state legislature to vote *against* the mayor's requests in the legislature, which in Massachusetts virtually governs the city. "Even when the governor is a Democrat," says Banfield, "the mayor of Boston does not get much from the state." Neither, of course, do Bostonians, the perennial victims of the interests of the Boston party organization.

In St. Louis, according to Banfield, Democratic ward bosses likewise fear an independent mayor and likewise have their legislative minions vote against the interests of St. Louis residents. They then blame this betrayal of their own St. Louis constituents on "rural interests" in the legislature, a tune sung so often in New York politics that the average New Yorker has come to believe that his city is squalid, his schools degraded, his streets filthy and his public transport foul because "upstate farmers" (12 percent of the statewide vote) want to see New Yorkers suffer. Persuading one segment of the citizenry to blame another segment for its troubles is a constant practice of party organizations. As will be seen, *divide et impera* is built into the very structure of machine politics.

What a party will do on the rare occasion when one of its "safe" officeholders dares to betray the organization is well illustrated by the brief Democratic governorship of William Sulzer. A Congressman from New York City, Sulzer was reputed a "liberal," but he was also, as Allan Nevins remarks in his biography, *Herbert H. Lehman and His Era,* "a member in good standing" of Tammany Hall. Since that combination of "liberal" sentiments and organization loyalty adds up to only one thing—a fake reformer—Charles Murphy, the boss of Tammany Hall (and hence of the entire state party), picked Sulzer for governor in 1912. This was Tammany's response to the national reform movement of the day. When Sulzer began campaigning on an antimachine platform—the single most popular issue in the country—Murphy was completely unconcerned. When Sulzer won the governorship, party politicians were "predicting," according to Nevins, "a stage encounter between Sulzer and Murphy of the paper shield and tin sword variety." Having been nominated as a fake reformer, Sulzer was fully expected to govern like one. When the state legislature passed a primary election law that left organization control of the nominations completely intact, Sulzer, to the amazement of the organization, denounced it as a fraud and vetoed it. At that point, according to Matthew and Hannah Josephson, who also recount the Sulzer story in their biography, *Al Smith: Hero of the Cities,* "Murphy decided to show him who was master." To destroy Sulzer's chance to win widespread popularity, New York's Democratic legislators were asked to block the governor's proposed program of reform with those two famous Tammany-liberals, Al Smith and Robert Wagner, "leading the interference." When Sulzer still refused to knuckle under and began a full-scale effort to rouse popular support for his reforms, Murphy decided that more drastic action was required. He had the Democratic legislators *impeach* the Democratic governor for routine fiddling with some campaign funds, and Sulzer was eliminated.

The Sulzer affair illustrates one of the fundamental perils that perpetually menace organization control over parties. Had it not been for a nationwide, articulate reform movement, a movement that had brought all kinds of nonregulars into active political life, Sulzer would not have dared bid defiance to Tammany Hall; given an apathetic, confused and divided electorate, his chance of defeating the organization would have been nil from the start. As it was, the party organization had to resort to impeachment, a sort of nonlethal assassination.

What was true in New York in 1912 is true in this Republic at all times and places. The grass-roots political activity of the citizenry and its inseparable adjunct, the entry into public life of nonorganization politicians, is a constant threat to party organizations. It spurs political ambitions outside their control. It opens new avenues to public renown. It encourages outsiders to enter party primaries and gives them a chance to win. It opens to officeholders themselves the opportunity to win public support on their own and thus render themselves independent of the organization. It is therefore the perpetual endeavor of party organizations to discourage and even squash grass-roots movements. After Dr. Francis Townsend's old people's social security movement began showing political strength in 1935, according to the New Deal historian William Leuchtenburg, "Republicans and Democrats seized the opportunity [of a scandal] to unite to scotch the Townsend menace." What made the mild Townsend movement a menace was not its program but its existence as a spur to political activity outside party ranks.

The moment Republican and Democratic leaders saw Senators and Congressmen scrambling to address peace rallies during the October 1969 Moratorium, the two national party syndicates again closed ranks like a drill team. Spokesmen for the Democratic opposition became spokesmen for President Richard Nixon's Vietnam policies. Hubert Humphrey pointedly paid a visit to the White House to demonstrate his support of the Republican President, and the Democratic Speaker of the House, John McCormack, had a House resolution passed to do the same. Uniting against the peace movement at the exact moment when it began attracting elected officials, the two party organizations then "took the Vietnam war out of politics," as the newspapers put it, for the duration of the 1970 election campaign, although every poll showed it was uppermost in the minds of the voters. The party organizations did not do this because they were afraid of the peace issue; what they feared, as always, was the independent activity of free citizens. Not until the peace movement was dead did organization Democrats come out against the war. When New York's Republican Senator Charles Goodell persisted in courting antiwar voters in defiance of the party leaders, Republicans from Nixon down to Governor Nelson Rockefeller's Republican county chairmen eliminated Goodell by throwing their endorsements, and their campaign funds, as well as their influence with the press, to the Conservative party's Senate candidate James Buckley—which is the only reason he won 39 percent of the vote. Why did the Republican organization do this? In order to "have it understood by example that the man that . . . did not stand by the organization got punished." Or, as Voltaire famously remarked, "to encourage the others."

From the point of view of party organizations, all such stratagems are merely self-protective measures, but they require truly pervasive control over public officials and political life. To eliminate Senator Goodell, the New York Republican organization had to exert strict control over numerous Republican county leaders, Republican state legislators, the Republican press and Republican sources of campaign money. Similarly Boston and St. Louis party managers must have city legislators so completely subservient that they will vote, year after year, against the interests of their own constituents. In general the great majority of state legislators must be docile minions of the state party organizations, or the organizations would be unable to protect themselves from independent governors, from insurgent primary challengers, from grass-roots political activity and other perennial political perils.

As V. O. Key has observed, describing party devices for keeping control of party members would fill an encyclopedia, for not only are these means numerous, but they also vary from state to state. Yet all these varied instruments of control would come to nothing if the majority of state legislators had to win popular support to gain reelection. A legislator who is truly vulnerable to defeat every time he runs for reelection cannot be entirely obedient to a party organization, for he dare not serve the organization's interests where they conflict sharply with those of his constituents. In proportion as he must win and hold popular favor, an officeholder becomes "unreliable." No matter how keenly he fears the organization's punishments and looks forward to its rewards, an elected official cannot be relied upon by the organization to commit electoral suicide. What is more, it is just when the organization is most in danger that he will prove most unreliable. Instead of helping the party organization prevent an independent reform governor from making a record, for example, he might well make his own record locally by siding with the governor. Since a legislator would be vulnerable to defeat if the other party tried to defeat him, party control of elected officials, hence organization control of parties, *cannot coexist with normal two-party competition in all the legislative districts of a state.* There is only one way a given state party organization can maintain itself in power, and that is to divide up most of the state's legislative districts with the opposition party and make them separate local one-party strongholds. The two state party organizations do not have to come to any formal agreement about this; the division arises by virtue of each party organization following its *own* interests, the minority as well as the majority party.

Suppose a minority party in a state is confined to a local bastion where the party is tightly controlled by a small ruling oligarchy or machine, for instance, the Vermont Democrats in a few "ethnic" towns, New York Democrats in New York City, Tennessee Republicans in East Tennessee, and so on. Nominally, of course, the party exists at least pro forma in *all* legislative districts of the state (it usually has to or a third party might fill the vacuum), yet if local bosses can ensure that the party loses in the legislative districts outside the bastion, they reap inevitable and indispensable advantages. Instead of being lively independent competitive coalitions striving to elect independent state legislators, the perpetually losing party units will shrink into little patronage gangs held together not by the prospect of victory, but by the crumbs of patronage and graft that the bosses in their bastions supply them with. They become, in consequence, the obedient tools of the bosses in all the state party's concerns and deliberations. The local bosses in the bastion, together with their patronage clients in the losing districts, form the core, the foundation, the *sine qua non* of organization control over the entire state party, and it is the bosses in the bastion who control the state party. It is they who wield the power. In Missouri, the Kansas City Democratic machine plus the losing Democratic leaders in the Republican districts control the Missouri Democratic party. In Tennessee the Democratic bosses of Shelby County (Memphis) control the state party by virtue of controlling their party clients in Republican East Tennessee. Whenever an independent challenges the Shelby bosses in a statewide primary, the East Tennessee Democratic leaders deliver the vote to the Shelby organization's choice. In Pennsylvania before 1952, the Allegheny County (Pittsburgh) machine, along with its patronage clients in Philadelphia, controlled the state Democratic party, just as the New York City bosses, by virtue of controlling county leaders in the upstate Republican strongholds, easily control the New York State Democratic party. It is obvious, therefore, why the minority

Democrats in Kansas, Nebraska, Minnesota, Wisconsin and other Western Republican strongholds did not during the 1930s "intensify efforts to capture state governments," to quote V. O. Key. If they had built up competitive party units in the numerous Republican districts of those states, they would have lost control over their respective state parties, the equivalent to suicide in party politics. Given the choice between being one among many in a victorious state party coalition and remaining the powerful boss of a minority party machine, the bosses have again and again chosen the latter.

The losing efforts of the minority party do not, of course, take place in a vacuum. By confining itself to its strongholds and not competing elsewhere, the minority party automatically gives the majority party its necessary majority. Far more importantly, it gives the leaders of the majority party the necessary condition for controlling their party's numerous legislators, namely noncompetition in the elections. A legislator who faces token opposition—if any—from the other party has little to fear from the electorate. With no one prepared to expose and attack his record, he can betray with considerable impunity the interests of his constituents. On the other hand, he has a great deal to fear from party leaders, for his reelection depends entirely on carrying the party label. Since the organization can elect virtually anyone it puts up, what appeal the incumbent has to the voters—if any—gives him little hold on the renomination. The incumbent in an uncontested district has very little reason to defy the party leaders and very good reasons to obey them.* Since they were usually chosen in the first place for their qualities of compliance, state legislators rarely give party

---

*The same principle holds true for Congressional seats. Party control of Congressmen is made possible primarily by the party organizations' practice of not competing seriously for Congressional seats. How widespread this noncompetition has become is well-attested by a single fact. In 1970, a year of widespread unrest and popular discontent, 384 Congressmen ran for reelection and 375 of them won. This is usually attributed to the "built-in advantages" of incumbency, but the only advantage an incumbent has is token opposition from the other party. In the nineteenth century, when party organizations were weaker and electoral competition consequently more keen, incumbent Congressmen usually lost.

organizations much trouble—which is why our state legislatures are so uniformly corrupt.

The common bond of interest between the minority party bosses and the majority party bosses is therefore clear and obvious. As long as the minority party bosses can retain control of their party—and therefore confine their electoral efforts largely to the party stronghold—the majority party leaders can control their far more extensive party. The majority party leaders therefore have every reason to protect the power of the minority party bosses, since it is by virtue of boss control of the minority party that the majority party can be controlled at all. What the minority party bosses need to maintain their power and their control over their party is equally obvious: they need just what the majority organization needs: token electoral opposition in *their* party bastion, and that is precisely what the majority party bosses provide them. Mutual noninterference in their respective party bastions is the reason both parties retain bastions at all. It is not electoral competition which characterizes the relation between two state party organizations, but strict and pervasive collusion. That collusion does not necessarily require conspiratorial plotting in smoke-filled back rooms. It springs up automatically between two state party organizations by virtue of powerful bonds of common interest. Neither party organization could retain control of its party *unless* the two party organizations were in collusion. As Senator Robert La Follette rightly remarked in 1912: "Machine politics is always bipartisan." It is because it has to be.

2.

The System of Collusion

State party bastions are one consequence of two-party collusion, a collusion so tight in many states, and in almost all the large ones, that the two party organizations actually form a single ruling oligarchy. These bastions, however, are not arbitrary divisions. They are, for the most part, districts whose inhabitants *did* strongly support one party or the other at a much earlier time in our history. As party organizations gained control of their parties, their mutual cooperation simply froze the earlier pattern of partisanship. Each party organization ceased to compete seriously where the other party had been strong, for only through mutual cessation of electoral competition can party organizations maintain themselves and so retain their power. This is the reason for "the long persistence of county patterns of party affiliation" in so many states, to quote an essay by V. O. Key, Jr., and Frank Munger in *Democracy in the Fifty States*. It is also the reason these partisan patterns often reflect Civil War party divisions: it was in the decades immediately after the war that bipartisan machine politics began taking hold in one state after another. In New York State, according to Allan Nevins, collusion sprang up in 1861: "Just before the war, a bargain had been made between Tammany Democrats and the Seward-Weed Republicans for a division of the spoils, whereby Tammany managed the city vote. This corrupt alliance between city Democrats and upstate Republicans passed through various permutations, but it steadily regained substance." It is more substantial today than ever.

It is collusion which also explains why one district will be Republican and another district Democratic even when, according to Key and Munger, these "contrasting partisan patterns [occur] in essentially similar counties." Given the motives of state party organizations, it does not matter whether two districts have become virtually alike since the Civil War. Under two-party collusion, a district is permanently marked off as "Republican" or "Democratic," and the voters in these districts can only follow suit, which means, simply, that the majority of voters will not often support candidates who are put up to lose.

Machine bipartisanship also explains what "local tradition" and sociological "affinity" cannot begin to explain: why a state party which has a tiny minority in the legislature can still elect governors and Senators from time to time or even quite often. It is by confining its winning efforts to a restricted set of *legislative* districts that party bosses control the basic units of the party. With that foundation laid, minority party bosses can afford to win statewide elections by putting up credible candidates, which is why "local tradition" or "affinity" will "weaken" from one line of the ballot to the next, these traditions and affinities being merely the apparent result of one party or the other deliberately trying to lose.

Historically, the Democrats have long confined themselves in the North to districts where the preponderance of voters were Irish or Catholic or immigrant or poor or urban. This historical choice has been deliberate. As the first machine party in the Republic (it became "mechanized," so to speak, in the 1840s), the Democratic machine found it safest to direct its appeal to the voters who were the easiest to control, people whose common denominator, politically speaking, has been their ignorance of the possibilities of free political action and a consequent gratitude for small favors. Glowing tales are often told of the charitable functions of Democratic ward heelers in city slums, how they would pat troubled immigrants on the back, give out turkeys and bags of coal at Christmas and make people feel they "belonged"—to what? one is tempted to ask. The slum ward bosses *did* do a great deal for the poor, the ignorant and the oppressed as long as they remained poor and ignorant and oppressed and thus grateful for small hand-

outs, pats on the back and occasional empty gestures of reform—
"shows of action," as Tammany Hall called them.

At the same time the Democrats have been less than eager to
extend their winning efforts to districts and states where the voters are
not as manageable. This is why the Democrats have usually been a
tiny legislative minority in Northern states possessing few cities, few
immigrants and large numbers of unruly farmers. By confining themselves to safe voters in these states, they have condemned themselves,
of course, to a lowly minority status, notably in the Western states.
Interestingly enough, in the few states where the minority Democrats
have consented to become a legislative majority in recent years—in
Massachusetts and Rhode Island, for example—it was partly because
ethnic or Catholic voters had long since become an overwhelming
majority of the population. Under these conditions, becoming the
majority party, though a perilous assumption of new responsibilities,
was relatively free of risk, particularly since Republican leaders retired
from all-out competition. The retirement of the leaders of an ex-
majority party illustrates once again that the fundamental purpose of a
party organization is to remain a party organization. From the point
of view of the organization, it is incomparably better to become a permanent minority party than to try to cling to majority status by competing in a large number of districts.

Since it is in the interests of each party's bosses to protect the other
party's bosses, neither party will try, if it can help it, to make permanent inroads into the other party's normal voters. The last thing the
majority party's leaders want is to hurt their fake opposition. As John
McCooey, the Democratic boss of Democratic Brooklyn, said to
Fiorello La Guardia in 1933 (the source is Ernest Cuneo's biography
of La Guardia): "I assure you that my most difficult problem is keeping my Republican opposition in the running." Insofar as minority
Democrats in Republican-controlled states restricted themselves to
certain narrow categories of voters, it was the permanent practice of
Republican leaders to keep these voters in the Democratic ranks, like a
man feeding scraps to his dog. As long as Massachusetts Democrats
confined themselves to Irish voters, for example, the state's Repub-

licans deliberately spurned the Irish vote. Not only did they not put up Irish candidates, they deliberately flaunted Yankee attitudes in order to antagonize Irish voters and so sharpen their "affinity" for Democrats, a quite necessary policy, since the Democrats' Irish bosses perpetually betray their Irish constituents. This policy was not due to any inherent nativist sentiment, since Massachusetts Republicans frequently put up Italian candidates in order to win the Italian vote, a vote which the Irish Democratic bosses for many years did not want, since the entry of Italians to party ranks would have threatened their political power. In party politics the voters themselves become political footballs. In Middle Western states, where the minority Democrats relied on the support of beer-drinking Germans, Republicans would regularly recement these voters into the Democrats' ranks by espousing prohibition laws. In New York City, whenever Tammany was tottery, Republicans regularly antagonized the city's Irish voters by rigidly enforcing Sunday "blue" laws. Today they keep New York City voters loyal to the Democrats by openly betraying the interests of the city in the legislature. They do this, they can only do this, with the full cooperation of Democratic legislators, who then blame their own acts of betrayal on "rural interests" and "extreme conservatives" in upstate New York. In Indiana, Ohio and Illinois, Republicans maintained Democratic support in the southern "Democratic" districts of these states by regularly abusing their Southern-descended inhabitants as "copperheads," "traitors" and even "degenerates," and did so until the turn of this century; when minority Democrats in the Middle West seemed to be losing their needed Catholic vote, Republican leaders would come to their rescue by proposing antiparochial school laws.

Setting one segment of the citizenry against another—Protestants against Catholics, rural people against city people, "natives" against "ethnics," one ethnic group against another, blacks against whites, downstaters against upstaters—is thus built into the very structure of two-party collusion. Yet the prevailing myth about the parties makes a truly vicious inversion of this practice. On the false assumption that parties are ceaselessly trying to win elections, political scientists and historians conclude that the parties, those "translators of public opinion," are merely voicing the spontaneous bigotries of a bigoted electorate. New York Republicans protect New York City's Democratic bosses by deliberately disfavoring New Yorkers, and this ancient collusive arrangement is attributed to antiurban bigotry in upstate New York where city dwellers outnumber farmers and neither is politically represented at all. Boston and St. Louis legislators betray their constituents at the behest of their party bosses, and this betrayal too is attributed to rural prejudice, for, according to the prevailing party myth, it cannot be laid at the feet of party bosses, since their one alleged motive is to court their local voters. The citizens are thus blamed, are asked to blame each other, for what party bosses in their own interest perpetually do against them. Since political fictions breed more fictions, the prevailing political myth carries this even one step further. The parties have actually been *lauded*—by Walter Lippmann, for example—for keeping a divided nation together. The truth is, the American people would be less divided if the parties were less united.

Mutual noninterference is the essential but not the only aspect of two-party collusion. When the situation demands, the cooperation between "opposing" party organizations becomes more intimate. Where patronage, for example, is the necessary cement of boss control, the ruling party will provide it to the bosses of the minority party in order to help them remain bosses. In Democratic Kentucky, "Republicans in their avidity for favors," Gladys Kammerer reports in *Democracy in the Fifty States*, "invite the Democratic Governor to attend their caucus for a reiteration of his bargains." Since the disposal of judgeships is an indispensable patronage tool (they are needed to satisfy aging hacks at the point where even a hack may become unreliable—when his political career in the party has come to a standstill), the ruling party distributes this patronage to the minority party under cover of bipartisan nominations. Both parties nominate the same candidate—which guarantees his election—while behind the scenes one party boss or the other makes the actual selection. Not long ago, a *New York Times* editorial suggested that judicial corruption would be lessened if New York's judges were appointed—but they already are.

Reapportioning of legislative districts provides another opportunity for collusion. To the mutual satisfaction of both party organizations, for example, incumbents who have won where they are not supposed to are gerrymandered out of office; an insurgent's supporters will be split into five different districts; two independents will be put in the same district, thereby eliminating one; party hacks will be protected; those groomed for higher office will be given safe districts so they can win "impressive" victories in the next election and become "front-runners" for higher office—as if their whole careers were not put-up jobs. These actions, of course, are part of the whole system of rewards and punishments by which party bosses keep elected officials in line. The threat or promise of redistricting is itself a powerful weapon of organization control, and the minority party only wields it because the majority party obliges. Yet these maneuvers are invariably described in the press as prime examples of two-party *competition*. In 1970, for example, a troublesome New York Democratic Congressman named Allard Lowenstein, leader of the "Dump Johnson" movement, was shifted into a Republican district to ensure his defeat. The press described this as an effort by the state's ruling Republicans to gain an extra Congressman. The more important motive was the Democratic bosses' wish, which their Republican allies met, to get rid of a political nuisance, just as in 1971 the Republicans eliminated reform Democratic state legislators in New York City and in 1972 two reform Democratic Congressmen with little "partisan" Republican advantage except the inherent advantage of strengthening the other party's organization.

Another form of collusion is made available to the party bosses by state election laws. Based on the assumption that the parties are unsleeping rivals, the election laws in most states give the parties responsibility for policing elections and operating the electoral machinery. If the two parties were in competition, this would work well enough, but where they are in collusion electoral fraud and chicanery can be practiced with impunity on each party's unwanted candidates. The victim may complain, but his losing party will not go to the trouble and expense of backing his claims for him. The fact that gross election fraud has been declining is usually taken as proof that the "bad old days" of machine politics are over, but in truth it proves the very opposite. Insofar as party organizations can monopolize politics, insofar as they have the ambitions of public men under control, their need to commit fraud decreases proportionately. Open electoral fraud is a sure sign that party bosses are in trouble and, as with Governor Sulzer's impeachment, have to resort to desperate measures. The truth of this—it is simply common sense—is more general. It takes a sharp challenge to a party organization to expose its real political interests; a party organization does not have to dump elections when only safe hacks can win nominations. On the other hand, nothing exposes collusion more quickly than the ambition of a politician who wants to win where his party wants to lose.

In New Mexico, Democratic bosses control the state party largely on the manageable Mexican-American vote (this is also true in Texas), which the minority Republicans make no effort to win. In 1966, however, an ambitious politician named David Cargo won the Republican governorship nomination and, to the dismay of the party regulars, made a strong and successful bid for Mexican and black votes. After winning the election, Governor Cargo then tried to broaden the Republican party and weaken its losing bosses. This was the necessary condition of his political survival. A genuine political maverick has only two choices: to surrender to the organization or destroy it. As a result of his efforts, Cargo not only won almost the entire vote of the state's black people during his 1968 reelection, he was able to put up Mexican candidates for local office who, in one county, won almost every election. In 1970, the Republican regulars, undermined by all this success, struck back at Cargo and his followers with the help of an enormous infusion of patronage and money from President Nixon. After defeating Cargo in the Republican Senate primary (state law prevented him from running a third time for governor) with national party money and a "law and order" candidate, the organization, according to *The New York Times,* ran "a heavily financed, well-organized and aggressive campaign that was built around conservative principles and highlighted repeated visits to the state by top national Republican figures including the President and Vice-President." As a result of this extraordinary election campaign, which was heavy with racist overtones, minority group voters deserted the Republican ticket, the Republican candidate for Senator lost, the Republican candidate for governor lost and local Republican officeholders were swept out of office. According to *The New York Times*, "a once-growing organization was shattered." Translated from jargon into reality, a winning, uncontrolled party was now back in the hands of its shattered party organization which had to inject racial and ethnic antagonisms into state politics in order to regain control. Another example of how the parties hold a divided people together.

In New York, to cite another instance, the state Republican organization protects the Democratic bosses of the city by the usual methods of nominating inept candidates, providing no campaign funds, raising no public issues, sabotaging local Republican candidates who show an unseemly desire to win, keeping local Republican clubs in the hands of leaders who want to lose and so on. The Republican organization has done this so thoroughly that in the borough of Brooklyn most of the three million inhabitants are scarcely aware that there is a Brooklyn Republican party. The borough is ruled by a potent Democratic county machine which, like all political machines including Mayor Daley's Cook County organization, owes its existence to such fake opposition.

Occasionally, an ambitious New York Republican will defy the party organization by trying to win the mayoralty, as La Guardia did in 1933 and twice after, as John Lindsay did in 1965. Should that unwanted victory threaten the local Democratic machine, the Republican state organization will become the determined enemy of New York's Republican mayor. During Lindsay's first term he was continually harassed by his fellow Republican, Governor Nelson Rockefeller, who was simply carrying out the elementary machine practice of preventing an independent officeholder from making a record with the voters. In 1969, the Republican organization successfully unsheathed yet another party weapon: it threw a local Republican hack into the mayoral primary to contest Lindsay's renomination and eliminate him. This was the first such contested Republican mayoral primary in twenty-five years; when New York City Republicans put up a *losing* candidate, there is never a contest. The previous primary was occasioned by the state party's efforts to repair the damage which twelve years of La Guardia's rule had inflicted on the New York City Republican organization. That year, for example, Governor Thomas E. Dewey replaced La Guardia's New York party leader with one Thomas Curran, who knew what was expected of a New York City Republican chairman, namely nothing. When the local Republicans in 1953 put up a hotel manager for mayor, New York politics was back to normal, at least on the Republican side of what Theodore Roosevelt once described as the "bipartisan combine" in New York State.

An unwanted party victory will sometimes destroy bipartisan arrangements permanently but not bipartisanship itself. When Joseph Clark won the Philadelphia mayoralty as a Democrat in 1951, he brought into being a winning, open reform coalition that completely submerged the old losing Philadelphia Democratic boodle gang. Such an open party in so large a city sharply imperiled the Pittsburgh machine's control of the Pennsylvania Democratic party. Fortunately for the party organization, a Democrat subservient to the state boss, David Lawrence, became governor of Pennsylvania in 1954. Since it was no longer possible to return the Philadelphia Democracy to its former abject state, Lawrence had only one option: to make sure that the Philadelphia party ceased to be an open reform party. Through his agent in the statehouse, Lawrence distributed three thousand jobs to the Philadelphia Democrats and gave complete control over their distribution, not to the victorious reformers, but to one William Green, a hack Philadelphia Congressman, who was then able to create a citywide Democratic organization. Given a choice between a large uncontrolled reform party unit within the state party or a second city machine, Lawrence, like any other state boss, chose to create and share power with a rival city boss. The reason is simple: although two local bosses in a party may vie for supremacy, their competition is sharply restricted by a compelling common interest—both want to remain party bosses and both have a common interest, therefore, in all the various policies that strengthen organization control of politics.

The interests of the Pennsylvania Republican organization were identical with those of Lawrence. The Republicans' ancient city machine had been broken. They could only regain control of Philadelphia through actual competition with the Democrats. Such a large, competitive and, therefore, unreliable Philadelphia party would have imperiled the Pennsylvania Republicans' statewide organization, so they simply junked the Philadelphia party by turning it into a losing clique. According to Banfield, Philadelphia Republican ward heelers became Philadelphia Democratic ward heelers, telling evidence that the Republican bosses had no wish to retain their services. What neither party organization could afford was competition in a large city.

Genuine third parties also expose collusion, for as soon as such a party emerges—e.g., the Minnesota Farmer-Labor party, the Wisconsin Progressive party—the two major parties invariably unite against it. If a minority party actually wanted to win, it would have no reason to unite with the threatened majority party of the state. Under the system of collusion, however, the minority party has every reason to help the ruling party, since any threat to that party's bosses threatens the system of bipartisanship and thus the interests of the minority party bosses as well. The two major parties come together, therefore, to crush the common enemy of the one ruling state oligarchy, which consists of the bosses of the majority party and their junior partners in the opposition.

Although they have identical interests, majority and minority state parties are nonetheless quite different. Confined to a few districts, dependably served by a large number of losing local patronage gangs, bearing little responsibility for governing, the minority party organization is the machine party par excellence. That the Northern wing of the Democratic party has consisted largely of such state parties is, as will be seen, one of the most important facts about the national Democratic party. The majority party, by contrast, is more difficult to control. Its winning districts are far more numerous, its dependent patronage districts correspondingly fewer. As the winning party, it attracts more ambitious men; as the governing party, it attracts more controversy. Insofar as it is spread out over a wide geographical area, as

Republican parties are in the Northern states, it must encompass, one way or another, a wide diversity of interests and sentiments. Compared to the compact minority, it is far more often beset by serious—as opposed to token—primary challengers and by uncontrolled reform factions. As V. O. Key has pointed out, in many states the contest between the majority party's regulars and its uncontrolled elements is the only real electoral competition that state parties, despite themselves, provide. The contest, however, is usually one-sided, because the regulars of the ruling party have the minority party on their side. Where the minority party is large and influential, as in New York, Pennsylvania and Illinois, the majority party leaders have little or nothing to fear from insurgents. Where the minority party is negligible, on the other hand, the contest is often not so one-sided. The success of Republican insurgents in the prairie states was due in large measure to the smallness and inconsequence of the collusive Democratic minority.

In addition to specific acts of collusion, minority parties help the ruling regulars in many ways, first and foremost by simply being a fake opposition. The minority party will raise no political issues and will subject the ruling party to no serious attacks on which the ruling party's reformers and insurgents can mount a serious challenge. This is one of the chief reasons why no-issue politics characterizes so many states despite the pervasive authority which the United States Constitution grants to state governments (in 1960 only eighteen state legislatures even bothered to meet regularly). Anything that stirs up the electorate, anything that rouses their interest in politics, is harmful to party organizations and, most directly, to a state's ruling party. Hence the absence of issues which the minority party helps to secure. Party insurgents not only have to challenge their party's bosses, they have to *create* the public issues on which to make their challenge, a difficult and expensive task in the face of dead silence from both party organizations.

The state legislature is one place to raise important public issues, but here, too, the majority party's insurgents are up against a wall of collusion, a "double machine," as Connecticut's bipartisan legislature has often been called. Working in tandem, the majority party regulars and the minions of the minority rig the legislature against them. It is the common practice in many state legislatures for the minority party to throw its votes for Speaker of the House and other key posts to the regulars' candidate whenever the majority party's insurgents have a strong candidate of their own. In these legislatures, William Buchanan notes in *Democracy in the Fifty States,* "members of the losing majority faction are likely to wind up with fewer spoils than the members of the minority party." As an anonymous New York Democratic legislator remarked—and the remark fits all collusive legislatures—"With enemies like the Democrats the Republicans don't need friends."

When a majority party insurgent mounts a serious threat to the regulars, minority party bosses have been known, where election law permits, to call out their faithful to vote against him in the *other* party's primary. In Minnesota in 1918, when the insurgent Charles Lindbergh, Sr., ran for the Republican governorship nomination, Democratic bosses urged Democrats to vote against him in the Republican primary. When Lindbergh lost the primary and decided to run as an independent candidate in the general election, the Democratic bosses once again came to the rescue. Not only did they endorse the Republican candidate for governor, but they made sure that their own candidate made no visible campaign in order not to split the state's stand-pat vote.

In Virginia, whenever an insurgent Democrat threatened the candidate of Senator Harry Byrd's statewide machine, Senator Byrd would also call on Republican leaders to get out a primary vote for his man. In the 1949 Democratic governorship primary, for example, an insurgent Democrat named Francis Pickens Miller made a powerful appeal to Virginians by calling for the overthrow of Byrd's "dictatorship" and a return to representative government. Badly shaken, Byrd asked the Republicans to send out their faithful against Miller, who narrowly lost the primary by 24,000 votes. For years, whenever a Byrd machine candidate was weak, Virginia Republican leaders would put up a weaker one. In 1964, for example, a Byrd machine candidate for Congress won very narrowly over a Republican. Two years later political observers—the "authoritative" *Congressional Quarterly,* among them—predicted a hotly contested fight for the seat. Instead the Republicans put up nobody.

The irresponsible power which a fake opposition can bestow on the rulers of a majority state party is well illustrated, in fact, by the politics of Virginia, where the Byrd machine for decades bent every instrument of government to its service and, in consequence, left Virginia with worse schools and poorer public services than any state of comparable wealth. Byrd was able to do this precisely because the Virginia G.O.P. was *not* a negligible party but a sizable collusive one. In statewide elections, the Republicans regularly polled 35 percent of the vote without even trying, and they didn't. Since fewer than 13 percent of the electorate even bothered to vote during the reign of Harry Byrd, the potential anti-Byrd support was enormous (unless it is supposed that voters don't vote because of deep contentment). Republican bosses, however, did nothing to attract it or even to encourage it to vote. It had its 35 percent of a tiny voting electorate and sat on it for decades.

Thanks to the silence of the Republican opposition, the one public issue in Virginia was "fiscal integrity," which meant in practice lauding Harry Byrd for not borrowing money for state public services. This was one reason so few Virginians bothered to vote; the less a government can do, the less political interest the electorate has. Indeed the chief reason for Byrd's famous pay-as-you-go financing was to keep Virginians apathetic. The other reason, equally self-serving, was that lack of state funds kept Virginia governors from making records and so winning independence of the machine. No other principle was involved, least of all fiscal integrity, which, in fact, left Virginia's counties bankrupt. In 1950, for example, Byrd's cheese-paring budgets, combined with increasing affluence, left the state treasury with considerable surplus funds. Even the most docile machine legislators began wondering aloud why *this* money, the fruit of integrity, might not be used for public improvements. Since public improvements excite public interest, the Byrd machine rammed through the legislature a new tax law which provided that any year's surplus would automatically result in a proportionate tax reduction the following year and so be eliminated.

To veil their collusion, Virginia's Republican bosses blamed their knavery on the people. They argued that any effort of theirs to increase their vote would attract *black* people and, given the alleged prevalence of racism in Virginia, would cost the party the *white* supporters it already had. This alibi was entirely mendacious. The main Republican voters over the years were, and are, the so-called hillbilly Republicans of mountainous western Virginia, who are largely indifferent to racist politics and strongly inclined to suspect that racism is just another trick against them. Racist politics has often cost the Republicans their white support. It was in 1920, for example, that Republicans first announced that henceforth they would be a white-only party, the official excuse being that the party was "bowing to public opinion and political expedience." This knuckling under to alleged racism was so expedient that in the 1921 elections the Republicans suffered their worst defeat in Virginia history. In 1953, on the other hand, a Republican from western Virginia named Ted Dalton managed to win the Republican nomination for governor and, to the dismay of the Republican regulars, made an all-out effort to win. Dalton canvassed the state, calling for repeal of the racist poll tax and an end to the circuit-court judge system, the governmental basis of Byrd's centralized control of Virginia's county governments (this destroyer of local democracy actually paraded himself in the Senate as a "Jeffersonian"). The racist response of Virginians was so great that Dalton, though losing, did the best any Republican candidate for governor had done this century, polling 45 percent of the vote. In 1969, another moderate, antiracist Republican named Linwood Holton made another all-out bid for the governorship and won it. In short, were it not for Republican collusion, there would have been no solid Democratic Virginia, no racist politics and no Byrd machine. If the substantial Republican parties of Tennessee, North Carolina and Virginia had not been collusive during this century, there would not have been, there could not have been, disenfranchisement and segregation of black people in those states. At this writing Governor Holton's chief enemies are the regulars of the Virginia Republican party and their ally in the White House, Richard Nixon, who in 1970 refused to endorse Governor Holton's Republican candidate for Senator and threw all his support to Harry Byrd, Jr., would-be heir to his father's broken Democratic machine.

But enough. There is no point, I believe, in multiplying examples of bipartisan politics in the states. The prevailing doctrine about powerless, competitive parties is completely false and untenable. The one, unswerving principle of state party organizations is to do all in their power to maintain themselves, for the organization is the source of political power to those who control the organization. The automatic and inevitable consequence of that principle of action is collusion between the two party machines in a state, for without it neither party organization could long survive.

In saying this, I realize that an important question might well arise in people's minds: why is this collusion not glaringly obvious to all? The answer to that question is itself supplied by collusive politics. When Senator Robert La Follette wrote in 1912 that machine politics is always bipartisan it *was* obvious to many people. Insurgent political action had made it obvious. By 1912 party organizations had been attacked for years by insurgents and third-party movements in almost half the states. Whenever such an attack was made, the two party organizations had had to close ranks in the full glare of the public light. They were betraying their own candidates so regularly, supporting opposition party candidates so openly, that it required no elaborate chain of reasoning to demonstrate to the citizenry that machine politics is bipartisan. Opposition to political machines exposed the collusion between them for all to see.

Without such opposition, however, collusion ceases to be obvious. What actors in the public arena will expose it? A Democrat beholden to a collusive machine party? A Republican beholden to a collusive machine party? A Democratic newspaper? A Republican newspaper? The American press is still far from total corruption, yet even to a good journalist "news" is what politicians say, and collusive politicians do not talk about collusion. In general, conventional political thought echoes routine political action. If a state's fake opposition party never raises a serious public issue, voters will eventually forget that state politics is even capable of generating such issues—and who remains in public life to jog their memories? If a state government does nothing for thirty years, voters will readily believe that state governments have lost their importance—and who will remind them that the Constitution grants and no one has yet taken away the states' constitutional quota of broad responsibility? When collusive parties are unchallenged, the routine results of collusion appear to be natural phenomena and not the result of political action at all. The aversion to Democrats of voters in normally Republican districts readily appears the result of "local tradition" or sociological "affinity" as long as the losing Democratic organization can prevent local Democrats from trying to win. Indeed, it is the explicit and constant endeavor of the party organizations to make the results of their deeds appear the consequence of social "forces" and "tendencies" and even Marxian "laws" of history. In short, when political activity is monopolized by collusive party organizations, collusion itself is well hidden. This is not to say that Americans do not suspect the existence of collusion. Millions of Americans harbor that suspicion, but it is confirmed neither by frequent acts of blatant collusion, for the party bosses are little challenged, nor by any eminent public men, for men who would do so are kept from eminence by the party organizations. So the suspicion festers in the hearts of many Americans as a private, embittering grievance and expresses itself, if at all, only in a refusal to vote.

One consequence of collusion in the states, however, is apparent to all: the corruption of state government in America. When Nixon proposed in 1971 a plan to return Federal tax revenues to the states, the standard argument against it was that state governments are too corrupt to be trusted, while the standard argument for it was that revenue-sharing would effect an improvement in government. The corruption itself was generally acknowledged. Yet there is nothing inherently corrupt about state governments. Before World War I, there was not a single genuine reform that did not originate with the government of a state—almost always a state where insurgents had broken the power of a state party organization. State governments today are exactly what state party organizations have made them, namely instruments bent to serve the interests of state party organizations. The matter, however, does not rest there. The corruption of state politics is not confined to the states alone. Self-serving, collusive state party organizations are the preponderant elements in the national party syndicates, and the union of these elements does not produce, by a sort of alchemical transmutation, national "handmaidens of democracy."

3.
The National
Democratic Party

E arly in 1910 President William Howard Taft found himself presiding over a rapidly splintering Republican party. In one Western state after another—led by Wisconsin and Oregon—Republican insurgents were overthrowing state party bosses and putting themselves at the head of a great national movement for reform. In the 1910 spring primaries President Taft, using all the enormous influence of his office, intervened massively on the side of regular Republicans in the rebellious states. The result was a massive failure: scarcely a single Taft-backed regular won a party primary in those states. With the 1912 election in the offing, Republican insurgents were a dire threat to Old Guard control of the national Republican party. Compromise with the insurgents, Taft and the party regulars decided, could only strengthen them further. In the winter of 1910–1911, therefore, national Republican leaders began sending out the word to local party bosses—no deals with insurgents and reformers, no efforts at harmony for the sake of winning. Instead, the party leaders made it clear that they had no intention of trying to win the Presidential election in 1912. Their sole purpose was to renominate Taft, whose popularity was nil. "We can't elect Taft," was the typical comment of a Kansas regular, "but we are going to hold on to the organization, and when we get back we will have it and not those damned insurgents." President Taft said the same thing himself: "I can stand defeat if we retain the regular Republican party as a nucleus for further conservative action."

The point is obvious: winning *Presidential* elections is no more the basic purpose of the national parties than winning local elections is the basic purpose of most state parties. Rather, it is control of the party. From the point of view of national party leaders, the only alternative to controlling the national party is total political disaster. Any President of the United States can, if he chooses, virtually destroy every state machine in his party. If every office is a potential menace to party organizations, no office is more menacing than the most powerful office of all. This is one of the most important single facts about national party politics in America. The would-be rulers of a national party, therefore, cannot afford to take chances. They must control Presidential nominations so tightly that no man they cannot trust in the Presidency has the smallest chance of gaining it. They must also prevent serious insurgent threats from arising, for even a serious, *failed* challenge to a national party's rulers can damage their rule; it will expose, if nothing else, that the purpose of a national party convention is not to "pick a winner" but to pick a candidate who serves party interests—even if he happens to be a loser.

National parties resemble state parties in this, that the prevailing doctrine about parties describes what party leaders are perpetually striving to avoid. Nominally, each national party is a coalition of independent state parties concerned with party success in state and local elections and with enjoying an independent voice in choosing a Presidential nominee. Were most state parties independent competitive parties, the national syndicate of state parties would be exceedingly difficult for any permanent ruling clique or oligarchy to control. In fact, however, the majority of state parties—and those of most of the largest states—are collusive, boss-controlled organizations, and it is they who control the great majority of delegates at national conventions. These boss-controlled units of the national party are united by a powerful common bond of interest—they wish, at the very least, to remain boss-controlled parties, and they share a common need to ensure that no one will win the Presidential nomination who will not protect their organization and its power.

The ruling bloc of the national Democratic party has been called many things in its long history: "The Dixie-Daley alliance"—James Reston of *The New York Times;* the "Boston-Austin axis"— Representative Richard Bolling, Democrat of Missouri; "The bosses and the bollweevils"—Senator Charles Goodell, Republican of New York. The various names point to the same thing: the permanent alliance between Northern state parties controlled by city machines and the Bourbon oligarchs who predominate in the Southern states. Together they control the national Democratic party, dictate the party's choice of Presidential nominees, determine the party's policies, decide the party's national issues. Under Democratic Presidents, their interests shape the policies of national administrations. In Democratic-controlled Congresses, they and their minions determine what legislation will pass.

How, it will be asked, can the Bourbons and the Northern city bosses be permanent allies when they are, for the most part, determined ideological adversaries? The Bourbons are obstructionists, apparently opposed to trade unions, to welfare legislation, to civil rights, to Federal programs, to Federal bureaucracies, to Federal infringement of the rights of states, opposed, in short, to virtually everything that the liberal wing of the party supports, and city machine politicians make up a large proportion of the Democratic party's professed liberals. In Congress it is notorious that big-city liberals propose precisely the kind of legislation which Bourbon legislators perpetually block. To all appearances the Northern city machines and the Southern Bourbons are not allies but antagonistic wings of a national party sharply divided along sectional and ideological lines.

The mutual enmity is taken for granted. It is the staple of most political writing. Yet what, after all, is the evidence of it? Chiefly this, that Southern Bourbons in Congress block the reforms which Northern Democrats propose. There is an obvious begged question, however, in this: the tacit assumption that most Northern and big-city Democrats actually want their reform proposals enacted and that the Bourbons by their independent power frustrate these genuine desires. There is, however, an infallible way to test this assumption: if we see the Northern liberal wing of the party trying to increase its power at the expense of the power of the Bourbons. Politically speaking, there is no other evidence. To say you want something done without trying to gain the power to do it is tantamount in politics to not wanting it done. What then does the Northern wing of the Democratic party do to increase its power at the expense of the Bourbon obstructionists? The answer to that question is: less than nothing. Virtually all the power which the Bourbons enjoy is freely given them by their alleged "antagonists" within the Democratic party.

The national power of the Southern Bourbons is principally lodged in Congress and derives from their well-known control over the Congressional committee structure. When Democrats control Congress (which they have done for all but four years between 1930 and 1972), Southern Bourbons are the chairmen of the most powerful committees and subcommittees. This gives them, to a remarkable extent, the power to shape legislation, to determine what issues will be aired before the public and to decide what abuses will be investigated and which ignored. It also gives them enormous power over their fellow legislators, since the Bourbons, by their control of the key committees, can grant or withhold favor to more lowly fellow legislators. They can help or hinder them in making a record with their constituents, and so their power breeds more power.

Yet the Bourbons since 1930 have been a distinct minority of the Democratic contingent in the House and Senate. How many Bourbon Congressmen are seated at any time would be difficult to determine precisely. Tom Wicker, in his useful book *JFK and LBJ*, observed that of some one hundred Southern and border-state Congressmen in 1961, only about sixty could be relied upon to vote openly against a major reform proposal. For the Senate the figure would be about fifteen. Since a party controls the House with a minimum of 218 members, whenever House Democrats are in control, the Bourbons are outnumbered by almost three to one. During the 1930s and the 1960s they have been outnumbered by as much as *four to one*. Yet they still hold on to their positions of power. Their durability is well illustrated by the career of William Colmer of Mississippi, a highly influential member of Congress and a Bourbon segregationist. In 1946, when Republicans gained control of the House, Colmer lost his seat on the powerful Rules Committee, a Bourbon-dominated committee which was able to gut Democratic reform legislation from 1937—when there were 331 House Democrats—until 1964. In 1948 he deserted the national ticket and campaigned for the "Dixiecrat" candidate for President, Strom Thurmond. Yet despite his apparent disloyalty, despite the fact that his political enemy, Harry Truman, was sitting in the White House, Colmer was given back his coveted seat by House Speaker Sam Rayburn. In 1960 Colmer once again deserted the national ticket and openly campaigned against John Kennedy. Once again, despite the presence of his alleged enemy in the White House, despite a non-Bourbon Democratic contingent of some two hundred Congressmen, Colmer retained all his privileges. In 1967 he became chairman of Rules. In short, given every reason and every opportunity to crush an influential Bourbon, the non-Bourbon Democratic majority elevated him to the highest of Congressional stations.

Similar examples abound in the Senate where Richard Russell of Georgia, leader of the Senate Bourbons, wielded enormous power until his death in 1971 regardless of how many non-Bourbon Democrats held seats. Russell's ascendancy was commonly attributed to his statesmanlike comportment and high repute, but this is childish. Senator Robert Kerr of Oklahoma, a powerful border-state Bourbon, was called the "uncrowned king" of the Senate in 1962, despite being a domineering bully and one of the most avaricious boodlers in Senate history. Kerr was king despite his unstatesmanlike comportment and, more importantly, despite a Democratic Senate contingent of sixty-five and a Northern liberal Democrat in the White House who was allegedly using his great office to "get this country moving again."

To the obvious question, how does the Bourbon minority get its power, the conventional answer is the seniority system, that curious dispensation by which Bourbons always end up on top and Northern reformers on the bottom of the legislative hierarchy. By virtue of seniority the most senior aspirant to a committee seat receives the committee assignment; the most senior members of a committee become the chairmen of the committee and its subcommittees. Since Southern states are one-party states, so the story goes, Bourbons are assured of reelection, accumulate seniority and eventually wind up in control as the "Establishment," the "club," the "ruling oligarchy" in Congress. Even if this were true—which it is not—it doesn't explain why the non-Bourbon majority doesn't scuttle the seniority system, since it is only a party arrangement which the majority is free to alter. The truth, however, is more graphic yet. Even under the seniority system, Bourbons would not enjoy the power they wield in Congress. Somebody else has to *give* it to them.

In the Senate, as former Senator Joseph Clark pointed out in *The Senate Establishment,* Bourbons maintain their power, not by strict seniority, but by ignoring seniority whenever it is inconvenient. It is a well-known fact in the Senate that Bourbons are put on the best committees as soon as possible while legislators who show signs of independence will have to wait for years, or forever. On the powerful Senate Appropriations Committee, there were in 1966 eight Bourbons among the eighteen Democrats, and they commanded most of the influential positions. On the other hand, according to Stephen Horn's *Unused Power: The Work of the Senate Committee on Appropriations,* only two members could be described as independent reformers, William Proxmire of Wisconsin and Ralph Yarborough of Texas. Yarborough had long been kept off the committee even though he was the senior Senator bidding for a seat, while three of the eight Bourbon members were given seats in their freshman year—Russell, Richard C. Byrd of West Virginia and A. Willis Robertson of Virginia. It is not seniority but its *discretionary* use which gives Bourbons their power in the Senate. This discretionary power is in the hands of the Democratic Steering Committee, which gives out the committee assignments every two years. Since this committee is controlled by Bourbons, the result, as Horn observes, "is perpetuation of party control in the Senate by the most senior members and especially the senior Southern conservatives." According to Clark, the Steering Committee made its assignments "in a manner which entrenched the control of the establishment over the committee structure of the Senate." The real key to Bourbon power in the Senate is Bourbon control of the Steering Committee. This gives them the power to bring into the Senate's ruling club every Bourbon Senator "almost with the taking of the seat of office," to quote William S. White.

In the House, the conventional workings of seniority would not alone give House Bourbons their power either. Allegedly the sixty-odd Bourbons derive their power from continual reelection in one-party districts. Yet most liberal Congressmen from New York, Chicago, Kansas City, Boston, Pittsburgh and other Democratic bastions also come from one-party districts and do not even have to face a primary fight. What is more, these delegates from the Democratic city machines—which is what they are—actually outnumber the Bourbon contingent, yet they are incomparably weaker. The magic of seniority fails to elevate them because they are usually put on the least important committees. If a freshman Democrat from Brooklyn is assigned to the Post Office Committee and a freshman Bourbon to a seat on Appropriations, the subsequent influence of these two legislators will scarcely bear comparison, despite their equal seniority.

In the House, the committee-assigning agency is the Democratic membership of the House Ways and Means Committee. Like its Senate counterpart it is controlled by Bourbons and chaired, at this writing, by Wilbur Mills of Arkansas.

This brings us to the heart of the matter. Bourbons do not control these assignment-making committees by accident. In a Democratic Congress the members of the Democratic Steering Committee are appointed by the Majority Leader of the Senate; the Democratic members of the House Ways and Means Committee by the Speaker of the House. Every two years, the Democratic Majority Leader turns over this crucial committee-assigning power to Bourbons and pro-Bourbons. Every two years the Democratic House Speaker has turned over the same power to Bourbon Congressmen, even when the opportunity to do otherwise is great. In 1955, when there were five Democratic vacancies on Ways and Means, Speaker Rayburn gave three seats to Bourbons. Every Democratic Majority Leader, every

Democratic Speaker of the House acquiesces in and connives at the biennial restoration of power to the Southern Bourbon minority. And who elects the Majority Leader in a Democratic Senate? The entire body of Democratic Senators, a caucus in which Bourbons are outnumbered by more than two to one. Who elects the Speaker in a Democratic Congress? Again, the Democratic caucus, in which Bourbons are outnumbered by at least three to one. The Bourbons do not "win" power. Every two years the Northern machine wing of the Democratic party unfailingly votes in secret caucus to *bestow* power on the Bourbon enemy. It is as simple as that. The city machines are, in the words of Representative Bolling, the Bourbons' "secret ally."

How many non-Bourbon legislators have sided with pro-Bourbon legislative leaders such as Rayburn, John McCormack and Carl Albert in the House, with Scott Lucas, Ernest McFarland, Alben Barkley, Lyndon Johnson and Mike Mansfield in the Senate? The answer is— as many as are needed to ensure the election of such leaders every two years. If the votes of Tammany-liberals are needed they are always forthcoming. When Sam Rayburn of Texas began, in 1937, his twenty-five-year career of protecting Bourbon power in the House, his chief supporters for the House Majority Leader post—the next step to Speaker—were Frank Hague of the Hudson County, New Jersey, machine, "Boss" Edward Kelly of the Chicago machine and the bosses of the Pittsburgh and Tammany gangs, whose Congressional fuglemen voted accordingly.

The only complication in this alliance is covering it up. In 1961, when Senator Clark moved that the Democratic caucus confirm the committee appointments made by Mike Mansfield, the new Majority Leader, Mansfield, blocked the move. It would mean, he told Clark, washing "our dirty Democratic linen in public." It certainly would. In 1971 the House Democratic oligarchy faced an independent bid for the Majority Leader post from Morris Udall of Arizona. His chief opponent was Hale Boggs of Louisiana, the Bourbon choice. In a straight man-to-man contest, the Northern Democrats would have had to vote for Udall, a fellow liberal, and Boggs would have lost. Miraculously, however, three other Northern Democrats jumped in as aspirants for the post. The Northern wing could then split its vote four ways and hand Boggs the victory. This sort of maneuver is invariably attributed to the inherent disunity of Northern liberals, but there is nothing inherent about it. When a reporter asked Udall what caused his defeat, his answer was simple: "the big-city boys." As Jim Folsom, the anti-Bourbon former governor of Alabama, once put it: "The Yankees and the Southerners give each other hell up in Congress and then they get in the back room over cocktails and say, well, we put it over on the folks again. It's been going on for a hundred years."

So far from being political antagonists, the Northern city machine parties and the Southern Bourbons are the closest of political allies, so close that no power has yet appeared in this Republic strong enough to divide them. The bond between them is like the bond between local chiefs within a state party: the survival of each would be imperiled if they did not make common cause. United they control the national Democratic party, united they control Presidential nominations, united they can ensure that Democratic administrations and Democratic Congresses do everything needed to protect their interests. United their power is enormous. Since 1932 the destiny of the American Republic has largely been in the hands of men who have earned their trust.

Any independent politician who seriously threatens either wing is invariably the enemy of both. When Senator Eugene McCarthy made his insurgent bid for the Democratic Presidential nomination in 1968, the two wings of the party smoothly united behind Hubert Humphrey. Northern liberals derided McCarthy for calling for a "weak Presidency" and repudiating the centralizing traditions of New Deal liberalism. Instead of supporting McCarthy for precisely those ideological reasons, the Bourbons supported Humphrey, the alleged epitome of that New Deal liberalism they profess to abhor. Bourbon principles had nothing to do with the matter, control of the party everything. McCarthy was a genuine anti-boss candidate, Humphrey a party hack.

Party politics is invariably circular: the ruling bloc of the national

Democratic party must perpetually use its power to protect that power. It is the abiding policy of the wings of the national syndicate to help each other retain local power. As will be seen in a later chapter, the Bourbons serve the interests of the Northern bosses precisely by blocking their reform proposals. On the other hand, it is the abiding policy of the Northern machine wing to protect Bourbon rule in the South, for if that rule collapsed, the Northern city machines would be doomed, hapless rumps of an uncontrolled national party. Whatever the Bourbons need to maintain their hegemony in Southern states, therefore, the Northern party bosses provide them. What makes this pro-Bourbon policy particularly urgent is that Bourbon control of Southern states has always been fragile.

The chief circumstance surrounding Bourbon rule is that most Southern states—Virginia, North Carolina and Tennessee excepted—have been one-party states, states whose local Republican parties have been so negligible they are not even useful as a fake opposition. This does not make these states easier to control than collusive two-party states, but just the contrary. Without the help of a sizable collusive opposition, it is impossible to maintain a party machine, for at least half the state's voters would form a permanent antimachine opposition within the state party, forcing such a machine to collapse in short order. In the one-party Southern states, as V. O. Key has repeatedly emphasized, Democratic parties are not organizations. They are not even parties in the usual sense of the word. They are, rather, neutral political arenas within which all of a state's political activity takes place, everyone being a Democrat. Bourbon power, therefore, does not rest on controlling a collusive party organization, but quite directly on the Bourbons' ability to command the machinery of government through control of the state legislature, the necessary number of county governments, the election machinery (which can be used to determine who is allowed to vote) and, ordinarily but far from always, the governorship.

In a word, the Southern Bourbons must do what Northern party organizations do not have to do—actually *win* elections (Democratic primaries, in practice). The opposition to Bourbon Democrats are non-Bourbon Democrats who have no inherent interest in putting up losers. Such being the case the permanent danger to the Northern Democratic party bosses is that Southern voters will elect Senators, Congressmen and delegates to national conventions who are accountable to the electorate. Political men who are thus accountable cannot be reliable servants of a party's interests, for politicians, like other men, cannot readily serve two masters, in this instance their party and their constituents. The Bourbons and their Northern allies must do all they can to see that Bourbon officeholders are not subject to continuous effective political opposition at home from the citizens themselves. The task is far from easy.

The foundation of Bourbon power, as V. O. Key has shown, is the so-called black-belt counties—plantation areas for the most part—where the black population is concentrated and the whites form a local minority. The white leaders in these counties have generally formed a compact obstructionist bloc, whose power, privilege and prosperity have depended on the disenfranchisement, suppression and exploitation of black people, on the economic dependency of the poor whites, on general ignorance and illiteracy, in a word, on securing a peculiarly wretched status quo. Their vote forms the Bourbons' voting bloc, the only real equivalent in America to a European *class* vote. The Bourbon voters in the black-belt counties, however, are a minority of the population in every Deep South state. Even apart from black people, they are a minority serving a minority interest—their own. This is why the conflict between the Bourbon whites and the whites of the so-called white counties (where the black population is small) has been the central political struggle in the history of every Southern state.

Starting with a determined voting bloc on their side, a bloc with financial resources to tap, with considerable social influence and, usually, strong overrepresentation in the state legislature, Bourbon politicians have considerable leverage but no hegemony. Reasonably united, the non-Bourbon voters can destroy Bourbon rule as they almost did between 1892 and 1896 under the leadership of the People's party, which, as C. Vann Woodward observed in *The New York Times Magazine* in 1972, "struggled hard to unite black and white voters in the South against the racist propaganda of the old party," namely the ruling Democrats. The central policy of the Bourbons is to make sure that such a union does not reoccur by splitting, suppressing and even terrorizing the majority opposition.

In doing this, the Bourbons cannot afford to take chances. To prevent another Populist revolt of poor white and black farmers after 1896, the Bourbons (with the indispensable help of the Northern Democrats and the Republican party) passed laws and constitutional amendments disenfranchising black and poor white voters, which had the obvious advantage of depriving their enemies of the ballot. After that, they were able to pass, in the following decades, an elaborate legal system of racial segregation that made cooperation between blacks and whites a virtual crime. They did this not because the white majority was virulently racist but because, politically speaking, it was not racist enough. Without a formal, institutionalized racial system, as the Bourbons well knew, racism in the white counties would languish as it is doing today with the repeal of Jim Crow laws and the reenfranchisement of black people. Woven by law into the fabric of daily life, kept alive and perpetually incited, however, racism has been used by the Bourbons as their chief instrument of political control. It has enabled them to attack dangerous anti-Bourbons as threats to "white supremacy" and the "Southern way of life"; it has enabled them to pretend that the only issue in state politics was whites versus blacks rather than Bourbons versus everybody else. It has enabled them, therefore, to split the anti-Bourbon ranks, to intimidate ambitious men, to raise racist mobs against insurgents and in general to render the majority of Southerners politically ineffectual for long periods of time. The relation between racism and politics is graphically demonstrated by the fact that racist propaganda has always been less virulent in the two-party Southern states of Virginia, North Carolina and Tennessee. Given collusion in those states, active racism was far less necessary.*

---

*The extension of two-party collusion to the Deep South through the expansion of boss-controlled Republican parties is the future, I suspect, of party politics in the changing South.

Yet not even institutionalized racism has been sufficient to ensure Bourbon control, not even combined with disenfranchisement, control of the electoral machinery, legislative overrepresentation and a virtual monopoly of political money. To render themselves safe from non-Bourbon opposition, the Southern oligarchs have had to ensure, as far as they could, that the white farmers remained in economic subjection as tenants and sharecroppers and thus open to brutal economic coercion whenever they showed signs of political independence. For years, too, the Bourbons had to keep out of Southern states all but the most corrupt racist trade unions for fear that Southern whites would transform their union locals from mere collective bargaining agents into centers of political activity. To minimize the conditions for free politics, the Bourbons have made sure that local self-government is conspicuously lacking in the South, where local control of schools and township government is virtually nonexistent—the county being, for the most part, the smallest unit of government in most Southern states. In short, the Bourbon oligarchs have had to encourage all that corrupts, divides and degrades, and to suppress all that might liberate in order to maintain their hegemony. That and that alone is the meaning of the Bourbons' so-called conservatism.

Bourbon devotion to political and constitutional principles is absolutely nonexistent. Allegedly opposed to the extension of Federal power, Southern Bourbon powers in Congress once granted without dissent the single largest accretion of executive power ever enacted in the American Congress, namely Roosevelt's National Industrial Recovery Act of 1933 (see chapter 6), an act so grossly unconstitutional that the Supreme Court struck it down unanimously. Allegedly opposed to bureaucracy, the Bourbons almost never expose, from their seats of Congressional power, the actual corruption of Federal bureaucracies, the only really effective act of genuine enmity. Even the Bourbons' "states' rights" posture is completely spurious, since the most important intervention in the political autonomy of states is the one which the Bourbons never resist: namely the continuous and decisive interference in state politics by the national party syndicates. They do not because, among other reasons, without the constant interference in Southern state politics of the Bourbons' Northern allies, the Bourbon oligarchy would collapse in a trice. So dependent are the Bourbons on help from the Democrats' Northern wing that they can be described, with little exaggeration, as native headmen set up by the Northern bosses to keep Southern states in line, as the British used to set up native headmen for the indirect rule of their colonies.

The help which the Northern Democratic bosses provide is easily summarized: it consists of whatever the Bourbons need to maintain their hegemony. Take, for example, the Bourbons' use of racism as an instrument of political control. What have the national Democratic bosses done about eliminating it from the South? The answer is they have done everything they dared to maintain it. In 1912, when the Jim Crow system was still so new the Bourbons feared that the North would not tolerate it, Josephus Daniels, a North Carolina editor and politician, announced publicly that "the Southerners" (i.e., the Bourbon oligarchy) were "seeking a national policy on the subject of the race question, for they know that short of a national policy they will never be secure." After appointing Daniels as his Secretary of the Navy, President Woodrow Wilson helped give the Bourbons what they sought: in 1913 his Administration instituted racial segregation among Federal employees in Washington, thus making racism a Federal institution as a first step toward making it that "national policy" which the Bourbons rightly regarded as the basis of their security. It remained a national policy under President Franklin Roosevelt, who made sure that his huge legislative majorities did nothing to impair Jim Crow in the South. To quote Basil Rauch's *History of the New Deal, 1933–1938,* a friendly account: "The President had never suggested or supported the numerous proposals for repeal of the poll tax by Federal enactment or any other reform *which might reduce the supremacy of the Bourbons*" (emphasis mine). Roosevelt, in fact, twice blocked anti-lynching bills that had passed the House with large majorities.

When the grass-roots civil-rights movement began growing in strength in 1960, John F. Kennedy promised civil-rights legislation but submitted none to Congress as long as he could hold out. Instead he appointed segregationist judges. In the famous confrontation with

Governor George Wallace at the University of Alabama in 1962, the whole scene was arranged so that Kennedy would look "good" in the North and Wallace, the diehard segregationist, would look "good" in the South. Why make a segregationist look good? Why not humiliate him absolutely and demonstrate to Southerners what they know today, that the segregationist cause was dead and its leaders impotent? Because that is exactly what Kennedy did not want to do, the beneficiaries of segregation being the Bourbon oligarchs whose power Kennedy, like every other organization Democrat, was dedicated to protect.

Only the 1965 Voting Rights Act stands out as a genuine act in favor of political equality for Southern black people, and that was forced out of President Johnson and the Democrats by overwhelming, angry and popular demand. As Evans and Novak point out in their biography of Johnson, the President thought he had successfully *put off* civil-rights agitation for years with the politically empty 1964 Civil Rights Act. He only acted in 1965 because it became impossible not to. The Democrats hardly deserve credit for a law which the citizenry forced from their unwilling hands and which they have since done their best not to enforce.

Apart from suppressing political equality in the South as long as they could, the Democratic bosses contribute to the oppression of Southern black people through the less visible mechanism of the Federal bureaucracy. Agriculture Department programs are routinely administered so that destitute black farmers can get no benefits. According to a 1969 *New York Times* story, the Farmers Home Administration deliberately "withheld from blacks" information about obtaining home loans. When Congress in 1965 passed an agricultural law which had the unforeseen effect of helping black farmers obtain crop support payments for the first time, Johnson's Secretary of Agriculture, Orville Freeman, scuttled the provision by administrative order. Such practices explain why four million rural black people are destitute in the South. It has been standard Federal policy since the beginning of the New Deal farm program to keep black farmers impoverished. The reason for doing so is not economic but political: the poor are easy to control.

Since economic dependence is the second key to Bourbon control, the national Democratic party has done what it could to keep Southern whites poor as well. Federal minimum wage rates are kept so low, for example, that they benefit few people except sweated Southern laborers, whose employers, conveniently, are given widespread exemptions from the minimum wage schedules. During the New Deal era, when a few reformers in the Department of Agriculture tried to help Southern sharecroppers, Roosevelt had them fired at once. He had no intention of making what he termed "a social revolution" in the South, by which he meant weakening the Bourbon hegemony, which would be a political revolution indeed.

The national Democratic party helps the Bourbon oligarchs in innumerable ways, but its single most important contribution to Bourbon rule in the South is granting Bourbons power in Congress, for it allows them to take care of themselves—to make sure the Federal bureaucracy acts in accordance with their wishes, to distribute legislative favor to local Bourbons while withholding it from anti-Bourbons and so on. Liberal Democratic administrations assist here, too, since they usually pour Federal patronage into Bourbon hands while withholding it from anti-Bourbons. According to Tom Wicker, President Kennedy "channeled ample patronage southward, provided defense contracts in profligate supply . . . and spread flattering attention on Southern leaders" who returned the favor by blocking the legislative program which Kennedy was allegedly trying to pass.

Kennedy, in fact, was assassinated in Dallas on a trip to succor the Bourbons, in this instance the Texas Bourbons, who were facing a monumental defeat at the hands of anti-Bourbon Democrats. The declared purpose of that trip was to bring the two warring factions together, but as Robert Sherrill observes in *The Accidental President,* this was the last thing the Texas insurgents wanted. A liberal President preaching unity would simply give the trimmers in the anti-Bourbon coalition their pretext for quitting the fight just when victory was at hand. Nor was this the first time Kennedy had come to the rescue of the ruling gang in the Texas party. As Sherrill points out, the Bourbons in 1961 were desperately in need of a governorship candidate to put up in 1962 against a tenacious anti-Bourbon Democratic challenger named Don Yarborough. To help the Texas Bourbons groom a candidate, Kennedy appointed an obscure Texas political operator named John Connally as his Secretary of the Navy. Burnished for one year with high office, branded with the liberal Kennedy label, Connally narrowly defeated Yarborough by fourteen thousand votes out of one million cast. Had Kennedy sent Yarborough as much as a telegram in his praise, Yarborough would probably have won, which is exactly why Kennedy did not. Kennedy died in Dallas doing what every Democratic President has been doing for a century: protecting the power of the Bourbons. He did leave a "legacy," but it certainly was not his—the legacy of the "Boston-Austin" axis, alias the national Democratic party. As the late Malcolm X put it with brutal concision: "A Dixiecrat is a Democrat and a Democrat is a Dixiecrat."

One more example, particularly grotesque, and I will have done with the two fictitious wings of the national Democratic syndicate. One of the standard myths about the national Democratic party is that the Northern wing needs Southern Bourbon support to elect presidents. Consequently, it is said, they are compelled to compromise with the Bourbons in all decisions of the national party. This is quite untrue, since, even if every Southern Bourbon fell, a Democratic Presidential candidate would still carry many Southern states. Truman, Kennedy and Johnson were all elected without benefit of a solid South; Roosevelt would have won all four of his elections had every Southern state gone Republican.

In 1948, the myth that Northern Democrats, to survive, must accommodate themselves to Southern Bourbons was publicly blown to smithereens. For various reasons, among them Henry Wallace's third-party candidacy and the influx of black people to Northern cities, the national Democratic bosses found it necessary to introduce the first civil-rights plank in the party's history. This act provoked what the Northern Democratic wing has always pretended to dread: the Southern Bourbons bolted the party. Not only did Bourbons sit out the 1948 elections, Strom Thurmond of South Carolina ran as an independent Dixiecrat candidate in several Southern states, a folly most

Bourbons were shrewd enough to avoid. Thurmond polled a paltry 22 percent of the vote and captured but two states on his own. Truman, of course, won the election. The alleged need to placate Bourbons had been exploded—it would seem—forever. The Northern wing of the party, now freed from its ancient bondage, could be expected in 1952 to propose an even stronger civil-rights plank and to nominate a devoted civil-rights advocate. Instead, party bosses did the opposite. For months before the 1952 convention, "party unity," "party harmony" and "reconciliation" were announced as the order of the day. According to the Democratic bosses, the Southern Bourbons had to be accommodated to prevent another split. As a result a negligible civil-rights plank was approved and the Presidential nominee, Adlai Stevenson of the Cook County machine, announced to Southern Bourbons that he was a "states'-righter" on the issue of civil and political liberty. In other words, having exposed for all time in 1948 that the Bourbon wing had no hold over the national party, the Democratic bosses, with impudent tongues of brass, turned around and pretended that they had more to fear from Bourbons than ever. The reason for the pretense was obvious. Had the Democrats passed a strong civil-rights plank and nominated a strong civil-rights candidate, the Southern Bourbons would have had one of two alternatives, each equally damaging. They could either bow to the national party bosses or make another embarrassingly ineffectual "bolt." Either way, the Northern party bosses would have exposed for the second time what in fact they were trying to conceal, the ancient political lie that they have to accommodate Southern Bourbons for fear of Bourbon power—which in fact is nonexistent.

To add one further grotesquerie: if the Northern Democrats had wished to reconcile Southerners, as opposed to Bourbons, they had in 1952 a particularly strong Southern Presidential aspirant on hand, Senator Estes Kefauver, who had won numerous Presidential primaries but who labored under one truly insuperable handicap: he was an independent public man.

Continuous interference by national party bosses in the politics of the states is necessary to keep all important states under control of the regulars and machines. Working through Congress and national administrations, the national party syndicate supplies patronage, campaign funds and abundant political favors to party regulars, while withholding them from party insurgents and independents. What is more, they see to it that party spokesmen do not raise any national issues that might strengthen anti-organization factions in the states. McCarthy's failed bid for the Presidential nomination, for example, left state Democratic organizations saddled with angry dissidents in several key states, New York, Connecticut and Massachusetts among them. Like any major insurgency, McCarthy's had revealed even to the purblind that there is nothing amiable about a "colorful" national convention when the party bosses are threatened. Had the national spokesmen for the Democratic party—operating in Congress under a Republican President—been a vocal and searching opposition giving voice to popular discontent, they would have strengthened the hand of the insurgents immeasurably. Instead the national Democratic party offered virtually no opposition to the Nixon Administration. Tacitly agreeing in 1970, for example, that "law and order" was the issue of the day and that the country was "turning to the right" (the standard party pretext for inaction), Democratic party hacks lapsed into virtual silence for four years after 1968.

For the national Democratic bosses, the perennial peril to party control has always loomed in the prairie states where Democratic bosses for decades settled for minority status by self-confinement to city dwellers and other readily manageable voters in those states. Until quite recently, further expansion of Western state parties would have brought into party ranks too many unruly independent farmers, the bane of party machines since before the Civil War. By keeping the Western parties small, on the other hand, many of them could be turned into dependent gangs of boodlers and tools of the Eastern machines as the Democratic party has been for much of this century in Kansas, Nebraska, Wisconsin, Minnesota, Michigan, Oregon, Iowa, South Dakota and North Dakota. What the ruling Democratic bosses have done to keep them that way is well illustrated by two momentous actions of the national Democratic party: the Al Smith candidacy of 1928 and Roosevelt's patronage policies during the New Deal.

From around 1904, when the Democrats nominated Judge Alton B. Parker of New York for the Presidency, the party leaders pursued an active policy of retreating from the unruly Western states, where the Democrats had temporarily gained popularity through the candidacy of William Jennings Bryan of Nebraska in 1896 and 1900. One example of what the Democrats did to kill their own support in the West deserves passing mention here for sheer low comedy. In the mountain states, Mormons had for a long time been staunch Democratic voters. As a reward for their loyalty, the national party in 1904 made the "extermination of polygamy" a plank of the party platform. This was not only whipping a very dead horse, it drove Mormons, understandably enough, out of the party ranks. To make sure the numerous Idaho Mormons deserted the Democrats as their coreligionists in Utah were doing, the Idaho party boss included the elimination of polygamy in the state party platform, thereby winning the general contempt of Idaho voters and the permanent loss of Mormon votes. To nail down the coffin on the Idaho Democratic party, the party's leaders persisted in making the moral turpitude of Mormons their sole public issue in *two* more state election campaigns.

After 1918, when Western farmers began rebelling anew against state party machines under the auspices of the Nonpartisan League, an organization of independent voters, state Democratic parties turned their back so completely on the turbulent electorate of these states that by the early 1920s third-party NPL candidates had run ahead of the Democrats in South Dakota, Washington, Minnesota, Wisconsin and Idaho. By 1924, the Democratic party, even as a national party, could scarcely be called a major party west of the Mississippi. That year the Democrats' Presidential candidate, John W. Davis of New York, managed to poll a mere 16.5 percent of the vote in Iowa, 10.2 percent of the vote in Washington, 6.2 percent of the vote in California, 7 percent in North Dakota and 6.8 percent in Minnesota—true vegetarian candidate totals. In these and four other Western states, Senator La Follette, running as an independent Republican, ran ahead of the Democratic nominee. By 1928, however, the farm depression had deepened still further and the Republicans' refusal to help had become glaringly apparent to farm voters. Had the Democrats wished to recoup their fortunes in the West, the last person they would have nominated was the man they nominated unanimously, namely Al Smith, a Catholic, an "ethnic," a Tammany protégé and a "wet" on the Prohibition issue.

The strategy behind Smith's nomination can be described as an all-out Democratic machine effort to win over ethnic voters in the big cities *by virtue of* repelling voters in the West, thus killing two birds with one stone. What dictated the strategy was the fact that the Democrats, by turning their backs on the West, needed a counter-weight of safe voters in the East to remain a credible national party. Until 1928, the Democrats' urban vote had not been large enough for this, since Republican candidates for President generally outpolled Democratic candidates in the largest cities, no matter how city dwellers voted in collusive local elections. What is more, La Follette himself had made alarming inroads into the Democratic city vote in certain cities, Cleveland and Pittsburgh among them.

Simply as an emblematic figure, Smith, the Tammany Irish Catholic, was a perfect choice to win over ethnic voters and repel the Western electorate, but the Democratic bosses were not depending on emblems alone. During his campaign for the Presidency, Smith actually went out of his way not to appeal to the desperate, deserted farmers. As his admiring biographer, Matthew Josephson, observes, Smith "seemed not to be extending himself to woo western and southern provincials." That is putting it mildly. In the West, Smith's campaign manager, John J. Raskob, went one giant step further. According to Josephson, he "did not focus the party's efforts on the issues of interest to that section, but concentrated instead on Prohibition"—a strategy on a par with exterminating polygamy in Idaho. Smith's own efforts to antagonize rural voters even extended to his famous Tammany brown derby, whose net effect in rural areas was summed up by Sam Rayburn: "I never thought the brown derby helped."

Exacerbating every rural prejudice while ignoring every serious rural issue, however, was precisely the means which the Democrats devised to get out a large immigrant vote, most importantly the votes

of immigrants who had never voted before. It allowed Smith's followers to bring back tales of rural Protestant bigotry to the Eastern cities
and hold up Smith before ethnic voters as a martyr to American
"nativism." The legend of Smith's martyrdom is now embalmed in our
history books along with a host of other party lies. Yet had Smith and
the Democratic bosses discussed the issues of interest to rural voters,
does anyone doubt for a moment that the "bigot vote" would have
drastically shrunk? Thanks to the self-serving calculations of a national party machine, distrust, dislike and division between rural
Protestants and urban ethnic voters were immeasurably deepened and
sharpened. In truth, the Smith campaign can well be described as a
massive and partially successful effort to turn the entire Republic into
two separate party bastions on the model of an Eastern state. The
deliberate selectivity of Smith's appeal to the voters is strikingly
revealed by the results in Indiana. In that state, Smith actually did less
well than Davis had done in 1924, while urban Indiana Catholics
gave the majority of their votes to a Democratic Presidential candidate
for the first time in decades.

The most direct and concerted effort to keep minority Democratic
parties safe losing parties was made, however, by Franklin Roosevelt. As
I said before, quoting Professor Key, the repudiation of Republicans in
the West "certainly did not intensify efforts by the professionals to capture state governments." That is only part of the story, for in fact the
"professionals" had to make a particularly strong effort to lose. During
the 1920s the Democratic parties in the extreme Republican
strongholds of Iowa, Kansas, Maine, Michigan, New Hampshire, New
Jersey, North Dakota, South Dakota, Vermont and Wisconsin held on
the average only 16 percent of the seats in the lower house of the state
legislatures (the figures are Key's). Then came the Depression, and
Republican voters began casting their votes for Democratic legislative
candidates, whoever they happened to be. By 1934, the Democrats in
the ten Republican strongholds held 42 percent of the legislative seats,
a historic, if unwanted, resurgence. Little boodle parties suddenly
found themselves saddled with flocks of freshmen legislators and all
sorts of unwanted ambitions that threatened the regulars' control. Had

Roosevelt wished to help the newcomers and overthrow the boodlers, he could have done so readily. All he had to do was endow them with the patronage, favor and prestige which he had in unique abundance at the time. Instead, Roosevelt siphoned almost all New Deal patronage into the hands of the old losing boodlers. A 1935 *Fortune* article supplied a list of state Democratic leaders who had control of Roosevelt's patronage: in South Dakota, an assistant postmaster general; in Kansas, a commissioner of Internal Revenue; in Nebraska, a lobbyist; in California, the old losing gang; in Michigan, a national committeeman; in Vermont, a national committeeman; in Connecticut, Senator Augustus Lonergan, anti–New Deal boss of the state party—not the only anti-reform boss Roosevelt patronized. In short, the Roosevelt Administration made a massive effort to help losing party bosses maintain control of their parties in the face of unwanted electoral success. The results were soon felt at the polls. In 1936, when Roosevelt and the national Democratic party stood at the very peak of popular success, Democratic representation in the ten Republican bastions fell off to 38 percent. Two years later it was down to 20 percent or normal, and the local party bosses were once more out of danger. Keeping party politics "normal" in this way is one reason state parties have changed so little since the turn of the century.

In recent years the Democratic bosses' fear of winning in the West is no longer as acute as it once was—that millions of Western farmers have been driven from the land has much to do with this. It is still strong enough, however, to have helped dictate John F. Kennedy's nomination in 1960, a nomination with very close parallels to Smith's earlier candidacy. The immediate background to Kennedy's nomination was, on the one hand, the loss of the Catholic voters in the East and, on the other, another sudden accession of voters and elected officials in the unreliable West. As Theodore White wrote in *The Making of the President 1960*, the "drift of Catholics away from Democratic leadership was all through the 1950s the chief concern of Democratic party leadership. . . . How to bring the Catholics back . . . this had haunted Democrats ever since 1952." The obvious way, of course, is to nominate a Catholic for President. In the late 1950s, too, Western voters had begun to elect Democratic Senators, Congressmen and state legislators in alarming numbers—alarming, for example, to Speaker Rayburn, who ruefully remarked of the 1958 Democratic victors, "They'll be hard to handle." That Kennedy was not only a Catholic but a man from Boston machine politics made his candidacy doubly attractive to the bosses.

Nominating Kennedy took a fairly regular course. He had been groomed by party bosses for high office since as early as 1956, when his name was submitted for the Vice-Presidential nomination. Shortly after that, the Senate oligarchy gave him a coveted seat on the Foreign Relations Committee, passing over the senior aspirant, Senator Kefauver. At the opening of Kennedy's nomination campaign he was hailed as a fresh young independent, but to make sure party regulars were not confused by this, a few party bosses made it known publicly that they, too, approved of Kennedy. John Bailey of Connecticut, William Green of the Philadelphia machine, two New York City county bosses and the Ohio organization came out early for Kennedy. Opposition to Kennedy was token; his only real competitor was Hubert Humphrey, whom the bosses crippled by providing him with no money (in 1960 the party bosses had no wish to nominate any prairie state Senator, even a toadeater like Humphrey). White insists in his book that Kennedy won the nomination entirely through his own prowess. Kennedy's primary victory in West Virginia, according to White, enabled him to "club" the party bosses into submission. This is totally unfounded. Kefauver had won numerous primaries in 1952, but despite that the bosses clubbed *him* into submission. Party bosses always hail a primary victory as "decisive" when it confirms their previous decision. Otherwise it is held to be the nonsignificant result of "purely local factors."

Once given the nomination, Kennedy proceeded to inject the Catholic issue into the campaign, beginning on September 12, 1960, and party spokesmen kept it there for the duration, this being the best way to bring out the Catholic vote. Meanwhile in the West, the last lingering home of isolationist sentiment, Kennedy told the voters about America's slipping "prestige" in the world—the major "theme" of his campaign. The results of these efforts were predictable. Kennedy, in White's words, "brought back to the national ticket most of the Catholic Democrats who twice preferred Eisenhower." He and the Democrats were swamped in the Western states. Republicans regained control of seven state legislatures and one house of six others. They regained twenty-nine Congressional seats (while losing seven), chiefly in the West. Back to "normalcy," as President Harding once said.

After the 1968 Democratic national convention, however, the party oligarchy faced an uncommonly complicated task in restoring normalcy. The nomination of a hated President's stooge, Hubert Humphrey, had revealed with great clarity that when the bosses' power is threatened by insurgency, public opinion means nothing, the great issues of war and peace mean nothing, picking a winner means nothing, common decency toward fellow Democrats means nothing. In short, it brutally exposed before a national audience what the party bosses dread to see exposed—the real nature of party politics. The Democratic oligarchy had only one recourse for 1972: it had to demonstrate to the public that boss control of the national party was a thing of the past. Needless to say, the demonstration has been entirely spurious. Had the party bosses wished to overthrow themselves, they could have nominated Senator McCarthy in 1968 and saved themselves much trouble.

The demonstration that the days of boss rule were over (an announcement which party apologists have been making periodically for generations) was carried out, essentially, on three fronts. Firstly, since the need for internal party reform was made glaringly apparent by the 1968 convention, the party oligarchy set up a reform commission ostensibly to open the party and destroy their own power. Secondly, to lessen the dangers of openness the party leaders then spent the next four years trying to defeat, discourage and drive from politics the dissidents left over from the McCarthy campaign, which had, for a brief moment, turned liberals into insurgents. They did this, as I said, partly by dumping elections whenever victory might have strengthened or heartened insurgents—in Connecticut, for example—and partly by disappearing as a national opposition to the Nixon Administration.

Coupled with the effort to reduce the dissident cohorts in the party (and to dismantle the organized peace movement), the party oligarchs groomed—indeed invented—a safe, fake, anti-boss candidate to sop up the support of those who still remained to be appeased. This was Senator George McGovern, who had shamelessly demonstrated his willingness to serve the interests of the party oligarchs in 1968 by entering the race for the Presidential nomination after Senator Robert Kennedy was assassinated in order to keep Kennedy delegate votes from McCarthy. At the time, McGovern was described as a stalking horse for Edward Kennedy, which was an explanation humiliating enough but kinder than the truth, that he was a stalking horse for the party oligarchy. To establish McGovern's national reputation as an anti-boss candidate, the party leaders made him head of their reform commission, which indicates how well they trusted him; men do not give weapons to their enemies.

McGovern did not betray their trust. His commission recommended the abolition of some genuinely shabby party tricks, such as the practice in some states of picking convention delegates two to four years before the convention. However, his most heralded proposal— "near-revolutionary," *The New York Times* called it—was not even a minor improvement. This was the requirement that state delegations to the Democratic convention be comprised of women, blacks, Chicanos and young people in proportion to their ratios in the state population. This proposal was based on the fatuous notion that females, blacks, the young, et al., are inherently independent of boss control, apparently through genetic factors. Since females have been district co-leaders in the worst machine counties, since black and Mexican-American ward heelers have been prominent in machine politics for generations, since young careerists have never been lacking in party circles, only a Tammany liberal could call this a reform. In fact it is a reform which will probably make insurgency more difficult in the future. It is a great deal easier for party organizations to fill these nice numerical quotas than it would be for a genuine insurgent, strapped for funds, living off the land, scraping up active supporters whenever he can find them. One reason Mayor Daley "defied" the quotas in the

1972 Illinois primaries was that he could have conformed to them with ease, thereby exposing their fraudulence.

During his campaign for the nomination, McGovern gave equally decisive evidence of his usefulness to the bosses. Although his campaign organization was on the ground in thousands of local districts, McGovern made a determined effort not to step on the toes of a single local boss or give serious help to a genuine local insurgent except where it was unavoidable. Claiming to overthrow the bosses, the McGovern organization protected them where they live and where they matter, namely at home. Politically speaking, his grass-roots organization hardly bent a blade of grass.

Having invented a fake, anti-boss candidate to represent the dissident element among Democratic voters, the party oligarchy, significantly, put no obstacles in McGovern's path. They actually smoothed his way as best they could. Until his nomination was virtually secured, McGovern faced no serious public criticism, especially of the kind that would have alienated those supporters whom the oligarchs wanted him to win. The press did not point out, for example, that McGovern had voted in 1970 against reform of the seniority system in the Senate, that the party bosses themselves had appointed him to the reform commission, that the quota system was a farce, that his economic programs were a financial mess (they were actually praised for months for their masterful detail), that his Senate record was that of a dimly conventional liberal, that hurting a dangerous insurgent in 1968 was scarcely evidence of political independence. To their real enemies, the oligarchs are not so kind. The Democratic leaders also made sure that McGovern had no serious competition for the dissident vote. Two Presidential aspirants—Fred Harris of Oklahoma and Harold Hughes of Iowa—whom the bosses might have used to hurt McGovern in the primaries (a routine political maneuver) found campaign funds so short their campaigns died on their doorsteps.

Whether the party oligarchs expected McGovern to do as well as he did in the primaries cannot be known for certain. It is possible that they originally envisioned a Muskie-McGovern ticket, but when Senator Edmund Muskie fell apart, the party leaders made no effort to stitch him back together. On the contrary, they allowed two of their most faithful servants, the trade unions (see chapter 10) and Hubert Humphrey, to hurt and eventually kill the Muskie candidacy, the unions by refusing to endorse or help him, Humphrey by contesting with Muskie for much the same primary vote. The bosses' real friendship for McGovern, the alleged anti-boss candidate, was sharply revealed when the nomination campaign came down to a two-man race between Humphrey and McGovern. At that point, the party oligarchs stopped Humphrey in his tracks. As the symbol and embodiment of the "old politics" of 1968, the bosses' former standard-bearer was the last person the oligarchs wanted to see nominated. As a result, Humphrey's campaign funds, sufficient to hurt Muskie, abruptly dried up—for the California primaries he woefully lacked money, for the New York primaries he had none—and his old allies, the trade-union bureaucrats, deserted him; in Michigan, they refused even to put up a Humphrey poster. In New Jersey and New York, the party regulars wanted no part of Humphrey, the veteran regular. The reason is obvious. Only McGovern's nomination could be truly heralded—and it was heralded ad nauseam—as the final revolutionary overthrow of the bosses. That, after all, was the point of the whole exercise. If Kennedy's candidacy was reminiscent of Al Smith's, McGovern's nomination echoed that of William Jennings Bryan, who temporarily overthrew the Democratic oligarchy in 1896 by prior arrangement with the Democratic oligarchy, who desperately needed an apparently insurgent candidate to win over the Populist party, which was toppling the Bourbon hegemony. The McGovern nomination also resembled the 1964 nomination of Senator Barry Goldwater, who "captured" the Republican party by prior consent of the allegedly disorganized Republican bosses.

Just because they nominate a candidate does not mean that the party bosses want him to win. Far from it. If the Democratic bosses allowed McGovern the nomination because they urgently needed a fake rebel to lead an ostensibly reformed party, they had compelling reasons, nonetheless, to secure his election defeat. A victory, even for a fake insurgent like McGovern, could only make genuine insurgency more promising to many and encourage yet more newcomers to enter active politics. On the other hand, a defeat, especially a severe one, would strengthen the party oligarchy considerably. Newcomers to active politics would be crushed with disappointment, branded as losers and quickly returned to private life. The more stubborn or high-ranking among them could be readily "purged" in a post-election "search for scapegoats," a vindictive activity that can be carried out quite openly, however, since it confirms the myth that winning means everything to the party professionals. In the aftermath of defeat, the Democratic bosses would be able to claim that it is they, the loyal "regulars" (whose true hallmark is disloyalty to the party label), and not a band of "amateurs" and "ideologues," who alone know how to win elections. By a defeat in 1972 the Democratic party bosses would be able to efface from memory the all-important fact that it was they, not the "amateurs," who courted defeat four years before in order to stymie an uprising of "amateurs." Of the soundness of these calculations the Democratic bosses had ample evidence, most recently the fact that the national Republican organization became more cohesive than it had been in some years after it helped the Democrats crush Goldwater in 1964.

The Democrats' effort to defeat McGovern, conspicuously absent in the contest for the Presidential nomination, was obvious enough in the election campaign. From Bridgeport, Connecticut, to Cook County, Illinois, and beyond, virtually every urban machine "sat out the election" or "cut the top of the ticket." This involved such standard organization practices as not getting out the straight-ticket voters, diverting Presidential campaign funds into local organization coffers, keeping McGovern speakers off local platforms and McGovern's name off local posters, confirming and amplifying whatever suspicions the local electorate might harbor against the candidate. A Cook County ward-heeler spoke for Democratic ward-heelers throughout the country when he told an American Broadcasting Company interviewer during the campaign that McGovern is "gonna lose because we're gonna make sure he's gonna lose."

The elected servants of the party syndicate played their part, too, in

the dump. Democratic Senators and Congressmen who had earned rep-
utations as liberals, as reformers, as opponents of the Vietnam War kept
virtually silent throughout the campaign. This was an essential part of
the Democratic effort to isolate McGovern and make him appear an
extremist. As if to prove that McGovern's attack on Pentagon expenditures was grossly irresponsible, Democratic legislators who had themselves opposed Pentagon spending from 1968 to 1971 suddenly
switched sides and, in the middle of the campaign, voted overwhelmingly and without debate for an enormous defense appropriation. To
show that McGovern's views on Vietnam were extreme, a Mayor's
Conference which had called for immediate withdrawal in 1971 also
switched sides in 1972 and voted, under Mayor Daley's leadership, to
endorse President Nixon's Vietnam policies. Despite all this, the Nixon
Administration was ridden with enough scandals in 1972 to sink any
incumbent, but here, too, the Democratic minions in Congress came to
Nixon's rescue. When a journalist, Jack Anderson, disclosed that the
Administration had taken an enormous bribe from the International
Telephone and Telegraph Corporation, Senate Democrats dropped the
investigation as fast as they could. When it was discovered that high-
ranking Republican officials had ordered the wiretapping of Democratic
headquarters in Washington, D.C., Congressional Democrats decided
not to investigate at all on the grounds that the issue was already before
the courts, thereby showing a nicety of legal scruple which party politicians never manifest when they are trying to win elections. An
Administration wheat-sale scandal and a milk-pricing scandal were similarly shunted out of sight by the obliging Democrats. During the campaign Democratic legislators were so openly helpful to the Republican
President that the press began speaking of Nixon's "mastery" of
Congress, something which had hitherto gone unnoticed for the plain
reason that it never existed until the Democrats in Congress conjured it
up for the campaign.

Because the Democratic bosses were determined to defeat their own
candidate, their faithful allies, the AFL-CIO chieftains, conspicuously
refused to endorse Senator McGovern, thereby denying him millions
in money and manpower. Since McGovern was the first Democratic

Presidential candidate the AFL-CIO had ever refused to endorse, it also played a vital part in making the Democratic nominee appear an extremist, someone beyond the bounds of responsible politics. Lastly, the Democratic oligarchy employed the most venerable of all means for dumping elections: charging "dissension" in their candidate's campaign entourage. The merit of this charge is its self-proving nature. Should a high-ranking traitor in the nominee's circle—in this case former Democratic National Chairman Larry O'Brien—complain of "dissension," the very complaint "proves" that dissension exists, with the clear implication that the candidate is an incompetent bumbler. This was something nobody had noticed during McGovern's nomination campaign when the party bosses allegedly cowered in fear of his "smooth-running" organization.

Without the party oligarchy to shield him from the light, Senator McGovern was mercilessly exposed for what he was—a poltroon, a hypocrite, a sheep in plastic wolf's clothing. "A 'hack' himself," as his friend and biographer Robert Sam Anson rightly observed, McGovern, when he saw the party bosses run away from him, could think of nothing better than hot pursuit. Were he a different kind of man, the bosses, of course, would not have nominated him. On the organization level, McGovern fired or sidetracked numerous followers whom local party bosses deemed persona non grata. He routinely assigned followers from one state to run his campaign in another, thereby preventing potential insurgents from building a local power base during the course of his campaign. Whatever the local Democratic satraps ordered, McGovern carried out; whatever harmed them he remedied. Under the slightest pressure from his fellow Democrats there was scarcely a reform proposal he did not retract, a firm affirmation he did not renege on from the moment when, after promising "1,000 percent" support of his running mate Senator Thomas Eagleton, he cut the ground from under Eagleton's feet. Having laid claim to unstained "sincerity," McGovern gave clear signs of boundless hypocrisy which he proceeded to confirm day after day. When he told the Governor's Conference in September 1972 not to worry about his program because Congress would dispose of it anyway, he virtually announced in public that his program was wind. Behind this suicidal expediency lay McGovern's sole notion of election strategy: the effort to prove to the party bosses that even if he, a fake insurgent, were elected President he was willing and able to betray his followers, to scotch insurgency, to jettison his reforms and to give the party machine every aid and sustenance, in a word, that he would be a President whom the oligarchy could trust and hence a nominee whom they could afford to see elected. No other Presidential candidate was ever so willing to destroy his own public reputation out of deference to the power of the party bosses as the candidate whom the bosses had paraded before the public as the man who had destroyed their power.

Blessed with an exposed poltroon for an opponent, two national parties for allies and the inestimable boon of four years of non-opposition (which made a mean-spirited blackguard appear a "statesman," a man of uncertain temper appear the coolest of helmsmen, a scandal-ridden Administration appear the fount of law and order), President Nixon won a curious kind of landslide victory. Generated neither by hope in the victor's future deeds nor gratitude for his past ones, the landslide election brought out the smallest percentage of Presidential voters since 1948. Since Democrats, despite the landslide, gained two Senate seats, captured seven of eleven governorships and lost a negligible thirteen seats in the House almost entirely through reapportionment (i.e., collusion at the state level), the 1972 elections demonstrated how efficiently a party oligarchy can "cut the top of the ticket" and how much power it wields.

One final point: it might well be asked why Taft and Nixon, Kennedy and Wilson intervened on the side of the party regulars and oligarchs, why Roosevelt protected losing Democratic bosses in so many states as well as Bourbon obstructionists in the South, and, more generally, why any President of the United States, once elected, does not turn against the party bosses who nominated him. There is no theoretical answer to this question. It is a fact that they have not done so and the practical reason is obvious. Had any of these Presidents ever shown antagonism to party power, or favor to the kinds of reforms and policies that would weaken party power, the party bosses would not have nominated them in the first place. The whole purpose of party organizations at every political level is to sift out, sidetrack and eliminate men of independent political ambition, men whom the party bosses cannot trust. Every act of every party organization is taken in order to secure this very capacity to eliminate the unreliable and to reward the faithful. It should hardly be surprising, therefore, that, given party organization control over politics, independent men rarely sit in the higher seats of public trust, least of all in the Presidency.

What the private thoughts of party politicians are is open only to speculation. Doubtless every loyal party servant believes to some degree or other in the virtues of the party system. Absolute cynicism is rare, and men are inclined to overlook the failings of that which has raised them to eminence. Mayor Daley, who knows as much about the corruptions of party politics as any man alive, reportedly defends the party system because it allows poor boys such as he was to achieve power and prominence. Other party politicians doubtless invent other spurious apologia for the party system they serve, but whether they believe them or not is susceptible to no proof. We can judge the character of public men only by what they actually do; we do not judge their actions by presumptions about their character. It is true, nonetheless, that any American President *might* betray the party organizations. This is exactly why party bosses must try ceaselessly to control Presidential nominations and party nominations all the way down the line. I said this, of course, at the outset, for like party politics itself, every account of party politics describes a circle.

4.
The National Republican Party

In their aims and intentions the rulers of the national Republican party differ not at all from those of the Democratic party. Yet the two major parties are very different nonetheless. Whereas the geographical wings of the Democratic party always act in unison, the sectional split in Republican ranks—the split between East and West—has been on occasion a genuine threat to regular control of the national party syndicate. Moreover, that split reflected in the past some of the most fundamental issues in modern American history, the issue of the trusts, for example, with Western Republicans opposing trusts and monopolies and Eastern Republican bosses conspicuously fostering them. Decisive conflicts of this kind were fought out almost entirely within the Republican party, whereas unlike that party, the Democratic machine rarely has dangerous issues permanently forced upon it.

The Democrats, for the most part, can turn issues on and off like tap water according to changing organization needs. Between 1896 and 1900, as I said, the Democratic party, forced to save the Southern Bourbons from the Populist party, transformed itself overnight into the party of William Jennings Bryan and "agrarian radicalism." In 1904 the same leaders who had nominated Bryan for the Presidency turned around and nominated a New York corporation lawyer, the antithesis of agrarian radicalism. In 1924, to take another example of a Democratic *volte-face,* agrarian Democrats—Protestant, anti-Tammany, anti-city—appeared to be making, according to conventional history books, a "last-ditch stand" against the Northern urban wing of the party at a "strife-torn" national convention. Yet a mere two years later, the word was out that the Tammany Catholic Al Smith would be the nominee for 1928, a nomination which he won without a contest. The "bitter" representatives of agrarian unrest, seemingly so potent in 1924, had disappeared without a trace in 1928. That is because agrarian interests had not attended the national convention in 1924, a Democratic convention being chiefly—1972 excepted—a conclave of party bosses and their henchmen representing themselves.

The Republican party is not quite so self-contained a syndicate of bosses, regulars and professionals. At times it has had to give voice to issues of gravest importance even when they threatened the regulars' control of the national party. Republican party bosses, however, have not risked their power through an altruistic wish to represent public sentiment. Far from it. Republican regulars, as I said, deliberately dumped the 1912 election—the surest way not to represent public sentiment—in order to "hold on to the organization . . . and not those damned insurgents." The reason divisive issues have been forced upon the Republican party, the reason that that party differs even now from the Democratic party, is due chiefly to its geographical spread.

Outside the South and the Border states, the Democratic party, as a winning party, appears on the map as a series of *pinpoints.* Its bastions are, for the most part, concentrated urban masses. Republican state parties, in contrast, are spread out over most Northern states. The political significance of this is great. Republican state parties must encompass the citizens of scores of counties and hundreds of townships, each with its own local politics and civic leaders, political activists and officeholders. Since the Republican party is the winning party in these areas, the politically active, influential citizens are chiefly Republicans and inevitably take part in local party activities.

No such problem arises for parties which predominate in cities, since cities lack local governments and local political institutions. The mayor of New York is a local official only in the sense that almost eight million New Yorkers enjoy no government more local than his. The city dweller is a member of an almost undifferentiated political mass. If he is politically inclined, his means of distinguishing himself outside party ranks are exceedingly limited. If he enters party ranks he enters as a supplicant bidding for favor. The members of a local Democratic club in a large city tend to be conspicuously *humble* party workers at best and petty boodlers at worst. Independent citizens, influential in their own right, are few.

Forced by its geographical extension to accommodate these active local citizens, Republican state parties in the North are saddled with party members other than workers and boodlers, namely a *rank and file* of active, influential citizens interested in the Republican party for reasons other than favors. Confined to city bastions, on the other hand, the Democrats in the North have no substantial rank and file of citizens permanently attached to the organization. Senator McCarthy's 1968 insurgency was dangerous, even in defeat, precisely because it turned so many liberal voters into local party activists. With some important local exceptions—certain New York City districts, for one; several university towns, for another—the chief permanent outriggers of the Democratic party organization are not citizens, but trade-union officials, "ethnic spokesmen" virtually appointed by the party organization, and, frequently, the Catholic Church hierarchy. This, as White has rightly pointed out in his account of the 1960 elections, is why the "Republican party is completely different from the Democratic party." Whereas the Democrats are chiefly party "professionals," the Republican party, in his words, consists of "an organization wing" and a restive "citizens' wing."

Burdened with an extensive rank and file of citizens external to the party organization, Republican regulars have been forced to provide them with something equally external to organization politics: some satisfying, unifying and more or less permanent political *principle*. This is because the only thing that can coalesce a plurality of citizens, in contrast to mere clubhouse boodlers, is a principle which they all agree to share. Moreover, the more varied and independent are the members of a state party's rank and file—the more they begin to approximate a coalition of free citizens—the more basic the unifying principles must be. Historically, the only political principles that have successfully united an extensive and varied plurality of citizens in this Republic have derived from the Republic itself. They have been, and perhaps must be, principles which appear, at least, to square with the preservation and enhancement of self-government, with equality of privilege and equality of right. This has certainly been the case with the Republican party's principles. Republican bosses, however, have no more interest in acting upon republican principle than the Democratic machine does. They may support the principle of equal privilege and equal opportunity, but it is the interest of party organizations, as will be seen, to dispense special privilege; they may speak for representative institutions, but party power consists precisely in controlling the representatives whom the citizenry elects.

This then is the central fact about Republican party politics: insofar as the Republican party has a citizens' wing, it must pose as a party of republican principle; insofar as it is controlled by party organizations, it perpetually betrays those principles. From this central condition the differences between the geographical sections of the Republican party in part derive. In the Eastern states, where Democratic parties are sizable and bipartisan cooperation makes organization control of Republican parties that much more secure, Republican state bosses do not suffer the consequences of betrayal; the stronger a party organization is, the weaker is its rank and file. It may be so weak that it becomes, to all intents and purposes, a mere flock of the faithful who do what the regulars say. In Western states, however, where the collusive Democrats have been small boodle parties and Republican organizations that much less secure, such betrayals have time and again proven costly; it is the rank and file in these less cohesive parties which rebels against the organization in what White has rightly termed "the old civil war between citizens and regulars" in the Republican party. Insofar as their rank and file remains influential, Western state parties must appear to uphold political principles while Eastern state bosses, in general, have been under much less constraint to do so. Since the

Western bosses have no more interest than the Easterners in acting on the principles they pretend to espouse, it was long the common practice of many Western Republican bosses to let their stronger Eastern allies carry out the betrayals, just as the Northern Democratic bosses allow the Southern Bourbons to obstruct their reforms. For the sake of the rank and file, Western Republican bosses long had to uphold the republican principle of "no entangling alliances," yet they usually connived with the Eastern "internationalist" wing to nominate adherents of a forward foreign policy whenever the Democrats were about to prosecute such a policy. They let the Eastern bosses nominate Charles Evans Hughes in 1916 while Woodrow Wilson was preparing to bring America into the First World War; they helped enact an elaborate charade in 1940 to nominate Wendell Willkie when Roosevelt was trying to bring America into the Second World War; they let Thomas Dewey be nominated in 1948 after the Truman Administration had inaugurated its Cold War policies. During the 1920s, to take an example from another sphere, Western Republican organizations had to denounce trusts and monopolies while supporting Calvin Coolidge of the Eastern wing, whose Administration was busily forming cartels and monopolies.

A party which must both uphold and betray general political principles is somewhat limited in its capacity to act, either as a governing party or as an opposition. In general, ever since the great Republican insurgency of 1910–1912, Republican oligarchs in opposition have done their best to muffle or even falsify party principles. So far from wishing to expose Democratic actions that go against those principles, they prefer to let the unhampered Democrats carry them out, whereas principled opposition to Democratic administrations would only arouse the rank and file and better the chances of Republican insurgents. As a governing party in the nation, the Republicans have been forced, by and large, to do as little as possible, since they cannot—or could not—betray party principles too blatantly or too frequently. The Eisenhower Administration, for example, was an eight-year holding operation. Since they never act upon principle either, the characteristic consequence of a Republican administration is usually the sharp loss of support in Western states (this happened under Taft, under Hoover, under Eisenhower in 1958 and under Nixon in 1970), Western voters being describable in general as a plurality of citizens who perpetually hope a national Republican administration will do something republican but who usually find their hopes blasted.

The first four years of Spiro Agnew's vice-presidency perfectly epitomized this alternation of hope and disappointment in Republican ranks. In order to win a favorable response from "Middle America" (while cowing the press), Agnew attacked the mass media chiefs, in his first important address, as irresponsible monopolists—which they are—and pointedly asked what gave them the right to decide what the citizenry would see or hear on television. Monopoly privilege, as Agnew well knew, is still a battle cry in this Republic. Attacking it, however, is also a politically dangerous act. As *The New York Times* complained editorially, Agnew's remarks would encourage Americans to ask who gave the New York banks their control over the nation's credit, who gave the great foundations their influence over intellectual endeavor and similar inconvenient questions. It would indeed, and that is why Agnew swiftly dropped the subject of privileged monopolists. As a result, his popularity, according to all polls, began to drop steadily after the opening speech in 1969 that brought it swiftly to its peak.

As the governing party in the 1920s, the Republicans perfectly illustrated the problem they have with their "principles." Although the great Western Republican insurgency had been thwarted by the First World War, opposition to the trusts, a principle which the Republican party had long professed to uphold, still survived in the West and Middle West and still had a voice in the Congressional farm bloc. Arthur Vandenberg of the Michigan Republican organization was still compelled, for example, to attack what he himself called "economic oligarchy," and other state Republican organizations were under similar compulsion. The reason so many Americans opposed the trusts, however, was the very reason both party organizations had been fostering the trusts for two decades and more: monopoly wealth is privileged wealth, and privileged wealth is always allied to those who can dispense and protect special privilege, namely the wielders of irresponsible political power. Monopoly is the buttress of the party bosses.

Caught as always between its principles and its interests, the Republican oligarchy tried to paper over the dilemma as best it could. On the side of principle, it attempted to falsify the antitrust issue entirely. Throughout the 1920s (and to this day) it was the constant effort of the Republican hierarchy to pretend that the real economic issue in the Republic was not the trust issue at all. The "real" issue, they said, was the conflict between the economic status quo—the new monopoly economy—and government ownership of the means of production. Borrowing from Marxist usage, Republican bosses and spokesmen described this new status quo as "capitalism," a term which conveniently—for the Republican hierarchy—embraces both the monopoly economy which Americans opposed and the non-monopoly economy which the party oligarchs opposed. The only alternative to "capitalism," they said, was "communism," which President Herbert Hoover contrasted to "rugged individualism" while personally forming cartels. By sheer mass propaganda (and the 1920s were the first era of mass propaganda), the Republican party hoped to obliterate from men's minds the traditional American opposition to monopoly by inventing the spurious alternative of communism, which had no political following in America and was about as dangerous to the Republican hierarchy as a dynastic marriage in Serbia. In fabricating this spurious alternative, the Republican oligarchs, be it noted, were adapting Marxist ideology to their own purposes—not for the first time, either. Their sole justification for insisting that communism, rather than an antitrust policy, was the real alternative to the status quo was the specifically Marxist theory of history which holds that communism is the necessary historic successor to capitalism. This justification was purely ideological, for the *actual* history of the United States, as opposed to a *theoretical* history, involved an actual political struggle between the great majority of Americans who opposed monopoly capitalism and a small number of men—the party leaders—who were fostering it.

Although Republican leaders tried to falsify the principle they were betraying, they still dared not provide the new trust economy with any legal and administrative foundation, a foundation which many corporation managers, J. P. Morgan, for example, had been pleading for since the turn of the century. That would have been *too* open a betrayal of principle. Instead, Republican administrations simply provided the trusts with windfall tax favors and let them do as they pleased, while themselves virtually retiring from view. The famous silence of Calvin Coolidge was a political necessity as well as a personal quirk; the less Republican leaders said in public the less blatant their betrayal of principle would appear. In practice they let corporation managers and bankers speak for them, for the first time, I believe, in American history; J. P. Morgan, at any rate, was distinguished in his own day by his discreet silence. What resulted from this haphazard policy is of course well known. Licensed to do as they pleased, allowed to soak up as much surplus wealth as they could command, the corporation managers beggared the nation, reduced consumer demand for their products to the disaster point, and the whole haphazard system came tumbling to the ground—trusts and all. What the Great Depression demonstrated to Republican party bosses was that if they governed the nation, which they had done since the Civil War, they could not manage the trust economy they themselves had largely created. On the other hand, if they took the legislative steps needed to maintain the new monopoly economy they would antagonize the rank and file, strengthen insurgency and imperil their control of the national party. Indeed, by late 1930, Hoover and the national Republican bosses, meeting in Washington, were once again fearful of another East-West Republican split. As with the renomination of Taft in 1912, the party bosses did not renominate Hoover in 1932 in order to contest the Presidential election. What they did instead was transform the Republican party for some time into a passively fake opposition.

The truth is, the Roosevelt Administration by 1936 (see chapter 6) had achieved by legislation what Republican bosses had never dared to do as a party constrained by principle, i.e., by a rank and file. Roosevelt had used governmental authority to restore price-fixing and so salvage the trusts. He had restored to the nation's discredited bankers their control over the nation's credit. He had created a number of regulatory agencies and other bureaucracies which would, as will be seen, protect the monopoly capitalists from competition while hiding that protective policy from public scrutiny. He had begun to solve the "farm problem" by means of legislation that would eliminate small farmers, the persistent bane of Republican organizations. This was the so-called First New Deal, the Second New Deal being chiefly the Social Security Act of 1935.

Roosevelt's landslide victory in 1936 has largely obscured the fact that his Administration's popularity had been drastically shrinking during his first Administration. By 1935, Americans had been marching out from under the two-party system by the millions, some into Huey Long's Share Our Wealth clubs, some into Father Charles Coughlin's restive following, still others into Dr. Townsend's old people's movement. These mass movements, needless to say, were not evidence of public satisfaction either with the First New Deal or Republican opposition to it. Had Republican bosses in 1936 wished to return to national power, they certainly had disaffected voters to appeal to. What is more, they had a great deal to oppose in the Roosevelt Administration, for not only had Roosevelt virtually dissolved the Sherman Antitrust Act, not only had he saved the creditors in a nation of debtors, even his one genuine landmark reform, the Social Security Act, was financed—and still is—by a savagely regressive tax bearing almost entirely on the poorer half of the citizenry. As the party of principle, the Republicans certainly could have put Roosevelt on the defensive; as a party organization they had no interest whatever in doing so.

Whether the Republicans could have elected a President in 1936 is beside the point. The point is, they deliberately offered token opposition. Their candidate, Alfred Landon of Kansas, was himself no formidable figure, but Republican bosses were taking no chances. Even a fairly tame party standard-bearer develops a keen appetite for votes in the course of a Presidential campaign. To cripple Landon and repel voters, the Republican bosses took over the direction of the entire Landon campaign, putting it under tight centralized control and virtually dictating its terms from party headquarters in Chicago. Drowning out hapless Landon's efforts to win votes with "positive" programs, improved social security, for example, Republican party bosses devoted themselves to increasingly shrill declamations about America going "down the road to dictatorship," which it certainly was not. Roosevelt himself had no trouble filling the political vacuum which the Republican hierarchy had deliberately left him. In a truly remarkable reelection effort, he attacked "economic royalists," promised to crush the power of vested interests and in general ran the very campaign which the Republicans could have run against him, since Roosevelt, by restoring and virtually legalizing the trusts, had done more for the "economic royalists" than any single President had ever done.

What the national Republican party offered in opposition to "New Deal liberalism"—to licensed trusts, to trust-protecting bureaucracies, to government-controlled industrial unions (see chapter 10), to the expulsion of small farmers—was *nothing*. From 1932 until virtually the present day, the national Republican bosses have largely served as the silent partners of the ruling Democrats, just as the Democratic bosses from the Civil War to 1932 had been the silent partners of the ruling Republicans. Since 1936 the national Democratic party has been licensed by its fake opposition to dictate the political issues that the voters will hear and to define the very meaning of reform.

The Republicans' self-imposed minority status has had a truly historic effect on millions of American voters and on the Republican party as well. It has literally created millions of "conservative" voters— particularly in the Western states—who are in no sense conservative. Given the Hobson's choice between New Deal liberalism and nothing, many voters have preferred nothing. Finding little in the public arena that resembles a republican principle, seeing liberal reforms that do not reform but instead promote more bureaucracies, seeing the government become increasingly remote and increasingly unaccountable, such voters have preferred inactive government to corrupting government, the status quo to the clear risk of seeing things made worse. This is not the conservatism of people genuinely wed to the status quo and to the protection of their privileges (there are, of course, plenty of these supporting both party organizations); it is the pseudo-conservatism of people with blighted hopes. It is no coincidence that the Western section of the Republican party which formerly provided the reformers and insurgents is now the obstructionist reactionary bloc. It is precisely those rank-and-file Republicans whose state parties were insurgent when reform was republican reform—antitrust, antimachine, anti–special privilege, anti–entangling alliances—who tend to prefer nothing as long as republican issues, issues pertaining to self-government itself, are kept out of the national arena. On the other hand, the Eastern wing of the Republican party, which had the task of obstructing reform when all reform was republican, has now become the "reform" wing now that so few reforms are republican. Conservatives despite themselves, Republican voters and rank-and-file Republicans in the Western and Middle Western states still haunt the calculations of Republican bosses. They are the sleeping dogs of the party whom the Republican oligarchy fears to this day to arouse. Nothing demonstrates this more graphically than the political stratagems of Richard Nixon during his first two years as President.

In 1968, party leaders found themselves facing for the first time in decades the resurgence of a grass-roots political sentiment which can only be described as republican, although it was far from articulate and indeed barely coherent. The Johnson Administration had largely brought it into existence. Millions of Americans had voted for peace in 1964 and got a war in Asia instead. Millions of Americans had voted for a war against poverty and got a poverty bureaucracy instead. They had heard Johnson's "Great Society" lauded as an unprecedented outpouring of reform legislation, yet no benefits were forthcoming and no grievances remedied. To millions of Americans the government itself seemed to have gotten entirely out of hand; it habitually betrayed its promises; it habitually lied; it habitually operated in secret. All this had become fairly obvious by 1968. Fretful party shills began writing about the citizens' "loss of faith in the democratic process," which was the shills' way of saying that Americans had lost faith in a blatantly *un*democratic process; what they wanted was not a dictator but "more participation in government" and "more control over their lives," as the cry then went. In short, by 1968 the republican issue of self-government itself—the citizen's voice in his own affairs—had entered the public arena. It had done so despite the party bosses and largely in response to their blunders. Such issues do not readily penetrate the Democratic syndicate, which characteristically made "compassion"—the rulers' pity for their subjects—the theme of its 1968 convention. The Republicans, being the party of republican principle, cannot ignore republican sentiment so readily; they had to promise more "participation in government" in their party platform. It is the Republican bosses, however, who are directly threatened by any emergence of republican issues, for the passive conservatism of their rank and file derives largely from the absence of any such issues from the public arena. The voters of 1968 were truly the "Silent Majority," of whom Nixon spoke so frequently, silenced for years by the collusive Republican hierarchy.

Nixon, however, had not been nominated by the party bosses to encourage, articulate or act upon republican sentiment, and from the moment he entered office, he pretended that such sentiment did not exist—least of all where it was most dangerous to Republican bosses, namely in that "Middle America" for whom he now professed to speak. By fiat he declared that the Silent Majority had only one issue on its mind, namely "law and order." By fiat he declared that the country was "turning to the right." By fiat he declared that a "conservative majority" was "emerging." Since the Democratic machine was saying the same thing at the time, the party bosses were in perfect unison for two years. These Presidential declarations were entirely mendacious. As party bosses well know, the electorate's demand for more representative government is not only not "conservative" (unless "liberal" is defined as *not* demanding it), it is a particularly pointed peril to the power of party bosses.

In 1970 the Nixon Administration began its law and order campaign in earnest by visiting more states and meddling publicly in more state elections (Nixon himself handpicked several Republican candidates) than any national administration had ever done before. This was

Nixon's all-out effort to lay down a national party line and prevent, partly by sheer noise, any overly ambitious Republican candidate from raising republican issues and giving voice to inchoate republican sentiments. More than sheer noise was involved, however. As Representative Paul McCloskey of California said of Nixon's 1970 campaign efforts, "Before the election he called in a bunch of us [Republican legislators] and told us that his polls showed that law and order, whatever that means, was the biggest issue, and campus unrest. He urged us to stress that. 'I'm not suggesting that you demagogue it,' he said and then he sort of grinned." Behind Nixon's urging, of course, lay the usual combination of a threat and a promise: campaign funds, patronage and favors withdrawn from the disobedient and bestowed on the compliant. Few Republicans took Nixon's urging more to heart than New Jersey's Nelson Gross. After winning the Senate primary as a moderate against an Old Guard Republican, Gross obediently followed Nixon's party line in the general election, inveighed against "radical-liberals" and lost. In Wisconsin the moderate Republican candidate for governor also followed the Nixon law and order line, also attacked "radical-liberals" and also got smashed on election day. In Idaho, Minnesota, Nebraska and South Dakota, incumbent Republican governors similarly went down to defeat. The Middle America for whom Nixon pretended to speak responded to his law and order line by repudiating Republicans in Republican strongholds. The truth is, law and order was a fake issue raised by Nixon for the sole purpose of drowning out other issues, and this it certainly accomplished. Whether Nixon truly believed it would win elections for Republicans can never be known, although it is difficult to believe he was foolish enough to think so. The real point is, he did not want Republican candidates to win any other way, least of all by articulating the inchoate republican sentiments of the voters in an effort to get themselves elected. Those critics—pseudo-critics, actually—of the party system who fault the parties for their excessive opportunism turn the political truth inside out. It is the opportunism of party candidates which the party organizations will often try to squelch.

After the 1970 elections were safely out of the way and his own reelection secure, Nixon then revived an Administration proposal about which he had been silent for almost two years, namely his plan to return $5 billion in Federal revenues to state and local governments and to remove from Federal bureaucratic control an additional $5 billion now distributed to localities through specific Federal grants. To an electorate whom he had just described as conservative, to a Middle America which was supposed to grow furious at the very phrase "radical-liberal," Nixon described his program as a "revolutionary" proposal to bring government "back to the people." Why did Nixon not feature this proposal, so well in accord with the republican sentiment of 1968, during 1969 and 1970? Precisely because it *was* in accord with it. The last thing Nixon and the Republican oligarchy wanted was to strengthen and articulate that sentiment and encourage Republican candidates to make it their theme in the 1970 elections.

Politicians frequently speak in code. When Nixon announced that a "conservative majority" was emerging in America, he meant it as a warning to Republican candidates not to try to win over millions of voters who had been growing increasingly disaffected with the Democrats—voters opposed to the Vietnam War, young people growing increasingly skeptical of liberalism, urban black people demanding local control of their schools in the teeth of Democratic machine opposition, and, most importantly, the newly enfranchised black voters in the Southern states. Agnew used a variant of the code when he insisted during the 1970 campaign that "we" were not going to let "radical-liberals" back into the "center." This was a warning to Republican officeholders that the party bosses did not intend, after three decades, to reswell the Republican rank and file with active political dissidents. (So determined was the Republican oligarchy *not* to expand party ranks that in 1972 when the Democrats were dumping the Presidential election, Nixon and the party bosses again made sure that Republican candidates did not benefit from the opportunity. This time Nixon did so, not by intense participation in state elections as in 1970, but by totally ignoring Republican candidates and starving them of funds. For openly complaining after the elections that the Republican hierarchy was trying to "batten down the hatches,"

Senator Robert Dole of Kansas was promptly fired as Republican National Committee chairman.) If law and order was Nixon's major effort to protect the party organizations from disaffected citizens in the West and Middle West, it also did the same for Republican organizations in the changing Southern states. This was the primary intention of Nixon's celebrated "Southern Strategy."

Until the 1960s, Republican party claques in the Deep South (the analogue of the Democrats' Western parties before the 1950s) were the subservient tools of the Republican party bosses. They were known collectively as the "Federal machine" in recognition of both this subservience and its cause: their absolute dependence on Federal patronage. Keeping Southern Republican parties in the hands of a few faithful boodlers has long been routine politics in the national Republican party. As long as black people were disenfranchised and racist politics prevailed, this was easy enough to accomplish. Black people, however, have been reenfranchised, and racist politics no longer prevails in much of the South. A nonracist reform-minded Republican stands a good chance of winning the votes of black people and white people together. In Virginia, as I already mentioned, an antiracist Republican became Virginia's first Republican governor. On a similar basis, Winthrop Rockefeller became Republican governor of Arkansas and Claude Kirk Republican governor of Florida. In South Carolina, an antiracist Republican reformer was elected mayor of Greenville, despite the state party's racist leadership headed by Senator Strom Thurmond. Independent political ambition, that perennial disrupter of party organizations, threatened the old losing patronage gangs in the Southern Republican parties.

At this point, early in his Administration, Nixon launched his Southern Strategy. The time was ripe, said Administration spokesmen, to build strong conservative Republican parties in the South. The operative word, the code word, was "conservative." Given the politics of the Southern Bourbons, a stand-pat Republican party is not likely to be strong since it is largely otiose. A winning Republican party is not likely to be conservative. To win, it must appeal precisely to those black and poor white Southerners whom the Bourbons do not represent. That is just what Nixon and the Republican hierarchy did not want Republicans to do, for it would threaten the boodlers' control of their state parties. Nixon's Southern Strategy was an effort, in part, to make it difficult for ambitious Republicans to make such an appeal by repelling black voters from the Republican label, an effort in which law and order, with its clear racist overtones, was an instrumental factor. More than the national party line was involved. What Nixon did in several Southern states was to intervene actively to hurt ambitious Republicans and to strengthen Republican regulars—his New Mexico intervention writ large. As with New Mexico, building a strong party had nothing to do with it; protecting party regulars, everything. In Florida, Nixon actively intervened to secure a Senate nomination for one William Cramer, leader of the state party's losing Old Guard. As a result of his efforts, Cramer lost, the Republican governor was unseated and the Democrats regained control of the state. In Virginia, as I said, Nixon openly refused to endorse the Republican governor's Senate candidate in an effort to weaken the winning governor's influence in the losing Virginia Republican party. In South Carolina, the Nixon Administration, siding with Thurmond's racist gang, nominated a racist candidate for governor who lost to a nonracist Democrat who won black votes, factory worker votes and the votes of former George Wallace supporters, precisely the vote which the Republican regulars had thrown away. In Arkansas, a Democrat unseated Governor Rockefeller. In Texas, Nixon's handpicked candidate for Senator, George Bush, ran a stand-pat law and order campaign and lost to a stand-pat Democratic hack named Lloyd Bentsen. Bush's only chance for victory in 1970 lay in winning over the supporters of former Senator Ralph Yarborough, who had been defeated by the Democratic oligarchs in the spring primary. However, as the Republican *Houston Post* complained, Bush "made no direct appeal to unhappy liberal Democrats." Nixon had not picked Bush to win a Texas election as a Republican reformer.

In addition to the major defeats inflicted by the Southern Strategy, Republicans in 1970 lost twenty-nine of their far from plentiful seats in Southern state legislatures. Indeed, the only important Republican victory in the South was William Brock's defeat of Democratic Senator Albert Gore in Tennessee, a victory largely provided by the efforts of organization Democrats of Shelby County (Memphis) and their party lackeys in Republican East Tennessee to defeat Gore themselves. In addition to the fact that leading Tennessee Democrats openly endorsed the Republican candidate, that the Democratic organization put up a woeful candidate for governor named Joe Hooker in order to weaken the Democratic ticket, that many Democratic party headquarters did not even put Gore's name on a campaign poster, proof of a dump was readily apparent in the balloting itself: it was in the regular Democrats' stronghold of Shelby where Gore lost the votes that cost him the election. (I cannot resist a further digression here. While covering the Gore campaign for *The New Yorker*, a political journalist named Richard Harris was faithfully recording the Democratic line on the upcoming election, namely that Gore was too liberal for Tennessee voters—although Kefauver was a far more genuine reformer than Gore and had won huge election victories in the state. At one point, however, a "farmer with a leathery face" came up to twit one of Harris's political informants. "The Democrats," he said, "couldn't have picked a worse man to run for governor if they'd looked in a lunatic asylum. They set it all up in East Tennessee to get Hooker nominated just so's they could knock him off and let him take old Gore with him." Harris's informant hotly denied this. "You don't know anything," he told the farmer. "No, except the truth," the farmer replied. "I come in here with some of the truth and it just tears you to pieces." The truth must have torn up Harris, too, since he ignored it entirely. He later informed *New Yorker* readers, in an article entitled "How the People Feel," that Gore lost because he was too liberal for Tennessee voters.)

In protecting Southern Republican parties, Nixon also helped the Democrats temporarily maintain the status quo in the South, but this is a far from isolated example of the coincidence of interests between national party oligarchies. When Roosevelt restored the trusts, the Republican oligarchs did not attack him; when Republicans describe the trust economy as "free enterprise," the Democrats do not expose their fraud. Whenever Democrats have launched an aggressive foreign policy, Republican "isolationists" have given it their silent support by letting the Eastern wing nominate "internationalists" to connive at that policy. As Daniel Moynihan, a Democrat, remarked after serving under Nixon, "The Republican party seems to be most protective about precisely those things which I think were worst in the Democratic administration during the last ten years." The truth is, neither party organization will attack the betrayals and abuses of the opposition party if that attack would seriously weaken the other party's *bosses*. The reason for this is obvious: if one national party organization fell apart, the other party's bosses would soon topple. An uncontrolled national party would no longer be in collusion in the several states, would no longer refrain from competing in the other party's bastions, would no longer keep serious issues out of state politics or carry out all the sundry acts of mutual assistance without which no state party organization could control its party. If the Republican hierarchy fell, the Northern Democratic machines would fall, and vice versa. On the national as well as the state level, machine politics is always bipartisan.

National party collusion means that neither national party will raise issues or initiate policies or launch partisan attacks which would weaken the other party's organization. It means that if either party raises issues or institutes policies that protect its own organization, the other party will not seriously oppose it, for what strengthens one party machine will probably strengthen the other. This is why both national parties will unite to snuff out a grass-roots movement even if, like the Townsend movement, it appears to be a threat to only one of them. This is the reason the Democrats let Nixon foist the law and order issue on the American people for two years while helping him "take the Vietnam War out of politics." Without such collusion between the two national parties, real issues could not be removed from the public arena or fake issues imposed upon it. Indeed there is *no* successful abuse of power carried out by either party's national administration, no betrayal of the common interest to a special interest, which does not depend for its success on the nonopposition of the other national party. The Democrats could not have taken steps to expel small farmers from the land had the national Republican party spoken in the farmers' behalf, or to launch a war had the national Republican party spoken for peace. Collusion between the two national party organizations means that, for all practical purposes, this Republic is now ruled by a single political oligarchy. Yet that collusion requires neither conspiratorial meetings nor constant plotting. It arises solely from the fact that neither party organization could survive without the other; that is the heart of the matter.

The political implications of national party collusion are vast, but let one example of it suffice here to suggest its scope and significance. That example is the oppression and degradation of black people carried out in the years after 1896. In the aftermath of the Populist revolt, as I said, Bourbon Democrats disenfranchised black voters and then instituted a legal system of racial segregation in order to protect their fragile hegemony. These measures grossly violated the Constitution, the Fourteenth Amendment, and the Republicans' own Voting Rights Act of 1869. The Bourbons could not have enacted these measures, would not have dared enact these measures, had the ruling Republican party protested, had the Bourbons even expected the Republican party to protest. Republican bosses and Republican Presidents did not protest. They saw their own Republican voters decimated by disenfranchisement, they saw their own winning party in North Carolina ruined by disenfranchisement, yet they let this unconstitutional degradation of American citizens pass unopposed. They even went further. They appointed judges who upheld those unconstitutional measures; they turned their Southern parties into "white-only" parties to give themselves an alibi for not defending the constitutional rights of black people in the South. They were as silent on the race question for fifty years as the Democrats were. Why did the Republican party bosses do this in defiance of every party principle and every party memory? Because, quite simply, if the Bourbon hegemony had fallen in the South, the Democratic machine would have fallen in the North, and without the national Democratic oligarchy there could be no national Republican oligarchy.

The historic degradation of black people in this century was the direct consequence of the collusive politics of two national party organizations united in their common interest in remaining party organizations. The invisibility of black people from the turn of the century until after 1954 was not due to white racism but to the bipartisan exclusion of black people from the public light and the public arena. The Bourbons needed a national policy on the race question and they got that policy, they could only have gotten that policy, through the connivance of the national Republican party. To suppose that the degradation of black people is but the reflection of white racism is to swallow one more time the mendacious presumption which I believe I have now laid to rest—that the party organizations, bent exclusively on winning elections, are the "translators of public opinion" and the "handmaidens of democracy."

The abiding principle of action of the party organizations, the principle which necessitates their collusion, is their constant and unremitting effort to remain party organizations and thereby control elected officials. That party organizations are constantly imperiled in this Republic, that their power, though great, is never secure, I have not yet shown. That the self-protective policies of the party organizations lie behind far more than the grafting and boodling side of politics, that they determine the most important acts in modern American history and shape the destiny of this republican commonwealth, that I have not yet shown. This remains to be done in the rest of this book, first by two major examples of the exercise of party power and then by more general considerations of the fruit of that usurped power.

PART II

THE PARTIES
V.
REFORM

5.
The Indispensable Enemy

When the 1936 elections were over, Franklin Roosevelt and his Administration stood at a unique pinnacle of power and promise. The President's victory was so great it overrode all sectional distinctions; in only two of the forty-eight states did he fail to win a plurality of the vote. Moreover, his victory was not a merely personal one. The voters that year sent 331 Democrats to the House of Representatives and 76 Democrats to the Senate, reducing the Republican contingent in the new Congress to an impotent rump. That reform of a broad and democratic kind would soon be forthcoming few people had cause to doubt. Although Roosevelt had offered no detailed program during the course of his campaign, he had expressed Populist sentiments which Americans had not heard in high places in many long years.

What happened shortly after the 1936 elections is well known. The apparently invincible President suddenly found himself blocked at every turn. An overwhelming Democratic majority, seemingly eager to follow his lead, split into warring factions; a coalition of Southern Bourbons and obstructionist Republicans, although numbering together no more than some 130 members, swiftly seized the legislative helm and blocked virtually all further reform. At the very height of its power and prestige, the New Deal came to a dead stop in one of the most remarkable reversals in American history.

Twenty-eight years later, another Democratic President, Lyndon Johnson, won a landslide election victory and found himself with yet another Congress dominated by lopsided Democratic majorities; 295 Democrats in the House, 68 Democrats in the Senate. He, too, had promised broad and sweeping reforms, among them no less a goal than a "war to end poverty," as well as a turning away from distracting foreign entanglements: he would not commit "American boys to fighting a war that I think ought to be fought by the boys of Asia to help protect their own land." Behind the President's evident wish to take care of the "unfinished business of the nation" lay, in fact, a great deal of unfinished business. Since the end of the New Deal in 1937 there had scarcely been a single major reform enacted in twenty-eight years—one-sixth the entire history of this Republic. During that period the Southern Bourbon-Republican coalition, which had arisen phoenix-like in 1937, had dominated Congress. It had frustrated Truman and Kennedy with apparent ease. It had subjected the Eisenhower Administration to the most muted criticism. It had given its full approval to just two major public policies since 1938—national defense and a forward foreign policy.

What happened? A few months after the election, Johnson's "Great Society" was deep in an Asian war; after a brief spate of trumpery legislation—the "poverty program," for example—Congress became balky and unmanageable. In 1966, Johnson's great legislative majorities were reduced and the Great Society was dead, the victim of the Vietnam War. Another reform President, another landslide election, another landslide Congress, another stunning reversal.

These two similar historic reversals share yet another common element. Each has been largely attributed to a gross Presidential blunder. The defeat of the New Deal, most historians agree, was due to Roosevelt's strangely misguided effort in 1937 to enlarge the Supreme Court, an effort which threw the Democratic ranks into confusion, turned reformers against the President and allowed obstructionists to defy him boldly thereafter. Why a politician as consummately skillful as Roosevelt should have committed so gross and clumsy a blunder has never been properly explained. To err, presumably, is human.

Johnson's gross blunder was his decision to wage an American war in Asia, a decision which not only thwarted his professed domestic purposes, but one which he made under no external compulsion, either political or military. It was a free and deliberate reversal of his own stated public policy. In February 1965, when the war began, all that had happened in Vietnam was the disintegration of another Saigon regime that had failed to inspire its army to fight. It was a case of the "boys of Asia" not doing what presumably they should have been doing. Had Johnson wished to keep America out of the war, he had only to adhere to his stated policy not to send "American boys" to fight in their stead. What he did, however, was the opposite. Because Asians were not fighting, he sent half a million Americans to do their fighting for them. A great many people have decried the Vietnam War, but no one can explain the decision. It has been called a "national aberration." It has been called a "gross miscalculation" based on blind adherence to "America's Cold War posture." It has been termed by Townsend Hoopes, a former ranking government official, "the story of an entire generation of leaders so conditioned by the tensions of the Cold War years that they failed to perceive in 1965 that the Communist adversary was no longer a monolith." But why Johnson and his advisers were so purblind is still unexplained.

So there it is: two national apogees of reform and two unexplained blunders that brought reform to a halt. What no one, to my knowledge, has suggested is that these blunders were not blunders at all, that each was the deliberately chosen means for achieving the very end it achieved: bringing reform to a halt. The reason for this is understandable. There appears to be no political reason why a reform President would deliberately frustrate his own promised reforms. The prevailing myth about the parties stands in the way of recognizing any reason. If the chief purpose of the parties is to pick winners, and elected officials, in consequence, are free to serve the citizenry in whose name they act, there is no political reason and motive. Why would a President who gained election as a reformer not want to enact reforms which would make him more popular yet? If the prevailing myth about the parties were true, whatever a reform President does that hinders reform cannot be deliberate and must be ascribed to a blunder, even though the blunder itself is inexplicable.

Yet there is a political reason for a reform President frustrating his own pledged reforms. It is none other than the ruling political principle in modern American politics—the preservation of party power, that power whose sole foundation is organization control of the political parties.

From what I have already said about the parties, it should be clear that the essential and inherent danger to party power is independent political ambition, the presence in public life and public office of men who ignore the interests and defy the dictates of party bosses and oligarchies. To preserve their power, party organizations must try constantly to eliminate the political condition that breeds independent ambition. That condition, in general, is the free political activity of the citizens themselves, their own efforts to act in their own behalf, to bring into the public arena issues that interest them and to encourage by their activity the independent ambition of public men. The political activity of the citizenry, whether within or without the major parties, whether it be as local as a village election, is always a danger to organization control of parties, and precisely because it strengthens independent ambition. There is in this Republic, however, one great wellspring animating citizens to act in their own behalf: their own understanding that by means of politics and government what is wrong can be righted and what is ill can be cured. In a word, political *hope*.

The very opposite condition, the condition safest for party power, is public apathy, gratitude for small favors and a deep general sense of the futility of politics. Yet there is nothing natural about political apathy, futility and mean gratitude. What lies behind them is not "human nature" but the citizens' belief that politics and government can do little to better the conditions of life; the belief that they are ruled not by the men whom they have entrusted with their power but by circumstances and historical "forces," by anything and everything that is out of human control; the belief that public abuses and inequities are somehow inevitable and must be endured because they cannot be cured.

The condition of public apathy and futility, however, is swiftly undone by reform and even by the convincing promise of reform.

Every beneficial law reminds the citizenry anew that the government—which is their government—can help them remove evils and better the conditions of life. Every law which remedies an abuse reminds the citizenry anew that other abuses can be remedied as well. Every beneficial law rips the cover of inevitability from public inequities and rouses the people from apathy. Reform in America does not bring passive contentment to the citizenry. It inspires active hope. The American people were far more clamorously hopeful after the passage of the Social Security Act in 1935 than they were in the wretched days of 1931, when the Depression was still being attributed to an inevitable "business cycle" and the "strangely phlegmatic response of Americans" actually "astonished" foreign observers, according to the New Deal historian William Leuchtenburg.

What is more, the national party that enacts the reforms does not benefit at all by the hope its reforms arouse. Far from it. The reforming party would find itself, among other things, attracting active citizens, ambitious men and hopeful idealists to every tight little political club of the party in every town and district and neighborhood. Such local incursions of the citizenry (which do not have to be great in size so long as they occur in many places at once) would seriously threaten and even destroy organization control of local parties. The reform party would gain in strength and election victories, but the party bosses would endanger their own power. This they have no intention of doing voluntarily. It is precisely to avert this fundamental danger that both major parties in America have a reform wing and an obstructionist wing; the one to promise, the other to betray. As a Republican governor of New York, Thomas Dewey, once remarked in the course of a lecture series, the two major parties cannot be realigned into a reformist party and a conservative party, for the reform party would always win. What Dewey did not say was that the rulers of the reform party would lose. Why then suppose that party bosses have any wish to see reform enacted if they can prevent it? Why not drop this baseless supposition? It is mere question-begging in any case. If we do, the blunders of reform Presidents become immediately intelligible as examples of the exercise of self-serving party power.

Before returning to Roosevelt and Johnson, it is worth examining the brief Administration of John F. Kennedy because it illustrates, with graphic simplicity, the political art of defeating one's own pledged reforms. The chief defeat in question was the Congressional tabling in August 1961 of one of Kennedy's major legislative proposals—a bill to provide Federal funds for public school construction. That defeat, according to Tom Wicker's account of it in *JFK and LBJ*, marked the moment when Kennedy permanently "lost" Congress and any chance of passing reform proposals. The important point is that Kennedy went about losing Congress with deliberate intent.

The school construction bill was scarcely an innovation since it narrowly failed of passage in 1960, but the Kennedy Administration proposed it anew, along with a minimum wage bill, as its two pieces of "must" legislation for 1961. Considering that Kennedy, in his inaugural speech, had promised to "begin anew," his program was notably stale. The school bill had been circulating in Congress for so long it had become, in Wicker's words, "as familiar in Congress as Sam Rayburn's bald head." Indeed, from the moment Kennedy took office he had been warning Americans not to expect too much from his Administration: his electoral mandate was slender; pro-Administration forces in Congress were beleaguered; the Bourbon-Republican coalition would have to be placated. It would be difficult, Kennedy spokesmen repeated again and again, to "get this country moving again" (except in regard to building missiles for a nonexistent "missile gap," "counterinsurgency," "confrontations" with the Soviet Union, putting a man on the moon and the like). Having prophesied trouble from Congress, Kennedy now proceeded by means of the school bill to prove the correctness of his "prediction."

After the bill's submission, Abraham Ribicoff, Kennedy's newly appointed Secretary of Health, Education, and Welfare, made the surprising suggestion that an education bill might well provide funds for parochial schools. Since Kennedy was the first Catholic President of the United States, this was an embarrassing remark for a member of his Administration to make. Moreover, any such provision would kill the bill, since legislators who would hesitate to vote against schools would gladly vote to uphold a constitutional principle. More significantly, Ribicoff's remark was completely gratuitous. Not only had the 1960 bill omitted any provision for parochial schools, no Catholic legislator had even proposed such a provision in 1960, nor had any Catholic prelate opposed the 1960 bill because it lacked such a provision. Federal aid to parochial schools was simply not an issue in 1960. Since Kennedy's obvious problem was not to woo Catholics but to ease the minds of many Protestants, all Ribicoff seemed to have done was borrow trouble for the man who had given him high office. When Kennedy, shortly afterward, avowed his opposition to parochial school aid in a strong and popular speech, Washington cynics thought they saw a reason for Ribicoff's apparently mischievous remark. It had given Kennedy an occasion to demonstrate to Protestants his strict adherence to the principle of separation of church and state. The cynics, as usual, were not cynical enough. What Ribicoff's remark and Kennedy's response to it had done was to create a divisive issue which previously did not exist.

The next development was more surprising yet. House Majority Leader John McCormack suddenly decided to bring pressure on Congress himself to include parochial schools in the funding. Oddly enough, this was something he had not thought of doing in 1960 when there was no Catholic in the White House. Acting, in Wicker's words, as a "sort of floor leader for the hierarchy," McCormack invited Catholic prelates to Washington, where he told them to pressure Catholic Congressmen to vote against any school bill that provided no parochial school aid. This the church hierarchy did, and "from that day forward," writes Wicker, "the Kennedy school bill was dead." "Why," asks Wicker rhetorically, "had the Catholic hierarchy chosen 1961 to push their case so strongly, when they had scarcely been heard from, in so many years?" Why put their case to the one President who was least likely to heed it? The answer to that is obvious. They were told to do so by the House Majority Leader, a lifetime servant of the Democratic machine, the Catholic Church's long-standing patron in urban Democratic bastions.

The real question is why McCormack acted as he did. If he were acting independently, it was independence of the most unruly kind. He was publicly defying and embarrassing the President of the United States, the leader of his own party, the first of his coreligionists in the White House, and the most important Democrat in his home state of Massachusetts. He was openly securing defeat for a "must" piece of Administration legislation and demonstrating that Administration's impotence in Congress at the very beginning of its existence. What is more, if McCormack were acting independently, it was the first and last act of independence in a half-century of undeviating party servility. Yet he was doing it in a cause so allegedly dear to his heart that he had not even seen fit to mention it less than one year before.

There is only one explanation of McCormack's sudden fit of independence: it was not independence at all. He was working from the start—like Ribicoff—with the approval and connivance of his fellow machine politician, namely President Kennedy, who now signed the bill's death warrant by going back on his public vow to oppose Federal aid to parochial schools. Bowing to McCormack's Catholic pressure—the one kind of pressure he had least to fear—Kennedy now declared that some form of parochial school aid was acceptable to him and that, as Wicker points out, was the end.

The actual death of the bill, however, did not even occur on the floor of the House. It occurred in the Rules Committee, where, to everyone's surprise, a New York City Democratic hack named James Delaney suddenly performed *his* first and last act of "independence." Instead of voting as expected with the Administration, he swung his deciding vote to the opposition and the school construction bill was killed in committee. "Hard-bitten members of the House were amazed," says Wicker, "that the White House and the Democratic party had not somehow been able to bludgeon or wheedle that single vote in the Committee on Rules." Not really very amazing, since they did not want it. "Nor, to anyone's knowledge," Wicker concludes, "was Delaney ever punished. Here, then, was a President, for all his Irish Mafia, who apparently could be defied with impunity." As Kennedy had predicted, Congress would just not enact reform and he had taken the necessary steps to prove it.

In arranging a Catholic opposition to his school bill, Kennedy was carrying out a basic political strategy for killing pledged reforms—the creation of what political observer Marvin Gelfand has termed "the indispensable enemy," the opposition required to prevent you from doing what you must appear to want done. The indispensable enemy may make an instant appearance, like the Church hierarchy whistled up in 1961 for the occasion. Or it may be a permanent presence, like the obstructionist wing of each national party which serves as that party's perpetual indispensable enemy. The enemy may even be a single individual, a tactical device which Kennedy now proceeded to employ in the Senate.

Had Kennedy really wished to press for reform in 1961, the Senate was the logical place to apply the pressure, for the Democratic majority was large and reform Senators more numerous than they had been in some time. Of the sixty-five Senate Democrats only about fifteen could be relied upon to obstruct reform at all times; of the thirty-five Republicans, some twenty could be relied upon to do so. The Bourbon-Republican coalition had become a distinct minority. Common sense dictated the strategy a reform-minded President would have employed in the Senate—to make every possible effort to split Republican Senate ranks and win over the votes of Republicans whose votes could be swayed toward reform. Instead Kennedy did the opposite. His Administration declared that it could not pass its programs in the Senate without Republican votes and—what was palpably untrue—could win them only if Senator Everett Dirksen gave his approval to Kennedy legislation. Accordingly, Kennedy made elaborate public efforts to win over Senator Dirksen and an "extraordinary rapport" was established between the two men, according to Neil MacNeil's biography, *Dirksen: Portrait of a Public Man.* Concurrently in the Senate itself, the newly elected Majority Leader Mike Mansfield "deferred so totally" to Dirksen, according to MacNeil, that Dirksen became, in effect, the acting Senate leader. Having given Dirksen this veto power, the Kennedy Administration now directed all its efforts to winning his approval by tailoring bills to his specifications and by "sacrificing" parts of them in order to win Dirksen's approval of some other part.

Oddly enough, this studious deference to Dirksen did not help Kennedy's program at all. Dirksen opposed all of Kennedy's domestic measures and carried the whole Republican contingent with him. That was precisely the point of Kennedy's strategy. By pretending that the entire Senate Republican contingent was represented by Senator Dirksen, Kennedy made the Republicans a unified body. Instead of trying to split them, he pretended that they spoke with one voice and—*mirabile dictu*—that of their leading obstructionist. Republican Senators who would have had to support reform measures could conveniently defer to Dirksen and let him bear responsibility for opposing reforms. As MacNeil observed somewhat demurely: "Kennedy's prospects for passing his legislation had been hurt by the unifying of the Republicans against him."

Having created an indispensable enemy in the Senate, Kennedy used him, first and foremost, to protect the parties from civil-rights agitation. In 1961, Kennedy had not proposed a civil-rights bill because, he explained, it would arouse Southern opposition to his "must" legislation—which the indispensable Bourbons scuttled anyway, a perfect example of fake expedience. When overwhelming public pressure forced the President to propose a civil-rights bill in 1963, Kennedy had his indispensable enemy ready and waiting. His Administration announced that no such bill could pass without the prior approval of Dirksen, who was given the power to rewrite the bill line by line (it became known in 1964 as "the Dirksen package"). The necessity of winning over Dirksen was blatantly untrue. By 1963 the party of Lincoln would have had an exceedingly hard time voting down in public a civil-rights bill, especially one with a strong voting rights provision, a provision which Dirksen proceeded to gut in private, thus saving Republican Senators from embarrassment and both party oligarchies from political equality for black people. It is more than likely, indeed, that Kennedy's entire effort to "prove" that Congress could "defy him with impunity" was directed largely toward providing himself and the Democratic machine with an alibi for not enacting civil-rights legislation. The indispensable enemy had other uses, however.

In order to pass the Test Ban Treaty in 1963, for example, Kennedy announced that he had been forced by Dirksen to "pledge" himself to piling up missiles. This was yet more mendacity. The Kennedy Administration had been building missiles at a fast pace since 1961. Kennedy also announced that he had to approve the Communications Satellite Act of 1962, which handed over to the American Telephone & Telegraph Company the rights to the government's own technological feats, after declaring his resolve not to do so, in order, he said, to win "conservative" votes for his Medicare bill. More mendacity yet. The Medicare bill was already dead before the Satellite bill came to a vote.

If anyone still believes that Kennedy's bestowal of veto power on Dirksen was merely an honest blunder, the 1962 elections provide an interesting revelation, for Kennedy let slip a golden opportunity to rectify it. That year Dirksen, the inveterate foe of Kennedy's domestic program—despite their "extraordinary rapport"—was locked in a close election contest with Representative Sidney Yates, a loyal Administration supporter. Kennedy came to the rescue of—Dirksen. Reducing his help to Yates to a derisory token gesture, Kennedy, in the middle of the campaign, ostentatiously invited Dirksen to the White House in order to get his counsel in an international crisis. He then let it be known that he considered Dirksen unbeatable, a Presidential prediction which was duly splashed across the pages of the Illinois press to the obvious detriment of Yates. As MacNeil remarks: "It was no secret that inside the Democratic hierarchy the defeat of Dirksen, if it happened, would be regarded as a political catastrophe for the Kennedy administration." A catastrophe indeed: Kennedy might have been forced to pass his program. Having set up their indispensable enemy, Kennedy and the Democratic machine were not going to let him go down the drain just to help an apparent friend win a Senate seat.

So much for the blunders of John F. Kennedy in his well-managed effort not to "get this country moving again" for a few years longer.

One more point needs to be made here: some people, I suspect, will object to the preceding analysis as grossly "conspiratorial" or "paranoid," as the cant phrases go. This is as good a place as any to clear the air. When it can be established that a number of political acts work in concert to produce a certain result, the presumption is strong that the actors were aiming at the result in question. When it can be shown, in addition, that the actors have an interest in producing those results, the presumption becomes a fair certainty. No conspiracy theory is required. It is common sense applied to the actual deeds of men without recourse to begged questions about the character of the actors, for in politics, as I have said, we judge the character of men by their deeds and not their deeds by presumptions about their character. On the other hand, those who make blanket condemnations of "conspiracy theories" base their own view on a farfetched theory indeed, namely that whatever those in high office actually do, they are essentially men of goodwill. According to this school of special pleading—the "King can do no wrong" doctrine suitably updated—it is entirely proper to praise an American President for skillfully engineering some desirable result, but to note the same skillful engineering of an indefensible one is to fall victim to "political paranoia" and "conspiratorial fetishism" on a par with subscribing to the *Protocols of the Elders of Zion*.

A good antidote to this infectious nonsense may be found in reading a speech delivered in 1858 by a man who would later become President of the United States. In that speech the orator describes in minute detail a complex series of acts taken by the then current party powers to legitimize the extension of slavery. He shows, for example, how those who passed the Nebraska Act of 1854 had put into it certain seemingly innocuous phrases which became, in his words, an "exact niche" for the Dred Scott decision, a decision which, he also shows, was well known in advance to the power wielders. After describing these and related actions in dense and remorseless detail, the speaker then concluded: "We cannot absolutely know that all these exact adaptations are the result of preconcert. But when we see a lot of framed timbers . . . joined together and see they exactly make the frame of a house or a mill, all the tenons and mortices exactly fitting . . . we find it impossible not to believe that [the ruling politicians] all understood each other from the beginning and all worked on a common plan." If, after reading this speech, anyone is still ready to denounce as paranoid the political analysis of political deeds, he will have to admit that Abraham Lincoln was suffering from "conspiratorial fetishism" and that when he called upon his fellow citizens, in his words, to "meet and overthrow the present ruling dynasty" he labored under the paranoid delusion that the dynasts had been acting together.

6.
Roosevelt Packs in the New Deal

If any President possessed both a mandate for reform and the means to effect it, Roosevelt surely did at the beginning of 1937. The specific nature of the expected reforms was as yet unknown, since Roosevelt had outlined no legislative program during the election campaign. He had attacked with mounting intensity "entrenched greed" and "economic royalists," he had promised a "struggle against private monopoly" and the power of "economic autocracy." In his Inaugural Address he had declared his deep concern for the "one-third of a nation ill-housed, ill-clad, ill-nourished." There seemed little doubt about his goals: first, to lift from the backs of the citizenry the private economic power of the great trusts and monopolies; second, to attack entrenched and long-favored special interests; third, to help equalize the benefits of the nation's wealth. Roosevelt, in short, had committed himself to genuine republican reforms, reforms that aimed to equalize the rights, the powers and the privileges of a self-governing citizenry. So matters stood on February 5, 1937, when, to everyone's astonishment, Roosevelt submitted to Congress not a program of reform legislation but a bill that would enable him to enlarge the Supreme Court by as many as six additional judges. The final tabling of Roosevelt's court measure five months later would mark the death of the New Deal.

That Roosevelt submitted his court bill for the deliberate purpose of thwarting reform will doubtless appear an incredible assertion, even more incredible than the conventional assertion that the most skillful of politicians had unaccountably committed the clumsiest of political blunders. What makes it appear incredible is the more or less explicit assumption that Roosevelt had been committed to such republican reform throughout his first Administration and had conspicuously led the fight to achieve it during Congress's two celebrated flurries of New Deal legislation, the so-called Hundred Days of 1933 and the Second Hundred Days of mid-1935. Before examining the court-packing "blunder" in detail, therefore, it is necessary to review Roosevelt's major actions during his first Administration. Only then will it become clear that this blunder joins foursquare—"all the tenons and mortices exactly fitting"—with a farrago of related Presidential blunders and with Roosevelt's New Deal as a whole.

The record of Roosevelt's commitment to genuine reform can be summed up briefly as follows: First, Roosevelt almost never fought for reform until it was forced upon him by overwhelming popular pressure, whereupon he saw to it that the reform enacted was as *minimal* as he could make it. This describes, in general, the so-called Second New Deal, the measures enacted during the summer of 1935. Second, the major legislation which Roosevelt proposed under no specific reform pressure cannot be called reforms at all. This describes, in general, the so-called First New Deal of 1933. In making these assessments I have leaned heavily not on extreme critics of the New Deal but on standard approving accounts of it, particularly those of Basil Rauch and William Leuchtenburg.

The legislation of the First New Deal began with the Emergency Banking Relief Act. If Congressional reformers had expected Roosevelt to strip from the discredited bankers their private control of the nation's credit, they were fatally disappointed. At public expense Roosevelt restored the bankers' power under the guise of "emergency" legislation. The Banking Act, according to Leuchtenburg, was "an exceptionally conservative document." According to Rauch, it was "a conservative solution, highly acceptable to bankers and businessmen, and *symptomatic of the policies of the First New Deal*" (emphasis mine).

It was "greeted with loud shouts of approval by all articulate conservatives," according to Raymond Moley, a member of Roosevelt's original "Brains Trust" and one of the architects of the measure. Further New Deal banking legislation would permanently consolidate the big banks' control over the nation's credit, control which the majority of Americans had vainly opposed for decades.

The First New Deal also included farm legislation aimed at relieving farmers of their chronic plight, which it actually did by the final solution of relieving them of their farms. The Agricultural Adjustment Act (reenacted in 1938) "furthered . . . the concentration of agriculture in large units and the displacement of tenants and sharecroppers," according to Rauch. It also created a "new class of migrant farm laborers [whose] lack of a fixed residence made them . . . uninteresting to politicians." For small farmers and tenant farmers, "New Deal policies made matters worse," to quote Leuchtenburg. This Roosevelt did quite intentionally, for his farm legislation, as Leuchtenburg rightly points out, "turned the power of decision over to the [government-sanctioned] Farm Bureau Federation, the Extension Service and the land-grant colleges—in short, the larger landholders." Under Roosevelt the Tennessee Valley Authority supplemented the same New Deal policy of driving small farmers off the land. As Leuchtenburg notes, the TVA farm program was deliberately administered "in the interests of the more prosperous white planters."

Confronted with a vast population reeling in debt, Roosevelt undertook a credit policy that is especially revealing. Resisting the "overwhelming" demand for inflationary measures, Roosevelt "pursued a policy," according to Leuchtenburg, "more ruthlessly deflationary than anything Hoover had dared . . . which still further eroded purchasing power." While the great majority of legislators clamored for inflation and even Hoover reportedly suggested that the Administration "repudiate all debts," the aim of Roosevelt's policies was to see that creditors were paid, as far as possible, in the hardest of deflated currency—a noteworthy aim for the alleged enemy of "entrenched greed." The Federal Home Owners' Loan Act was passed "amidst cries that the law bailed out real-estate interests rather than the homeowner." By the spring of 1938, as Leuchtenburg points out, the Home Owners' Loan Corporation would itself foreclose mortgages on one hundred thousand homes. Roosevelt's credit policies did offer some relief to debtors, but the chief thing about them is that they provided the absolute minimum that was politically possible and far less than Congress would have provided had Roosevelt not determined otherwise.

During the First Hundred Days, Roosevelt's most daring and far-reaching measure was reserved for salvaging the trusts from competition, for, in Rauch's words, "the collapse of the trade associations' codes brought businessmen to admit in desperation the need for governmental authority to bring order out of the chaos created by destructive competition." Roosevelt's response was the National Industrial Recovery Act, the keystone of the First New Deal and the final piece of major legislation of the First Hundred Days. The act authorized the government to give the trade association cartels— renamed "code authorities"—the legal right to fix prices, eliminate competition, limit production, determine minimum wages and maximum hours and enforce these with governmental powers of coercion. Since the "code authority" in each industry was controlled by one or two large trusts—the Steel Authority, for example, being the Steel Institute which was controlled by U.S. Steel—what Roosevelt's NRA did was virtually delegate to a handful of giant corporations the authority to control the economy and directly rule the citizenry. As Leuchtenburg remarks, "The NRA created a series of private economic governments"—exactly what the majority of Americans had been opposing for fifty years and more. Between the citizenry and their elected government, Roosevelt had inserted a thick layer of private power that was completely out of reach of those subject to it. The greatest single legislative blow to political liberty and representative government ever struck against the American people, Roosevelt's NRA was invalidated by the Supreme Court in 1935 in a 9–0 decision.

Passed by Roosevelt as the key to "recovery" from the Depression, the NRA had nothing to do with economic recovery and in fact "actually hindered it," according to Leuchtenburg. Its chief purpose was to reestablish the crumbling trust economy on a permanent legal foundation. Saved from competition, the restored monopolists did what monopolists are wont to do: they cut back production, fired employees and raised prices, thereby increasing unemployment and further reducing demand—as any economist could have told Roosevelt had he cared about recovery in the first place. One of the popular justifications for the so-called philosophy of the NRA, interestingly, was the claim that it would help eliminate sweatshops. In fact sweatshops could have been eliminated by enacting a strong wages and hours law, but Roosevelt blocked passage of such a measure from 1933 until 1938, when he saw to it that a bill was passed with sufficient loopholes to protect sweatshops.

So much for the First New Deal, which provided the absolute minimum benefits to the citizenry while taking the most far-reaching steps to salvage and protect entrenched privilege. That a stricken citizenry was nonetheless grateful is due largely to the fact that the apparent alternative to this meager slice was the Republicans' no loaf at all. That is how collusive politics works. Near the end of the First Hundred Days, according to John T. Flynn, author of *The Roosevelt Myth*, Roosevelt's policies were "cheered to the echo" at a Chamber of Commerce dinner while *The Wall Street Journal* and *Dun & Bradstreet* joined in singing his praises. He was the kind of reformer they could well appreciate. In the teeth of a fundamental collapse of so many corrupt institutions, in the face of growing popular hopes for reform and a Congress in which reformers outnumbered obstructionists, Roosevelt had done more for the privileged and less for the great majority of citizens than any of the privileged had thought possible on Inauguration Day, 1933.

To accomplish this and to continue accomplishing this required superbly skillful management on Roosevelt's part. On the supposition that he genuinely wished to enact genuine reforms, every element in that management must be accounted a blunder, for each served to strengthen the enemies of reform and weaken the power of those determined to enact it.

The heart of Roosevelt's strategy—or his central "blunder"—was his successful effort to keep Congress under control of obstructionists and party hacks and to funnel all legislation through them. This was a task made difficult both by the large number of reformers in Congress and by the size of the Democratic majorities. Each time the Democrats organized Congress, however—in 1933, 1935 and 1937—Roosevelt and the Democratic oligarchy saw to it that obstructionists sat in the major seats of power. In the House in 1933, the Democratic caucus gave Bourbons control of the three most important committees: Rules, Ways and Means, and Appropriations. The House leadership was similarly arranged. The new Speaker of the House in 1933 was former Majority Leader Henry Rainey of Illinois, who had demonstrated his devotion to reform in 1932 by siding with Hoover to block reform legislation and by proposing a Federal sales tax to balance the budget, a measure so grossly unfair even machine Democrats balked at it. That did not deter them, however, from raising Rainey to the Speakership. Behind the aged Rainey, who soon died, stood a bevy of Bourbon leaders-to-be, including William Bankhead of Alabama, who became Speaker in 1936, and Rayburn of Texas, who became Majority Leader in 1937. If Roosevelt opposed these arrangements, so inimical to reform, he showed no sign of it whatever. In fact they could not have been made without his connivance. In 1933, for example, there were two Democratic vacancies on the Rules Committee which the leadership elected by the party caucus managed to fill with two Bourbons. As Representative Bolling observes in *Power in the House:* "Someone saw to it that Rules was packed with Southern Democrats." That someone was Roosevelt, and respect for seniority had nothing to do with it. One of the newly seated Rules Committee Bourbons was Howard Smith of Virginia, its future chairman, who was given the seat after one term in the House, with the usual complicity of the Northern machine delegations. Bourbons would not "suddenly" seize control of the Rules Committee in 1937. Roosevelt and the Democratic oligarchy had planted them on the committee as early as 1933—the indispensable enemy waiting to be whistled up when needed.

Had Roosevelt wished to liberalize the Congressional leadership the opportunity was surely his in 1934 when 319 Democrats were elected to the House and 69 to the Senate. All Roosevelt had to do was mobilize the more than one hundred freshmen and sophomore Congressmen elected through the national repudiation of the Republican label, combine them with the many genuine reformers already in Congress and the scores of Tammany-liberals who would not have dared vote against reform in public and together they would have overwhelmed the tiny Bourbon contingent and swept them completely out of power. This was exactly what Roosevelt did not do. To make sure that the Democratic newcomers in Congress had no Presidential encouragement of any kind, Roosevelt refused to invite them even once to the White House during his first term, as the loyal Harold Ickes bitterly complained in his diary in February 1935. Ickes could simply not understand why the "Chief" would spurn the support of so many valuable allies of reform—another Roosevelt blunder. The truth is that Roosevelt, following the standard party practice of setting up indispensable enemies of the reforms he did not wish to enact, was the only reason Bourbons retained their power in Congress. They were still in the seats of power after 331 Democrats organized Congress in 1937—"not a good augury for a harmonious session," as *The New York Times* rightly observed.

Far from being an opportunity, the landslide Democratic majorities of 1935 and 1937 were a stark danger to the Roosevelt Administration. Lopsided legislative majorities always are, because they weaken the ability of the party oligarchs to control legislation. As Rayburn remarked in 1958 (the source is Evans and Novak's biography of Johnson) when a Democratic landslide was in prospect: "I'd just as soon not have that many Democrats. Believe me, they'll be hard to handle." What was true in 1958 was even more true in the clamorous days of 1935, when Roosevelt and the Democratic oligarchy, according to Bolling, were "worried about the unorthodox views the newcomers might have." An eagerness to enact reform measures was their major unorthodoxy.

To help safeguard oligarchic control over legislation, Roosevelt had to strengthen local machine control over machine Congressmen, for they, like other legislators, were under increasing pressure from the voters to press for reforms. Since the ability of local party bosses to control their minions depends on the cohesion of their organizations, Roosevelt poured Federal patronage into the hands of local Democratic bosses and virtually every enemy of reform in the Democratic party. As Leuchtenburg notes, "frequently New Deal opponents controlled the local WPA [Works Progress Administration] organization," but much more was involved than that. On the supposition that Roosevelt wished to strengthen the power of reformers, his alleged allies, his entire patronage policy must be considered yet another colossal blunder. In Connecticut, New Deal patronage flowed into the hands of Senator Augustus Lonergan, boss of the state party and a leading obstructionist. In Mississippi it went into the hands of Senator Pat Harrison, arch-Bourbon chairman of the Finance Committee, whom Roosevelt then turned around and professed to "fear." In Massachusetts, Roosevelt's patronage went to Senator David Walsh of the old anti–New Deal Al Smith gang. In Rhode Island it was put in the hands of the obstructionist Senator Peter Gerry to help him beat back reform Democrats led by the state's former governor. In Texas it went to the Bourbon wing of the state party; in San Antonio it went to the local machine enemies of the reform Congressman Maury Maverick. In California Roosevelt studiously shut out insurgent Democratic Congressmen and gave control of patronage to Senator William McAdoo of the California party's conservative wing. Enormous patronage was showered on the leading city machine bosses, conspicuously the Kelly-Nash machine in Chicago and Frank Hague's Hudson County, New Jersey, machine, although Hague himself was an open enemy of reform. "By 1940," according to Flynn, the city bosses "were among the most ardent Roosevelt men," and like their President, their minions always sided with Bourbon power in Congress.

What is more, Roosevelt had during 1934 used his power to help defeat a number of Democratic reformers—by giving heavy support to the Chicago machine against liberal Chicago Democrats, as Ickes again complained; by securing the Senate nomination for a Nebraska hack against the state's governor, "a type of populistic radical," as Raymond Moley correctly observed in his 1939 memoir *After Seven Years*, "with which the New Deal certainly had no sympathy." When Upton Sinclair captured the Democratic nomination for governor of California in 1934, "New Deal officials," according to Leuchtenburg, "forged an alliance between Democratic conservatives and the anti–New Deal Merriam," the Republican governorship candidate. When Roosevelt told the nation in a 1938 "fireside chat" that there were still too many conservatives in the Democratic party, he was speaking plain truth, but it was he who had kept them there and, in many cases, put them there. Either that or Roosevelt was the most egregious political bungler in American history.

The story of the "Second New Deal" is briefly told. Despite all that Roosevelt had done to put a brake on genuine reform, the lopsided Democratic Congress elected in 1934 still "threatened," in Leuchtenburg's words, "to push him in a direction far more radical than any he had originally contemplated." The threat was particularly pointed since what Roosevelt had "originally contemplated" was restoring, by sweeping measures, all the nation's shaky holders of corrupt privilege and corrupt power. To help prevent the Democratic majority from getting out of hand, Roosevelt and the Congressional leadership increased the number of signatures needed to dislodge a bill from the Rules Committee from 145 to 218 just three years after they had reduced it from 218 to 145; this would be yet another key element in the Rules Committee's future power to thwart reform legislation. To damp down unruly enthusiasm for reform, Roosevelt conveniently submitted almost no legislation to the new Congress and showed not the slightest propensity to fight for what he did submit. By June 1935 the New Deal was at another standstill, as Ickes and others loudly lamented. According to Leuchtenburg, Roosevelt "seemed to fear the conservatives less than the spenders and inflationists." That is putting it mildly. "Roosevelt's actions left his progressive followers in a quandary. They could not countenance his conservative posture." In mid-May, for example, a delegation of Western

Republican reformers had urged Roosevelt to take some action and pointedly told him, as Ickes reports, that he would get nothing done if he persisted in dealing with the Senate solely through Majority Leader Joe Robinson of Arkansas, Senator Pat Harrison and the rest of the ruling gang in the Senate, this "deference" to the Senate Democratic oligarchs being yet another of Roosevelt's alleged blunders as an alleged reformer.

Stall as much as he could, however, Roosevelt no longer possessed full power of decision. Having stirred the citizenry out of despondency, Roosevelt was now being threatened by men who were feeding on their hopes. "As the New Deal bogged down," in Leuchtenburg's words, "demagogues and radicals who feasted on the popular discontent of 1934 challenged Roosevelt for national leadership." The two key figures were Senator Huey Long and his Share Our Wealth following and Dr. Francis Townsend and his old people's movement, each of which was pressing hard on an already impatient Congress. Roosevelt's hand was forced. Suddenly springing into action on June 5, 1935, Roosevelt enacted the "Second New Deal," which was exactly like the first in one fundamental regard: it revealed Roosevelt's persistent attitude toward reform—to yield as little as political circumstance allowed.

The Social Security Act, for which the New Deal is celebrated, was not even a Roosevelt-initiated reform, but one forced out of him by the Townsend movement and by the country at large; in the 1934 elections *Republicans* had attacked Roosevelt for not submitting a social security measure. Even after submitting a proposal in January 1935, Roosevelt had given no signs of supporting it until he was forced into action in June. Passed in June by enormous majorities, the Social Security Act was, in Leuchtenburg's words, "an astonishingly inept and conservative piece of legislation. In no other welfare system in the world did the state shirk all responsibility for old-age indigency and insist that funds be taken out of the current earnings of workers." Fiscally, the Social Security Act imposed—and still imposes—a savagely regressive tax on the ordinary citizen, one which, thanks entirely to Roosevelt, puts a heavy burden on the ill-to-do and almost none at all on the affluent.* In short it was the *worst* measure he could get through a Congress far more reform-minded than he. That is what he needed Bourbon leadership for.

Another famous enactment of the Second New Deal, the Wagner National Labor Relations Act, was likewise not a true New Deal proposal, since Roosevelt had in fact opposed it until it passed the Senate 63 to 12. After that, bowing to necessity, he gave it his support. As politically corrupt as the trade unions are (see chapter 10), Roosevelt himself preferred an even safer form of trade unionism than that legalized by the Wagner Act, namely unions controlled by management; under the aegis of Roosevelt's NRA "codes," such company unions had flourished mightily in 1934.

The third major measure, the Wealth Tax Act, was explicitly intended to "steal Huey's thunder" by promising to redistribute the wealth more equitably—the "soak-the-rich tax," as it was quickly dubbed. Roosevelt, however, proposed it chiefly as a Tammany-style "show of action." After submitting the measure, says Leuchtenburg, "the President seemed remarkably reluctant to take the lead." When Roosevelt's Congressional henchmen began hinting that they would adjourn Congress without acting on the bill, Roosevelt gave no sign that he would fight adjournment. "He seemed wary of pitting himself against the conservative Harrison, chairman of the Senate Finance Committee," his patronage client. "It took a bold move by Senator

*No tax is considered progressive which takes the same fixed portion of everybody's income. The Social Security tax is sharply regressive because it takes a fixed portion of people's incomes up to a stipulated point; anything beyond that is untaxed. Conventional historians frequently quote with approval Roosevelt's allegedly "shrewd" explanation for burdening the have-nots so heavily. By making ordinary people pay, he said, future "reactionary" administrations would be unable to take Social Security away from them. This is pure mendacity. Even if the great mass of people paid nothing for their Social Security benefits, no administration would dare strip such a general privilege from the citizenry. Powerful "reactionary" forces were a bogeyman Roosevelt used again and again. The real reason Roosevelt chose to burden the citizenry was to discourage them from too keenly demanding the expansion of Social Security provisions, since any expansion hits them so hard. By means of a savagely regressive tax, another avenue of hope was closed down by Roosevelt and every one of his successors.

La Follette to turn the tide" by preventing the Democratic oligarchy from adjourning Congress. With Roosevelt "reluctant to take the lead" and "wary" of a man whom he virtually kept in office, the tax bill was then slaughtered in Harrison's committee, which was exactly what Roosevelt wanted. As a result, according to Leuchtenburg, "the share of the top 1 per cent even *increased* a bit after the passage of the Wealth Tax Act."

When Congress adjourned in August 1935, New Deal legislating was virtually at an end. Despite the "radicalism of his rhetoric," in Rauch's words, during his 1936 reelection campaign, Roosevelt had recommended no new reforms during that year, his *third* spell of inactivity in four years. According to Rauch, "the paucity of important new legislation in 1936 was . . . striking." Indeed, after the Second Hundred Days of 1935, Roosevelt himself had remarked that his program was "substantially complete"—a remark which in the event ought to be taken literally but never is.

This then was the situation when Congress convened in January 1937: a President whose deeds reveal his skillful determination to hold genuine reform to a minimum had committed himself in flaming words to reforms of the broadest and most liberating kind. What is more, if his campaign words had any meaning, they committed him to an antitrust policy diametrically opposed to the one sort of "reform" to which Roosevelt seemed genuinely committed, namely the creation of "private economic governments" by legislative enactment. On the issue of the trusts, two antithetical Roosevelt critics agree: Raymond Moley, who thought the NRA not far-reaching enough, and John Flynn, who deemed it fascism. Writing in 1948, Flynn argued that Roosevelt had proposed the NRA "not as a temporary expedient but as a new order....He had done his best to impose the dissolution of the antitrust laws on the country." Writing in 1939, Moley denied that "Roosevelt was won over to a policy of 'anti-bigness.' . . . he went no further than to ask for a thorough Congressional study of 'the concentration of economic power in American industry,'" in 1938. Knowing what Roosevelt's consistent policy had been during his first term in office, which alternative is easier to believe: that a President who had skillfully tried to thwart reform for four years would use the same skill to thwart it in the fifth year or that the same President, at the outset of his second term, was miraculously transmorphosed into a determined reformer of unsurpassed political ineptitude? An examination of the court fight itself makes the former proposition a fair certainty.

Roosevelt's purpose in launching the court fight was, quite simply, to inflict upon himself the worst kind of public defeat in the most dubious possible cause. His political reason for doing this will shortly become apparent. All the well-recognized blunders which Roosevelt allegedly committed in the course of the court struggle were neatly concerted to this end.

The first point about the court plan was the enormous political risk Roosevelt ran in submitting it at all; a more ill-timed proposal can scarcely be imagined at the outset of his second term. At best, any law enabling a President to name as many as six additional justices to the Supreme Court was bound to raise bitterly divisive questions about the separation of powers. At best, it was sure to look like a suspicious reach for judicial power on the part of a President already under attack from Republicans for harboring dictatorial ambitions. Whatever the merits of the plan, it could not fail to antagonize a good number of adherents of reform. Whatever its merits, it could not fail to give the opponents of reform an opportunity to cloak their opposition in constitutional garb. This much was predictable in advance.

Had Roosevelt wished to minimize these inherent political risks, it was imperative for him to persuade the citizens of the overriding public need for the plan, but Roosevelt did nothing to convince them of this. For one thing, he might have told the people that without an enlarged court they would be deprived of future beneficial reforms he was now requesting, but this Roosevelt did not do and for good reason; he had offered no program of reform legislation except the court plan itself. For another thing, Roosevelt might have told the people that without court reform, past beneficial laws were in grave danger of being struck down. This Roosevelt did not do either, and also for good reason: there was not, in February 1937, any clear-cut need to enlarge the Supreme Court to secure the validation of major New

Deal enactments. Historians, obligingly putting words into Roosevelt's mouth, have expatiated at length about the Supreme Court's threat to the Social Security Act and the Wagner Act. The facts are otherwise. The Social Security Act, resting on the Federal Government's acknowledged taxing powers, was not in any danger and was duly upheld in May 1937. The Wagner Act was allegedly threatened by a Supreme Court decision of 1936 invalidating a New York State wages and hours law. The decision was 5–4, however, and one of the judges who had voted with the majority did so on purely technical grounds. He could be expected in future to vote with the liberals and soon did. In any event Roosevelt could scarcely use the threat to wages and hours legislation as a reason for the court plan; he himself had blocked a strong wages and hours measure in 1933 and 1936. As for the NRA, which delegated legislative authority to corporation magnates, it could not be salvaged short of Roosevelt's naming ten flunkies from Tammany Hall to a nineteen-man bench.

Defenders of Roosevelt who argue that the President "really" wanted to protect New Deal enactments (without explaining why Roosevelt did not say this himself) inadvertently expose yet another of Roosevelt's "blunders" in presenting his court plan. If such protection was his real motive, his plan was grossly in excess of its putative purpose. Since the validation of New Deal legislation seemed to require at most the replacement of *one* anti–New Deal judge by a liberal (the key decisions were all 5–4), there seemed to be no earthly reason why Roosevelt would want the naming of *six* additional judges—except of course the most sinister reasons, and suspicion of these his plan duly aroused. Assuming that protecting past New Deal laws was Roosevelt's secret motive, and assuming in addition that he wished to *avoid* any unnecessary risk to his power and prestige, his most practical move would have been to submit no court plan at all but rather to work behind the scenes to persuade one anti–New Deal judge to retire. Interestingly, Roosevelt's opportunity to do this had come up the year before. In 1936, two of the conservative justices told Representative Hatton Sumners, chairman of the House Judiciary Committee, that they were willing to retire if their retirement status was improved by a new Congressional enactment. Hoping to liberalize the court by so simple a means, Sumners introduced the necessary bill, but the Roosevelt Administration beat it down. Clearly Roosevelt was not trying to avoid a grave political risk; what he had avoided was the opportunity not to take it. On the assumption that Roosevelt "really" wished to see past New Deal laws upheld, his court plan, with all its inherent dangers, with its vague and sinister purposes, was an entirely gratuitous undertaking. And if this were not Roosevelt's intention, then it still constitutes a gratuitous undertaking, for then it would have had no purpose at all.

These preliminary "blunders," however, were but the beginning of a whole charade of "blunders" which Roosevelt began committing in the course of the court fight itself. The first public action Roosevelt took to inflict trouble on himself was to trump up not a strong case for the plan but the worst possible case. Instead of arguing that he wished to "liberalize" the court, Roosevelt said only that his plan was needed to make the court more "efficient." The justices, he claimed, were old and falling behind in their work. Moley himself was puzzled over this "strangely transparent plan of presentation," which Chief Justice Charles Evans Hughes duly exploded a few days later by informing Congress that the Supreme Court, so far from falling behind, was completely up to date in its proceedings. If Roosevelt had wished to incite the gravest possible mistrust of his motives, the blatant duplicity of his argument served that purpose well. Assuming that the mistake was unintended, such egregious stupidity is beyond explanation.

To stir up further trouble for himself, Roosevelt dropped the court plan on Congress and the country without a single word of warning. Not only had he not disclosed his intentions in any public address, he had even kept it secret from the Democratic leaders in Congress, the very men whose prerogatives he had so delicately cherished at all other times. Between the secrecy of the plan and the transparently fake reason for offering it, "Roosevelt," in Leuchtenburg's words, "could scarcely have bungled the presentation of the Court plan more." In two easy steps, Roosevelt, the consummate politician, had ensured widespread distrust of his motives and widespread unpopularity for his bill, which grew more odious every day as well-known reformers publicly denounced it and headlines across the country condemned Roosevelt's "grab" for arbitrary power, just what he had contrived to make his court plan appear.

If Roosevelt had blundered thus far, the extraordinary thing about his ensuing actions was his absolute refusal to rectify his mistakes. Every opportunity which Congress offered for compromise, Roosevelt spurned as "defeatism." When Congress passed the Supreme Court Retirement Act in February 1937—Sumners' bill of the preceding year—the prospect of a conservative judge retiring did not prompt Roosevelt to relent. When the Supreme Court on March 29 upheld a Washington State minimum wage law and the most plausible pretext for the court plan was plainly crumbling away, Roosevelt, instead of relenting, took personal charge of the fight. He now staked all his prestige on the outcome, which was growing dimmer each day as every possible reason for the fight disappeared one after the other. On April 12, the allegedly endangered Wagner Act was duly upheld; on May 18, Willis Van Devanter, the conservative judge who had promised to retire, announced his intention to do so; on May 24 the allegedly endangered Social Security Act was upheld. If Roosevelt wished to "liberalize" the court, he had already won; if he wished to secure major New Deal enactments, they were now secured. Yet Roosevelt continued to prosecute the battle. According to Rauch, "Roosevelt's unwillingness to compromise now angered his supporters who were being forced to carry this unpopular cause." At the same time, according to Leuchtenburg, "men who had feared to oppose his economic policies . . . now had the perfect justification for breaking with the President."

On June 14, the Senate Judiciary Committee voted down the bill as a "proposal which violates every sacred tradition of American democracy" and *still* Roosevelt carried on the fight. By then "the Democratic party," according to Leuchtenburg, "was tearing itself apart. Still Roosevelt pushed on with the hopeless struggle." Not until July 22, after 168 days of wrangling, did Roosevelt finally allow the bill to die. The death blow had been struck three days before when Roosevelt's loyal protégé, Governor Herbert Lehman of New York, publicly denounced the plan, an act of "betrayal" which reportedly "angered" Roosevelt, who vented his fury several months later by securing Governor Lehman's renomination for office.

The defeat which Roosevelt suffered was not inadvertent. That a politician who in thirty years had made so few political errors should commit a farrago of childish blunders in the space of 168 days stretches credibility to the breaking point. He had done everything wrong and nothing right and had then proceeded to make everything worse. Even if we knew nothing of Roosevelt's intentions it would still defy credibility. Since we do know something of those intentions during his first Administration, it is difficult to doubt that Roosevelt had deliberately sought defeat. By inflicting on himself the worst possible rebuff in what he himself had made appear the worst possible cause, Roosevelt accomplished several things, each designed to help him prevent the enactment of reform.

The first thing Roosevelt's deliberately prolonged court fight accomplished was to tie up and virtually kill the first session of an unruly, reform-minded Congress. As Rauch puts it: "A more immediate and significant consequence of the bitter fight over the court plan was the failure of Congress to pass important laws....Such a result would have seemed impossible when the 1937 session of Congress opened." With the court fight Roosevelt had taken the great reform impetus that dominated Congress in January 1937 and sent it up a blind alley for almost six months. (I cannot resist citing here the "explanation" which Roosevelt's aide Harry Hopkins offered in 1937 for the lack of legislation. America, he said, had become "bored with the poor, the unemployed and the insecure." For sheer official effrontery, this remark, I believe, is unmatched.)

The second objective Roosevelt achieved by inflicting defeat upon himself was precisely to prove that Congress could defy him, a stratagem Kennedy would use later on in far less difficult circumstances. This paved the way for the sudden emergence of the Rules Committee in the summer of 1937 as the "third house" of Congress under the obstructive control of a new Bourbon-Republican coalition.

Openly defying Roosevelt, the coalition transformed Rules into "a slaughter house for legislative proposals," to quote Representative Bolling. The Democratic half of the coalition, of course, had been planted there four years before, thanks entirely to Roosevelt. Had it begun defying him before his defeat on the court plan, however, the collusion between Roosevelt and the Bourbons would have been glaringly obvious. Who would have believed for a moment that a half-dozen Congressmen could withstand a President who could marshal nearly three hundred votes against them in Congress and most of the people outside it? By suffering an abject defeat in Congress after exerting all his power, however, Roosevelt had proved that obstructionists in Congress could successfully thwart his will. Moreover, by giving his obstructionist "enemies" the opportunity to resist a President harboring "dictatorial ambitions," Roosevelt had given them a creditable cause. In short, what Roosevelt had done with his self-inflicted defeat was to demonstrate in the most graphic way possible that his indispensable enemy was powerful enough to prevent him from doing what he did not want done in the first place. Without such a defeat, nobody would have believed this possible, not even a professional historian.

The third goal Roosevelt achieved was to tie an albatross around the necks of all those vulnerable Western Democrats elected during the landslide years from Republican districts who loyally stood by him during the prolonged court fight. Due to the unpopularity of the court plan, this was one sure way of killing them off in the next election—and the lopsided Democratic majority with them—and it would work quite well. After spurning the newcomers for four years, Roosevelt had now contrived to turn their constituents against them.

Having blocked reform for one year, Roosevelt quickly set out to block it by more permanent means. He now began to trump up foreign dangers and overseas alarms, an effort which was certain, at the height of American isolationism, to breed further mistrust of the President, further distract Congress, further split reform ranks and put yet another nail in the coffin of Western Democratic Congressmen. Roosevelt began this operation by delivering one of his most unpopular speeches in the part of the country where it was certain to be most ill received. This was his famous "Quarantine the Aggressors" address given in Chicago in October 1937, referring to the Japanese attack on Peking. Having begun to recover somewhat from the long court fight, Congress and the country now heard from Roosevelt that warfare ten thousand miles away threatened the security of the United States. In Roosevelt's January 1938 message to Congress—still a radical Congress—reform legislation was virtually forgotten. The heart of the President's annual message was the need for national defense. "By the end of the year," notes Rauch, "this theme had superseded all others." Having foisted the theme on the country, Roosevelt now turned around in 1938 and regretfully announced that henceforth he would have to submit to the Bourbons on reform in order to gain their support for "collective security"—the indispensable enemy put to work once again.

To expose in detail Roosevelt's famous 1938 campaign to "purge" the Democratic party of its Bourbons would be to whip a dead horse. Suffice it to say that it not only failed but was arranged to fail. As Rauch rightly observes, Roosevelt, in his alleged campaign to unseat Bourbons, "did not appeal for militancy by the submerged groups" in the Southern states, namely the nonvoting poor whites, the only people who would have surely voted to unseat Bourbon legislators. Roosevelt's sole reason for the mock purge was to demonstrate that he really opposed the conservatives whom he had set up to oppose him. He had to allay any lurking suspicion of their mutual friendship after six years of continuous collusion.

In the 1938 elections, Republicans made a net gain of 75 House seats; the lopsided Democratic legislative majorities were finally killed off and the danger of reform at last overcome. The country, according to our historians, turned conservative in 1938, by which they mean that the people, having voted overwhelmingly for reform in 1936 and gotten nothing but "national defense," were turning increasingly to the only other available party. If that means Americans were becoming conservative, then liberal must mean the determination to blast public hope.

The praise that has been lavished on the New Deal had always rested, essentially, on a single specious argument—that whatever its faults and limitations, it was better than nothing at all; that driving small farmers into urban slums was better than no farm legislation; that a regressive Social Security tax was better than no Social Security Act; that Roosevelt's "activism" was better than Coolidge's "laissez-faire." But these were never the alternatives that *Roosevelt* faced; they were the alternatives the two party oligarchies offered the citizenry, but that is another matter. Roosevelt was neither bestowing reform on a reluctant conservative people nor dragging it from a balky conservative Congress. He had done the very opposite. He had held back genuine reform from a clamorous democratic people who in 1936 had responded with overwhelming favor to his republican campaign talk. He had suppressed an unruly, reform-minded Congress by saddling it with Bourbon overlords. Every piece of New Deal legislation bears the imprint of that purpose; every political move Roosevelt made was subservient to that purpose, was deliberately calculated to achieve it.

The history of Roosevelt's New Deal constitutes, therefore, the largest and most detailed confirmation of the proposition I have already set forth: first, that party organizations constantly endeavor to block reform and blast untoward hope in order to maintain themselves and their power; second, that they are powerful enough to choose for high office those who are willing to serve their interests. From 1933 to 1938 the fate of the party oligarchs rested entirely in Roosevelt's hands. Without his determination to protect party power and his extraordinary skill in doing so, it would have disintegrated rapidly—it *was* disintegrating rapidly. With one push from Roosevelt, the party oligarchs would have toppled to the ground. That Roosevelt chose to save them should not be surprising. The Democratic bosses knew very well to whom they had entrusted their power when they nominated Roosevelt in 1932. Had Roosevelt betrayed their trust instead of betraying the people's, the evidence of that betrayal would have been swiftly forthcoming. The 1936 Democratic convention would have been a bloodbath; instead it was a celebration.

That Roosevelt employed extraordinary means—notably the court-packing scheme—to protect party power should not be surprising either. In the larger context of the world's political history, his court-packing maneuver is merely a humdrum example of duplicity. The annals of politics are crammed with acts of the bloodiest villainy taken to gain and hold power. As Gibbon famously remarked, political history is a register of little else. It is not the business of free citizens, however, to judge their public men by any standard other than those of this Republic. By that standard, Roosevelt's duplicity was a heinous act of bad faith and betrayal. There is no doubt that Roosevelt saved the prevailing system of oligarchic power at some sacrifice to himself. It is no small thing for any President to accept a humiliating public rebuff as Roosevelt did in 1937. Such is the stuff of heroes, however, though Roosevelt was not a hero of the Republic, its citizens and its liberties. He was the champion of the party system, a very different matter. In any event the party bosses repaid him well for his sacrifice by letting him seek an unprecedented third term and play a very satisfying role, that of a "wartime leader."

Perhaps the most revealing remark ever publicly made about Franklin Roosevelt was made by Lyndon Baines Johnson in 1964. It was a remark which looked back to Roosevelt's 1937 duplicity and forward to Johnson's own, providing a dramatic link between them. The occasion, as Tom Wicker recounts it in *JFK and LBJ,* was a luncheon for reporters at the White House to discuss Johnson's landslide election victory over Barry Goldwater. Johnson quickly dimmed the reporters' spirits. He reminded them that landslide victories are tricky affairs, as indeed they are to the party oligarchs. "Roosevelt," he told the reporters, "was never President after 1937 until the war came along." Knowing that his task, like Roosevelt's, would be to block reform in 1965, Johnson was virtually telling the reporters that *he* was not going to thwart it by suffering rebuffs until "a war came along." He would kill reform by starting a war—and that is precisely what he did.

7.
Johnson Launches a War

The most striking thing about President Lyndon Johnson's decision to wage war in Vietnam is that had he followed his own official policy line he would not have waged war. According to Johnson's stated policy, the American Government was committed to helping a viable South Vietnamese government help itself against guerrilla rebels, but it would not try to salvage a regime so incapable of commanding the loyalty of its people that it could not get its army to fight. This proviso was based on a set of unimpeached facts: namely that the essential weakness of any Saigon regime was not military but political, that the strength of the Viet Cong guerrillas was indigenous to South Vietnam, that the conflict in South Vietnam was predominantly a civil war. Although Kennedy had drastically broadened the United States commitment to the Saigon regime, he himself had not crossed the Rubicon by committing the American Government to the limitless defense of any non-Communist regime in Saigon.

During the 1964 election campaign Johnson summed up his official policy on several occasions. On August 29, 1964, for example, he said that he had rejected advice to bomb "certain areas" because it "would enlarge the war and escalate the war, and result in our committing a good many American boys to fighting a war that I think ought to be fought by the boys of Asia to help protect their own land." And again on September 25: "We don't want our American boys to do the fighting for Asian boys . . . and get tied down in a land war in Asia."

In February 1965, when Johnson carried the nation into war, all that had happened in South Vietnam was that another Saigon regime was crumbling; Buddhists were rebelling, neutralist and antiwar sentiment, were surfacing in the city. The official policy, therefore, was clear. This was the time, if ever there was one, to disengage entirely from South Vietnam. The disengagement would certainly have been opportune. In Johnson's January message to Congress, he had announced his determination to work for a "Great Society" of "liberty and abundance for all," and he surely knew, in Wicker's words, that "a major war in Vietnam could do little to advance—it would actively pervert—both his domestic and his international purposes." Every schoolboy knows that war distracts the citizenry from domestic reforms, that it enables the enemies of reform to oppose reform as divisive in an hour of national peril. Johnson knew this as well as any schoolboy. In January 1965, according to Evans and Novak, he actually told his advisers that he would lose public and legislative support "if I have to send any more of our boys into Vietnam." This was understandable enough, since it was by upholding the restrained policy line against an apparently "trigger-happy" Barry Goldwater that Johnson had helped himself to his landslide election victory a few months before. Johnson certainly did not expect that an American war in Vietnam would make him *more* popular; no modern American President, not Wilson, not Roosevelt, not Truman, had gained popularity—to put it mildly—by starting a major war; a citizenry which had just elected a President who promised no Asian war was not likely to applaud him for launching one—and they did not. Three years after the bombing began, Johnson was so thoroughly detested by the American electorate that he was forced to leave politics, while the party which had nominated him and supported him lost some twelve million votes between the 1964 and the 1968 elections. Nor was Johnson's hand forced by any alleged fear of a public outcry if the South Vietnamese government fell to the Viet Cong. Quite the opposite was true. As William Bundy told Johnson in a January 1965 memorandum, the forthcoming decision to bomb North Vietnam presented "grave difficulties" just then, precisely because, in Bundy's evasive language, "the picture of South Vietnamese will is extremely weak." What he meant was that the more clearly Americans understood that "Asian boys" would not fight for a corrupt, inept and unpopular regime, the less they would tolerate American boys "doing the fighting" for them. So far from arousing popular sentiment for war in Vietnam, the imminent collapse of the Saigon regime in January 1965 was something of an obstacle to Johnson's launching it.

Given every apparent political reason not to wage war—the risk to his popularity, to his legislative support, to his "Great Society" program—Johnson decided to begin a war in a startling reversal of his stated public policy.

On the apologists' perennial assumption that every American President tries to do what he thinks will best serve the citizens' interests, Johnson's war decision has been ascribed to blunders of all sorts. It is often said, for example, that Johnson "sincerely," if mistakenly, believed that the fall of South Vietnam to the Viet Cong would pose a grave threat to the security of the United States, this mistake being due to Johnson's "blind" adherence to the Cold War doctrine first set forth by Harry Truman in 1947, namely that any Communist victory, "whether by direct or indirect aggression," threatens the security of the United States. It has been said, too, that Johnson mistakenly believed—despite his own official policy line—that the weakness of the Saigon regime was due chiefly to the "aggressive" deeds of the North Vietnamese regime. It has been said that he ordered the bombing of North Vietnam on the mistaken belief that it would be effective, and then "reluctantly" sent in combat troops when the bombing proved a failure, thus finding himself sucked, inadvertently, into a "quagmire." It has been said quite often that Johnson's actual responsibility for the war was small, that he was "caught up" in the "logic" of a "decision-making process" that began with Kennedy and Eisenhower and that the war, in consequence, was merely the culminating step in an inexorable process.

Each of these explanations, however, is thoroughly exploded by the actual government documents published in the now famous "Pentagon Papers," a massive study compiled at the behest of

Secretary of Defense Robert McNamara. What these documents reveal, first, is that as early as March 1964, Johnson and his principal advisers—McGeorge Bundy, Walt Rostow, General Maxwell Taylor, the Joint Chiefs of Staff, McNamara and Secretary of State Dean Rusk—began making all the necessary military and political preparations for war in Vietnam, preparations that would enable Johnson to launch a war at a moment's notice should he deem it desirable. What the documents reveal, secondly, is that this fixed determination to prepare for war corresponded to no fixed reason for doing so, that the several justifications the war plotters proposed were transparent pretexts which not only changed with changing circumstance, but were also in large measure concocted by the plotters themselves. Most importantly, the Pentagon Papers reveal that Johnson did not order the sustained bombing of North Vietnam in February 1965 because he sincerely believed that North Vietnamese "aggression" was the chief element in the South Vietnam conflict; he believed nothing of the kind. What the Pentagon Papers do *not* reveal, however, is any reason for Johnson's determination to go to war. They make his decision seem even more arbitrary.

We know from the Pentagon study that the 1964 war preparations were not drawing-board contingency plans in the usual sense of that term. They were carefully implemented and well-concerted operations carried out under Johnson's orders in accordance with a preconceived scheme outlined in March 1964. The scheme involved the waging of what the study terms "clandestine warfare" against North Vietnam during 1964 for the express purpose of provoking North Vietnamese reprisals in order to build up a case for North Vietnamese "aggression" and so accustom the American people to regard North Vietnam as the "real" enemy. It involved the deployment of air strike forces capable of carrying out what the war plotters called "retaliatory action" against North Vietnam on seventy-two hours' notice as the necessary complement to the provocation strategy. It involved the preparation of a Congressional resolution that would free Johnson from further need to consult Congress. This was to be submitted—and was—when the provocation strategy produced a suitable act of North Vietnamese "aggression." It involved the massive deployment of bomber planes capable of carrying out, after a suitable number of "retaliations for aggression," what the war plotters called "graduated overt military pressure" culminating in sustained bombing of North Vietnam. This was made ready to go into effect within thirty days of Johnson's ordering it, an order he was to give on February 13, 1965. No military rationale stood behind any of these preparations. They were determined entirely by the war plotters' need to prepare public opinion for an American war in Vietnam when and if Johnson ordered it. This was the reason the preparations were kept secret; if the electorate knew of them, they would have failed of their purpose.

These plans explode the nonsense that Johnson's war decision was a mere culminating step in an inexorable "decision-making process." The war plotters themselves did not think they were merely taking the "next step" in a "process." All their plans and preparations, which were, essentially, an elaborate effort to prepare public opinion, demonstrate what in any event is obvious, that they knew full well they were preparing to take a momentous step and make a sharp break with the past. The difference between 30,000 advisers in Vietnam and 500,000 combat troops, the difference between not bombing a small distant country and laying it to waste, are not the differences separating adjacent points on a curve. The war plotters knew that if Johnson decided on war he would not have been part of a decision-making process, he would have made a momentous decision, precisely the decision to wage war. One of the war plan's purposes, indeed, was to concoct a series of graduated responses from "one-shot" reprisals for "aggression," to stronger reprisals, to sustained bombing, to introduction of more "advisers," to their open deployment as combat troops and so on. These gradations were concerted elements in a common plan to make it appear that America had been dragged into its involvement one reluctant step at a time. To concoct the appearance of a "decision-making process" was itself a *decision* of Johnson's. The truth is, the very phrase "decision-making process" is a political lie; every decision is the antithesis of a process. Had Johnson decided not to bomb North Vietnam, no "process" would have bombed North Vietnam. It is as simple as that, and all the claptrap about decision-making is designed chiefly to veil the obvious. It is the lie of the courtier who blames the king's errors on his advisers, the advisers being replaced nowadays by pseudo-scientific jargon about "processes."

The Pentagon Papers also explode the notion that Johnson "sincerely" believed that a Viet Cong victory was so deadly a threat to American security that the grave step of war—and there is no graver political step—was necessary to avert it. If Johnson believed this, then his toadying advisers were too stupid to divine why he did so because they could not agree among themselves what grave danger the war was supposed to avert. In 1964 Johnson and his high-ranking flunkies held two basic reasons for waging war in Vietnam. These reasons were such that if the first were true the second was otiose, and if the second were important the first was clearly false. Early in 1964, the "domino theory" seems to have held sway among the war plotters. In a March 16 memorandum from McNamara to Johnson calling for a "program of preparations for initiating action against North Vietnam," this tenuous doctrine was in full flower. According to McNamara, if South Vietnam fell to the Viet Cong, "almost all of Southeast Asia will probably fall under Communist dominance. . . . Even the Philippines would become shaky, and the threat to India to the west, Australia and New Zealand to the south and Taiwan, Korea and Japan to the north and east would be greatly increased." (Now that Nixon has gone to China, unsettling Japanese politics, and has sided with Pakistan, giving Russia a strong influence in India, we can better judge the oligarchs' "fear" of falling Asian dominoes.)

In addition to saving Asia from total disaster, the war plotters, curiously enough, also advanced a second, altogether different, reason for war in Vietnam. To quote one of the lesser plotters, John T. McNaughton of the Defense Department, the chief reason America must bomb North Vietnam was to "avoid a humiliating U.S. defeat (to our reputation as guarantor)." This reason was frequently expressed as America's compelling need to demonstrate "resolution," to maintain our "prestige," to show our willingness to "honor treaty obligations" (which were nonexistent in the case of South Vietnam), to show the world we could "act like a great power." In other words America was to fight a war half the globe away in order to (a) save Asia, (b) save face. This is rather like a housebreaker explaining to the police that he entered his victim's home because he was fleeing deadly pursuers and *also* because he wanted to keep warm. When two such reasons are thus combined, common sense suggests that both are untrue. However, there were advantages in having two chief reasons on hand. Asked its opinion of the domino theory, the Central Intelligence Agency in June 1964 gave its forthright view that it was largely nonsense. After that it was eclipsed somewhat by the alternate doctrine that America had to defeat the Viet Cong, not actually to save Asia from Communism, but to show that we were honorable allies. In an important position paper dated November 29, 1964, the "domino effect," that is, total disaster, had fallen to third among the government's enumerated objectives in South Vietnam.

How little Johnson or any of the plotters actually believed in either of the first two reasons as a *casus belli* was demonstrated in spring 1965 when North Vietnamese army elements, in response to America's entry into the war, crossed the border into South Vietnam. As soon as this happened, the war plotters announced that the North Vietnamese army had actually "invaded" South Vietnam back in January 1965, which is to say, just before Johnson's decision to wage war. This "invasion" was now deemed retroactively to be the chief reason the President was forced into war. If using and concocting any justification for the war that Johnson thought would go down is evidence of sincerity, it is hard to imagine the evidence for duplicity.

Nothing reveals how fixed was the determination to prepare for war and how adaptable were its justifications than the way in which the war plotters met what McNamara had termed in March 1964 "the problem of marshaling the case to justify . . . military actions" against North Vietnam. The need to "marshal the case" arose out of the most fundamental political fact about the Vietnam War, namely that the plotters had no choice but to begin the war by attacking North Vietnam. Had they announced that they were going to war against Saigon's real enemy, the Viet Cong, they could not have justified doing so to the

American people. The electorate, as the plotters well knew, would not readily support a war to save a corrupt regime from its own native rebels. *Not* to do so was precisely Johnson's official policy, and that policy was the chief obstacle to war. The "enemy" of Saigon, therefore, had to become an "external aggressor." This was the only pretext for war that stood any chance of getting by with the American people.

Unfortunately for the plotters, there was no military or politically acceptable reason for bombing North Vietnam. All that the North Vietnamese regime actually did was train small numbers of South Vietnamese rebels to serve as a cadre in the guerrilla war. This return of South Vietnamese rebels to their own country would invariably be termed, in the councils of the plotters, "North Vietnamese infiltration," itself a lying phrase and a most important one. Since Hanoi had committed no aggression that could conceivably justify an American attack and since the plotters could have a war on no other basis than such aggression, they were now forced to concoct a variety of reasons—or the appearance of reasons—for the future bombing of the North Vietnamese "aggressors." Their problem was further aggravated by the CIA's judgment against the plotters' plans to conduct secret warfare against North Vietnam. As the CIA asserted in mid-1964, such action against North Vietnam would accomplish nothing, since "the primary sources of Communist strength in South Vietnam are indigenous." At this point, according to the Pentagon study, Walt Rostow came to the war plotters' rescue with his "theory" that the North Vietnamese government was "the root of the problem" in South Vietnam. Although it contradicted the facts, the judgment of the CIA and the entire foundation of Johnson's official policy, this "theory," according to the Pentagon study, quickly gained acceptance. This is hardly surprising, since Rostow had simply told Johnson what he wanted to hear—that is what Presidential advisers like Rostow are paid for. Johnson did not order the bombing of North Vietnam in February 1965 because he mistakenly believed that the North Vietnamese were the key to the fate of Saigon but because he knew that only by pretending that they were could he successfully palm off a war. The "blunder" was no blunder but a necessary pretext for war.

Having swiftly accepted the theory that North Vietnam was the root of the problem, the plotters now set in motion two sorts of actions to prove it. The first was to put pressure on the intelligence agencies—which are after all employees—to change their inconvenient opinion about the indigenous strength of the Viet Cong. In March 1964, Rostow ordered an underling to "come back from Saigon with as lucid and agreed a picture" as possible of North Vietnamese "infiltration." On November 5, William Bundy was happy to report that "we are on the verge of intelligence agreement that infiltration has in fact increased. . . . In general we feel the problem of proving North Vietnamese participation is less than in the past." Thus the plotters were preparing to go to war for a reason they had not even proved yet; the war was a conclusion in search of a premise. Bundy also suggested that when American forces take "reprisal action" such "action be linked as directly as possible to DRV [Hanoi] infiltration." This was to help impress upon the American people that "infiltration" was the key problem in South Vietnam. As far as the war plotters were concerned, the only problem in Vietnam was the American electorate.

The second effort to make appearances fit the Rostow theory was the strategy of clandestine warfare designed to provoke reprisals against American forces. If the reprisal was committed by the North Vietnamese, it would help prove that they were aggressors, the American provocation, of course, being secret. If the reprisals were carried out by the Viet Cong, however, the plotters recommended that American retaliation be directed against the North Vietnamese anyway to strengthen the public belief that the Viet Cong and the Hanoi regime were indistinguishable, since our bombers would make no distinction. This strategy of provocation, as the Pentagon study calls it, culminated first in the shadowy Tonkin Gulf attack of August 1964, wherein American destroyers were deliberately ordered into waters where secret raids against North Vietnam were in progress and in full knowledge gained from radio intercepts that a torpedo boat attack was imminent. Needless to say, Johnson was not trying to avoid an incident. After the apparent attack, itself the result of months of assiduous skirt-trailing, Johnson brayed loudly about the dastardly deed and submitted the resolution to Congress that freed his hand in the future. He also ordered a savage "retaliatory action" which had been made ready for just such a moment as well as the massive deployment of bomber forces capable of carrying out sustained air attacks on North Vietnam within thirty days' notice, the second major element in the war plan.

While Bundy and Rostow were still fabricating proof that North Vietnam was the "root of the problem," the plotters adopted what might be called interim reasons for bombing North Vietnam. Maxwell Taylor, our ambassador to Saigon, first justified the planned bombing on the grounds that it would bolster the political fortunes of the Khanh regime, whose survival, according to Taylor, was "50–50." Since the war plan was fixed and the justifications transient, Taylor's later cable of August 18 makes especially interesting reading. He notes his full agreement with the preparations for "a fully orchestrated bombing attack on NVN" because, as he had said before, it would help secure the Khanh regime. If the regime collapses, however, "we would have to restate the problem"—that is, think of another reason. In that case, he suggests, "our objective [would be] to avoid the possible consequences of a collapse of national morale." In short, America was to bomb North Vietnam because it was "the root of the problem," but until that was proven, the war plotters could justify the bombing on the grounds that it would gladden South Vietnamese hearts.

By November, however, any notion that bombing the North was contingent on political conditions in the South was entirely abandoned. Given the state of things in Saigon, all such pretexts were too risky; they were likely to disappear at any moment and leave the war plotters in the lurch. "It is impossible to foresee a stable and efficient government under any name in anything like the near future," General Taylor informed Johnson from Saigon on November 27, 1964. Having recommended the bombing for its allegedly beneficial political effects, Taylor, one would suppose, would now recommend that the bombing plan be jettisoned entirely. Such, however, was not the case, since Taylor's original arguments were mere pretexts anyway.

We can still bomb North Vietnam, he said, "if we justified our actions primarily upon the need to reduce infiltration." In other words, having learned from Washington that this was the new line, Taylor had promptly switched to it in the timeless manner of the time-server. The notion that Johnson was misled by his Kennedy-appointed advisers—the King can do no wrong—is patently absurd; a more spineless collection of high-ranking toadies can scarcely be found in American history. The new justification, the work of some months, was formally embodied in a November 29 position paper. According to that paper the primary reason for bombing North Vietnam was "to get Hanoi support and direction removed from South Vietnam." The CIA's earlier judgment that Viet Cong strength was indigenous had apparently been forgotten entirely. In fact it was not forgotten at all.

At this point—the end of November—Johnson's advisers (if echoes can be called advisers) agreed to recommend that the President commence the long-prepared air war against North Vietnam. Yet, astonishingly enough, not one of them believed the bombing would help. Taylor recommended the bombing war but said it would not save an independent non-Communist regime—infiltration "justified" it, but clearly infiltration was not crucial to the civil war in the south. The Joint Chiefs of Staff recommended the bombing, but they too agreed with Taylor that it would serve no military purpose. McNaughton argued that even if the bombing failed it would demonstrate that at least the U.S. Government had tried; McNaughton apparently believed that "honoring commitments" was the real reason Johnson wanted to wage war. Dean Rusk corrected the fatuous McNaughton. If the bombing failed, said Rusk, it would only make matters worse, from which he drew the conclusion that Johnson should order the bombing and make matters worse. Bundy averred that the bombing would not stop infiltration, would not bolster the Saigon regime, would not prevent a Viet Cong victory, but he too recommended the bombing.

Why did all these erstwhile advisers recommend a momentous course of action if they were so convinced it would serve no purpose? For one reason only. Because they knew that Johnson could not get by with a war in South Vietnam except against North Vietnamese "aggressors," and the best way to indicate the aggressor is to bomb him. Why then did they argue that the bombing would not work? Because it had been "justified" on the "theory" that North Vietnam was "the root of the problem," and this they knew was a lie fabricated for domestic consumption. The Viet Cong's strength was indigenous and that is why bombing the North would fail. Instead of using the truth about Viet Cong strength to explode the lie about North Vietnam's importance, however, Johnson's flunkies simultaneously accepted both the truth and the lie and drew from this irrational combination the dual conclusion that Johnson launch a war by bombing North Vietnam because it was the root of the problem and that he should introduce American *combat troops* to fight the Viet Cong—as they now suggested—because *they* were the root of the problem. Advice so patently shoddy would influence no one not already predisposed toward it. In accepting that advice Johnson proved only that he was determined to do so. Certainly he did not bomb North Vietnam because he thought the bombing would serve a military purpose; he knew it would serve no military purpose. Certainly he did not then introduce American combat forces because he discovered a few weeks later that the bombing was ineffectual. He bombed North Vietnam to begin a war to "punish aggression" and he introduced ground troops because a land war in Asia was exactly what he wanted. And the question still is why.

To review once again the conventional explanations: Johnson did not launch the war in Vietnam because he was caught up in a "decision-making process"; men do not concoct new lies because they are caught up in an old process. Johnson did not launch the war because he sincerely believed that a Viet Cong victory would prove so dangerous to American security it warranted the grave step of war; a President who tells the electorate one day that he is trying to save Asia, on another that he is "honoring commitments," on a third that he is "punishing aggression," on a fourth that since America was "in" there was no way to get "out," is sincerely convinced only of the grave danger of losing support for his war. Nor did Johnson launch the war because he was blindly persisting in a Cold War policy; he did not persist in a policy, he made a complete reversal of a policy, precisely a policy that would have kept him out of war. He did not launch the war because he sincerely believed that North Vietnamese aggression was undermining a friendly ally; that was the lie he concocted as his public pretext for war. He surely did not start the war to gain personal popularity or to avert unpopularity; every element in the war plan, every lie and every secret stratagem, was shaped by Johnson's clear understanding that it was popular aversion to a war that he had to overcome. What the Pentagon Papers reveal is that Johnson had a fixed determination to prepare for war, that he used pretexts for war so patently mendacious that any man not disposed for war would have redoubled his efforts to avoid one. What the government documents do not reveal is why Johnson in 1964 decided to make elaborate preparations for war and why he launched it early in 1965.

Yet Johnson's war decision, so apparently arbitrary by conventional political notions,* becomes entirely intelligible in the light of party politics and the perennial interests of the party oligarchs. I have tried to show by general considerations about the nature of party power that widespread public hope and imminent reform are grave dangers to party power. I have tried to show both by general considerations and by several examples that the grass-roots political activity of the citizenry is a sharp threat to party power. I have shown too that landslide Congressional majorities pose a threat to party power and I have shown in the specific cause of Franklin Roosevelt what a President who represents the party oligarchs will do to avert a major danger to their interests. Consider the situation which Johnson and the party oligarchs faced in 1964.

Long before election day it was clear that Johnson would win a signal victory over the egregious Barry Goldwater, whom the Republican

---

*There is, of course, an economic or Marxian explanation of the Vietnam War adapted from the more general Marxian explanation of imperialism. This explanation, which is based on the axiom that the only possible explanation of a political act is an economic explanation, I will examine in a later chapter on American foreign policy in general.

oligarchy nominated with every intention of sending him to defeat. Johnson was certain to have the public hopes of the nation, reviving after so many years, focused directly on his second Administration. Indeed hopes had crystallized around him from the moment Kennedy was shot, and he dared not blast them until he was safely nominated and elected, for he had been deeply distrusted by liberal Democrats and the country at large.* He was certain to have strong legislative majorities to enable him to fulfill those hopes. He was certain to face the first important grass-roots citizens' movement in thirty years, namely the democratic movement arising from and centered upon the black people's struggle for civil and political equality. The dangers this movement posed can scarcely be exaggerated. Not only were its numbers great and its membership varied, not only was it going from strength to strength and from success to success, it was, most importantly, one that united citizens around a republican principle and armed them with the authority of the Constitution itself. Neither an elite nor a mob, neither "left wing" nor "right wing" but a genuine coalition of free citizens, from sharecroppers to Back Bay ladies, the civil-rights movement was giving the Republic back its voice in the affairs of the nation. Party power, in short, faced its first major peril since 1936 and Johnson was assuredly a faithful party servant. Before he had become President through Kennedy's assassination he did not even have a fake reputation as a reformer. It was no secret that he had been the servant and beneficiary of the Bourbon wing of the Texas party. It was no secret that the Senate Democratic oligarchy had made him Majority Leader because it needed his superb parliamentary skills to ride herd on the Senate Democrats. It was no secret that as Majority Leader he had continually stifled reformers in the Senate and muffled their opposition to the Eisenhower Administration. He was the beneficiary and servant of the national Democratic machine and that machine was in peril in 1964, imperiled by what Johnson had

*Johnson certainly tried to win a sweeping election victory—with the help of a Republican dump. He seems to have thought that the larger his election triumph the more public support he could later "spare" and the freer his hand would be.

spent his whole Senate career obstructing, namely reform. When the elections were over, the peril had become greater yet. At the sight of lopsided Democratic majorities in Congress—295 Representatives, 68 Senators—hopes for reform ran high, and the civil-rights movement was more clamorous, more extensive, more determined than ever. The presumption is strong, therefore, that Johnson prepared for war in 1964 because he knew this would happen and that he launched it in 1965 because it did happen. The presumption is strong, that is, that Johnson launched the Vietnam War because he hoped the war would kill reform, that it would split and then reduce his Democratic majorities, that it would distract the citizenry from domestic concerns, that it would kill a grass-roots republican movement, that it would provide the means to suppress dissenters and insurgents in the name of wartime unity.

That the Vietnam War in fact put an end to Johnson's promised struggle for "liberty and abundance" there can be no doubt. Johnson's ability to pass reform legislation scarcely lasted six months, and most of the measures enacted were either trumpery or poorly enforced. By the summer of 1965 Congress was already balky. In September the apparently invincible President suffered his first "defeat" in Congress on his proposal for self-government for the capital city. In October the House voted against appropriating money for a rent-subsidy measure it had enacted in June. There was a war on and, perforce, Congressional leaders had to call a halt to further "experimentation." After mid-1965, as Wicker points out, there would be no more Great Society speeches from Lyndon Baines Johnson. In the 1966 elections, Republicans gained forty-seven House seats and the danger of reform was once again averted.

That Johnson knew this would be the result of his war can hardly be doubted. Throughout modern political history, rulers have started wars to suppress dissent and distract their subjects. War had certainly done this for Woodrow Wilson in 1917, mere war talk had done this for Roosevelt after 1937—as Johnson certainly knew. He himself told his advisers that he would lose support if he sent American troops to Vietnam. To suppose that Johnson sincerely believed that he could have a major war and major reforms is absurd. It is certain that Johnson launched the war in full knowledge that it would achieve the political results it so swiftly achieved.

What is more, and this is particularly telling, Johnson deliberately took steps in addition to war to achieve the same results which the war achieved, namely the frustration of reform and the reduction of another lopsided Democratic majority. Directed at the House of Representatives, this effort was designed by Johnson and the House Democratic bosses to inflict defeat in the 1966 elections on Congressmen first elected in the 1964 landslide. According to Representative Bolling, who describes these tactics in his excellent book *Power in the House,* the chief weapon used against the new members was to call on them to support controversial Administration measures that in fact stood no chance of passage; "walk-the-plank" votes Bolling calls them. The strategy depended on the fact that freshmen Democrats elected in a landslide from Republican suburbs and Western states are virtually the only incumbent Congressmen who face serious election competition.

The first of these "lethal" measures, as Bolling calls them, was the repeal of Section 14(b) of the Taft-Hartley Labor Act (which the party oligarchs had no intention of repealing) authorizing states to pass "right-to-work" laws. This is always a controversial measure in Western states and therefore well suited to damaging those perennial problems to the Democratic machine, namely Western Democratic legislators. Told by the House oligarchs that every Democratic vote on 14(b) was crucial, Bolling was "horrified," in his words, "to discover that the Democratic leadership was leading its yearlings to the slaughter without having the least assurance that the Senate would act favorably" on repeal. Since the Senate duly killed the measure, "the vote," according to Bolling, "served no purpose except to defeat a number of promising newcomers."

The second "walk-the-plank" measure was Johnson's controversial 1966 open-housing bill, which prompted his legislative aide Larry O'Brien to observe slyly that "some of our Democrats are going to vote for it and be defeated in November as a result." This time Bolling asked the Democratic House oligarchy point-blank if the bill were sure to pass the Senate. If not, he believed, a vote in its favor would again serve no purpose except to endanger the seats of the freshmen. The House leadership assured Bolling it would pass the Senate. It was later killed in a Senate committee.

In addition, as Bolling points out, Johnson and House Speaker McCormack deliberately scheduled House votes to bring maximum political trouble to the Congressional freshman. Not only did they bring up measures so that the new members could not return home during the year to mend fences, they contrived to delay the open-housing bill vote until a mere seventeen days before the elections, "another factor that sent the freshmen to their avoidable defeat." According to Bolling, "it reached a point where more than one new member came to me to ask if I believed the President and Speaker were deliberately trying to get them defeated." That is exactly what they were trying to do and they succeeded. After the Democrats lost forty-seven seats in the 1966 elections, says Wicker, "Republicans and anti-Johnson [sic] Southerners would control the House." That was the point of the strategy. If it is evidence of Johnson's genuine wish to enact reform, then suicide is evidence of a desire to greet the next dawn.

To sum up: the Vietnam War produced certain political results and Johnson surely knew that it would produce such results. In addition, Johnson deliberately tried to achieve the same results by means other than war, which suggests at the very least that he did not launch the war despite the results it achieved. I have shown, too, that the party oligarchs who nominated Johnson in 1964, and whom he had served so faithfully throughout his political career, had a compelling interest in achieving those results. I have shown, moreover, that the conventional explanations of Johnson's war decision do not begin to explain that decision; that his alleged blunders were not blunders at all; that the false justifications and false military reasoning were not errors of judgment but necessary pretexts for war. Johnson had been the enemy of reform throughout his career; he launched a war that thwarted reform when reform was imminent. The conclusion, it seems to me, is difficult to avoid, and again I must refer to Lincoln's House Divided speech in drawing it. We cannot know for certain, but we find it impossible not to believe that Johnson launched a bloody, brutal and needless war in Vietnam to thwart reform, to kill his Great Society, to reduce his landslide majorities, to stifle a grass-roots political movement, to blast political hope and protect the party oligarchs in yet another moment of political peril.

Why then has America been in Vietnam? Because the party oligarchs, through *their* elected representatives, control the government of the United States and use their control of the government in order to maintain themselves and their power. The protection of party power is no trivial matter of patronage and endorsements. It determines the actions of government throughout almost the entire range of government. It has shaped the most decisive events in our recent history: the defeat of a seemingly triumphant reform movement in 1937; the waging of a bloody and unjust war in Vietnam. Because of party power, Congress has been rigged and rerigged so that the enemies of reform control legislation and prevent the nation's highest representative assembly from representing those who elect its members. The blighting of public hope through the prevention of reform, however, is but one aspect of the oligarchs' unremitting effort to retain their great power. The party oligarchs are by no means wed merely to the status quo. To preserve their power, the collusive and self-serving party oligarchs actively promote in every way they can every kind of corruption, degradation and special privilege that strengthens their hand and stifles the citizenry.

As for Lyndon Baines Johnson, he committed only one genuine blunder: he thought he could get away with the Vietnam War. Doubtless he did not anticipate a military stalemate, doubtless he did not foresee the emergence of a powerful grass-roots peace movement and an insurgent antiwar candidate who would seriously challenge the Democratic machine. And since he started the war for the good of that party machine, he was bowed out of politics in March 1968 in order to save it again.

PART III

THE FRUITS OF
OLIGARCHY

8.
The Politics of Special Privilege

en rightly recognize the abuse of power in America. They see billions wasted yearly to sustain a bloated military establishment while millions are begrudged for the most ordinary amenities. They see poverty maintained in the midst of unparalleled wealth and wars declared for the most farfetched reasons. They see bureaucracy expand while public services decay. They see a thousand obstacles impede the simplest improvements while gross betrayals of the public trust are accomplished in a trice. They see a government expeditious in corruption turn into a Circumlocution Office when called on to remedy a common grievance.

People see the abuses but not the reasons for them. What they find so hard to understand is why apparently sane leaders should put first things last and dubious things first, not once in a while, but continually, regardless of their promises, their platforms, their party affiliations. To this fundamental political question the prevailing political ideology supplies two alternative answers, and between them and various combinations of them they monopolize established political discourse. The first is based, as I have said, on the proposition that the competing political parties are the "translators of public opinion into public power." Since the people, ostensibly, are well represented, they are held to blame, one way or another, for all unjust policies and inveterate abuses. We wage dubious wars because Americans are self-righteous jingoes; we have racist politics because most Americans are racists; we have poverty because most Americans despise the poor; we have giant corporations because Americans "admire bigness"; reform perpetually fails because Americans are essentially "conservative"; corruption flourishes because Americans are essentially apathetic. In this view, the parties are blamed for being too faithful to an inadequate citizenry; too willing to be merely popular; too craven to lead; in a word, too democratic and powerless.

In the alternative view, the faithlessness of politicians is generally recognized, but their faithlessness is held to be not of their making. In this view, that of economic ideology, "real" power is not in the hands of politicians at all. They are seen as mere servants of powerful special interests and dominant economic forces working behind the facade of politics. In this view, whatever moneyed interest profits from a particular political deed is held to have ordered the deed, so that if highways are built to the neglect of mass transportation, this is attributed to the power of the auto-makers; if war brings profits to large corporations, the war is attributed to the corporations' power. According to the ideology of economic power, no political act is explained until it can be attributed to the will of a powerful economic interest.

Although the first view is that of the apologist and the latter that of the "radical" leftist critic, neither the apologist nor the "radical" can actually explain what happens in America without borrowing each other's presuppositions. The apologist who tries to explain, for example, why the American economy is dominated by giant corporations despite the citizenry's historic opposition to trusts and monopolies will agree with the "radical" economic ideologues that big business is a result of autonomous economic forces more potent than the people's representatives. Those who hold that economic forces or dominant economic interests rule the American Republic, on the other hand, accept the apologists' assumptions about American politics. They too implicitly assume that politicians wish to serve the common interest; they infer from the fact that they do not actually do so that economic forces are bending politicians to their will, just as astronomers once inferred the existence of the invisible planet Neptune from perturbations in the normal orbit of Uranus. So, too, the ideologues of economic power infer from the fact that the two parties are collusive that economic powers rule them both, an inference based on the unwarranted assumption that the party oligarchs would naturally prefer to compete. The political analyses offered by a great many "radical" economic ideologues are shot through with apologist assumptions and vice versa.

This blending of apparently antagonistic viewpoints into a single comprehensive ideology is well illustrated by the writings of the late C. Wright Mills. After years spent uncovering the "power elite" in America, Mills concluded that corporation managers and generals make all our important political decisions. The political parties, he said, occupy the "middle levels" of power alongside trade unions and farm organizations. The reason for their reduced state, Mills believed, was that American parties are not "disciplined" national organizations capable of forcing their legislators to hew to a party "program." Instead, our legislators are independent of organization control and represent merely the parochial interests and sentiments of their local constituencies—as if a liberal Brooklyn Congressman were independently representing Brooklynites by voting in secret caucus for Bourbon control of Congress. As a result of America's lamentable *lack* of ruling party oligarchies, according to Mills, our independent legislators assembling in Congress are too weak to say boo to a general, an officer who owes his very rank to Congressional approval. Mills' picture of powerless, fragmented parties is, of course, the apologist or Junior Scholastics myth of American politics. The only reason Mills, a professed radical, swallowed such twaddle was that it enabled him to complete a circular argument, an argument, that is, which dresses up an assumption and puts it forth as a conclusion. Mills wished to "prove," ostensibly, that military and corporate power render self-government inherently futile. Being an ideologue, however, he assumed in advance that self-government is inherently futile in the face of corporate and military power. From this assumption it follows that Americans actually enjoy self-government but that it does them no good; the American party system provides Americans with would-be representatives who are prevented from representing them, not by anything in the party system, but solely by the power of corporations and generals. It follows from this that the American party system is a system for providing representative government, and proving this was simple enough for Mills: He simply accepted the apologists' myth of fragmented political parties which is given in civics textbooks to deceive American schoolchildren.

Politically speaking, the difference between Mills' "radical" view of American politics and the apologists' view is nil, for the two views share the central myth of the American party system, namely that the parties are powerless in themselves, that whoever is responsible for the deeds and decisions that comprise our history, the party oligarchies are not. That poverty might be sustained, foreign wars sought, bureaucracies established, special interests favored and the common interest betrayed by the party oligarchs for political reasons *of their own* is a possibility foreclosed by that central myth. That is why it is the central myth.

Yet, as I have tried to show, party organizations do wield great political power, for they control most of the nation's elected officials. It is the party oligarchs who provide our oligarchy-approved Presidents, Congressional leaders, Congressional committee satraps and most of our governors and state legislative leaders. It is the party oligarchs who groom the promising young politicians and provide the government with its elder statesmen. It is the party oligarchs who can now decide, for the most part, what issues will appear in the public arena.

I have endeavored to show, too, that the party organizations will use their political power to maintain their political power, will make momentous public decisions—will send men to their death—in order to do so in moments of peril. It remains to show that party power is perpetually and radically imperiled in this Republic, that the oligarchs' self-serving under these conditions abundantly accounts for the grave abuses of power in America; that to understand why things happen as they do in our times we must look precisely where the prevailing political ideology tells us *not* to look: at the party oligarchy itself.

The central fact about the American party system is simply this, that party power is power usurped from a self-governing citizenry, for it consists precisely in the ability of the party oligarchs to hold the citizens' elected representatives in thrall. From that fact of usurpation and what must be done to secure it, all the compelling reasons that underlie party politics ultimately spring. Because party power is usurped power it is great in proportion as the citizen's public voice is weak. Like two protagonists on a seesaw, the one cannot flourish save at the other's expense. Whatever strengthens self-government ("Allow all the governed an equal voice in the government and that and that alone is self-government"— Abraham Lincoln) weakens party power; whatever muffles the voice of the citizenry strengthens party power. That power and the liberty of self-governing citizens are inherently at odds. The capacity of free men to enter politics freely, to bring easily into the public arena issues of concern to them, to keep the avenues to public office and public renown open to other than party organizations, is, at one and the same time, the condition of republican self-government and a dire threat to the party organizations. In short, the radical and perpetual danger to the party system in America is the exercise of political liberty.

Yet the party oligarchs cannot destroy the essential conditions of political liberty, for these derive from and are secured by our republican foundations themselves. The party oligarchs cannot disenfranchise the citizenry (though they might if they could—witness the disenfranchisement of black people and poor whites in the Southern states); they can impair but they cannot destroy the right to free speech, a free press, the right to assemble, to petition and to all other constitutional immunities that secure against usurping government officials the citizen's permanent capacity to act in his own behalf. They can impair but they cannot destroy the Federal separation of powers, the autonomy of state governments, the local politics of self-governing communities, all the great constitutional forms and municipal liberties which make it difficult in this Republic—and in this Republic only—for any usurpers to monopolize politics entirely. The party oligarchs cannot destroy the essential conditions of political liberty because it would be suicidal for them to do so. The foundations of the Republic are the sole source of all legitimate authority; adherence to constituted forms is the sole reason Congressional enactments have the force of law and any elective office any authority at all. Were the foundations fragmented everything would crumble, including the party system itself.

The abiding strategy of American party politics is set by this inescapable condition. Unable to destroy the perilous forms of political liberty, the party oligarchs can only try—have no choice but to try—to empty those forms of substance, to reduce in any way feasible the ability of the citizens and the willingness of the citizens to act for themselves. It was, said Lincoln, the essential task of free men to uphold and enhance equal political liberty, to see that it is "familiar to all, and reverenced by all, constantly looked to, constantly labored for, and even though never perfectly attained, constantly approximated." It has been the abiding bipartisan principle of the party oligarchs to do the very opposite, to suppress whatever enhances liberty and to promote whatever weakens it. The grave abuses of power in America are the results of that unremitting effort, an effort to despoil what cannot be destroyed, an effort which might well be called the Hamiltonian tradition in America, after the first man of power in the Republic who tried to establish a permanent oligarchy in the teeth of political liberty.

The first and primary abuse of power which follows from that central effort is the oligarchs' favoring of special interests in general and their creation of the monopoly economy in particular.

The reason for both is rooted in a political truth first boldly applied in America by Alexander Hamilton himself—that a political oligarchy could survive in this Republic only if it could bring into its camp a substantial portion of the wealth and social influence existing in society at large. Through the private influence of such influential allies, the oligarchs would have at their disposal a prime requisite of their rule—a safe means to impinge directly on the minds of the citizenry and to shape them to oligarchic requirements. Men of wealth and influence would, as Hamilton expected, control in large measure the local newspapers and periodicals, reign over the church committees, sit on the boards of libraries and universities, dominate the local civic groups, groom the promising young men. Allied to corrupt rule yet immune to the electorate, they would be in a position to prescribe the expectations, shape the ideals and instruct the thinking of their fellow citizens and, through a thousand social filaments, tincture established society with a uniform and pervasive coloration serviceable to oligarchy. If, as

Jefferson said, free men must "know how to judge for themselves what secures or endangers their freedom," the influential, allied to oligarchy, would be bent, for example, on upholding the virtues of deference and trust in one's "betters." If, as Jefferson said, free men must be able to recognize the ambition of usurpers "under all its shapes," the influential would help teach the opposite, that the rulers have no ambition but to serve the common good, as circumstance, popular folly and the inflexible "laws" of society permit. The filaments of social influence have changed somewhat since Hamilton's day—a great foundation is a more influential agency than the chairmanship of a local library committee —but the principle remains the same. Only by commanding a substantial portion of the social influence in the country can a political oligarchy—Hamilton's or the party organizations'—hope to impair permanently the willingness of free men to act for themselves.

By allying wealth to oligarchic rule, the oligarchs would have money at their disposal for all the varied political ends that money can serve. For Hamilton, perhaps, this was less important than it is for the present-day party oligarchs. For them its importance is great. Party organizations, it is worth repeating, have no binding authority over their members; party bosses have no legal power to command and party members no compulsion to obey. American party organizations are, in Walter Bagehot's phrase, "jobbery parties" of self-seeking individuals. What renders party members submissive to party oligarchs in the end is the expectation of reward for loyalty and the fear of reprisal for independence. By commanding a substantial portion of the nation's political money, party organizations can dispense it abundantly to those who have proven their fealty and withhold it from elected officials who have proven themselves dangerous to the organization's interests. Whether the wealth takes the form of campaign funds or such equivalents as lucrative sinecures, legal fees, consultant positions, insider business deals and the like, the ability of party oligarchs to disburse it as they choose among party members adds greatly to the arsenal of rewards and punishments without which a party boss would be the boss of nothing but a handful of clerks and cronies.

Moreover, through such command over wealth, the oligarchs could not only provide themselves with money but make it difficult for a free opposition to secure any, whether for insurgent candidates or for grass-roots political activity, and thus they could seriously hamper the ability of the citizenry to act for themselves. This was well seen, for example, in late 1969 when the two party syndicates openly united against the peace movement. As soon as they did so the movement's supply of philanthropic money dried up with extraordinary rapidity. Under present-day party power, few wealthy philanthropists will support for long what both party organizations are determined to crush.

Obviously this is only the barest sketch of what wealth and influence can do to protect and enhance oligarchic power. A full account would be encyclopedic but hardly necessary. The contribution which wealth and social influence can make to oligarchic rule is great, obvious and beyond dispute. What is not obvious, what in fact is profoundly obscured by ideological thinking, is that the wielders, or would-be wielders, of oligarchic power do not automatically have the wealth and influence of the wealthy at their disposal. They must take active steps to bring wealth and influence into their political camp. The means of doing so are probably as old as politics itself. The wielders of corrupt power must make wealth and influence dependent on special privilege, must make corrupt privilege the very source and foundation of wealth and influence. The political reason for this is clear. Whatever form a special privilege takes, whether it be a private monopoly, an unjust subsidy, a loophole in the tax laws or any other politically created source of unearned wealth, a special privilege is a privilege granted at the expense of the many. It can be safely dispensed—and protected—only by those whose power is unaccountable to the many. In a free republic it can only be dispensed and protected by those who wield power usurped from the citizenry. By dispensing special privilege, the wielders of usurped power render its recipients dependent on corrupt usurped power itself, and insofar as they are dependent, their privileged wealth and influence is at the usurpers' disposal to be drawn upon as needed and exerted on demand. This is why the principle of equal privileges for all and special privileges for none is a fundamental maxim of the American Republic. Special interests thus vested with corrupt privilege are the clients, not the masters, the protégés, not the patrons, of those who wield irresponsible power. Privileged special interests do not exact the privileges they enjoy, they are given special privileges because the dispensers of privilege find it politically useful to dispense it. There is only one special interest in this Republic which enjoys political power and that is the party oligarchy itself.

The most important point about the politics of special privilege is that it is a policy of active corruption, a policy which requires for its success that the sources of wealth and influence be made as directly dependent on corrupt privilege as possible. This is well illustrated by the policies of Hamilton, who tried to ally to his political faction what he called the "considerate" people, chiefly affluent city merchants. At the time, many of them were fearful that extended political liberty would put their fortunes at hazard. Fearful though they were, however, Hamilton knew that the bare promise to protect them from the depredations of the have-nots would not render the "considerate" subservient to oligarchy. A merely passive policy would not provide them with a sufficient stake in corrupt political power, and since their fears were essentially ill founded, they would soon lose what stake they had. Knowing this, Hamilton proceeded to carry out at enormous political risk policies which actively bestowed on the "considerate" new corrupt windfalls at the common expense—by redeeming at face value, for example, government bonds which the "considerate," i.e., speculators, had purchased at one-tenth the price; by giving them shares in monopoly enterprise through the creation of a privately owned Bank of the United States, and so on. It was by virtually creating privileged wealth for them that Hamilton hoped to render the "considerate" the permanent allies of a permanent oligarchy. To put it in moral terms, Hamilton tried by his policies to engender and satisfy active greed as the buttress of oligarchic power. The party oligarchs, his sole true heirs, do the same thing for the same reason.

What obscures the active nature of the politics of special privilege is the widely held belief that wealth and influence are, per se, inherently on the side of the prevailing power. Historically the doctrine is false. When the monopoly-creating policies of the party oligarchs began to hurt small Midwestern manufacturers, whose wealth was not dependent on monopoly privilege, many of them put their wealth and influence on the side of insurgent Republicans, the avowed enemies of special privilege, monopoly and corrupt party power. The notion that wealth in America is inherently allied to the prevailing power is based not on what actually has happened in American history but on a general theory of history which holds that the only real alternative to the status quo is taking people's money away, that is, communism or socialism. If, in any given political community, communism *were* the sole actual alternative to the status quo, in the sense of forming the chief political opposition, doubtless the ideology would be true—private wealth, whether privileged or not, would side with the prevailing political powers. That alternative, however, is not the one America's party oligarchs actually face, although they often find it useful to pretend it is. Their constant endeavor is not and never has been to forestall a communist revolution but to stifle republican self-government. Such being the case in this Republic, private wealth, per se, is not automatically allied to corrupt power. The wielders of usurped power must make it so by making it dependent on corrupt privilege.*

The second point about the politics of special privilege is that privileged interests do not have power; the notion that power and privilege invariably go together is entirely false. Those who argue from the fact of special privilege that the recipients exacted it from servile politicians base their inference entirely on the assumption that the party oligarchs have no interest of their own in dispensing privilege and therefore must be considered under some compulsion to do so from economic forces external to them. Yet the party oligarchs have every reason of their own to dispense special privilege and certainly require no prompting, let alone coercing, from those they choose to favor.

*Socialists would doubtless argue that any system of private wealth is corruptly privileged, but this opinion, whether true or not, is politically irrelevant in America. From the start, Americans agreed almost unanimously to a system of private wealth and enterprise. In consequence, the mere possession of otherwise unprivileged private wealth is not a special privilege threatened by self-government.

Since privileged interests have no power, every effort by the ideologues of economic power (a doctrine much favored by "radicals," by "liberals," by "conservatives" and by the party oligarchs) to show how an interest actually exerts its alleged power over politicians ends up in absurdity or circular reasoning. A prime example of absurdity is to argue from the fact that the party oligarchs take bribes in return for favors that they are in thrall to the bribers, which is to say, that the men in a position to exact tribute are in thrall to the men forced to pay. Circular reasoning usually takes the form of arguing that a moneyed interest has power because money, per se, is power. A characteristic example of this kind of reasoning appeared in an August 1971 issue of *The New York Times Book Review* in which the reviewer, a professor of government, tried to show how a moneyed interest's "dollar power," in his phrase, got President Kennedy to alter an Interstate Commerce Commission ruling in its favor. The interested party, said the reviewer, exerted its dollar power by hiring a lobbyist for $150,000 who twice had audience with Kennedy. According to the reviewer, the reason Kennedy favored the lobbyist's client at the expense of the "consumers" (current cant for citizens) was that they, alas, had no lobbyist to speak for them. All they had was a President of the United States, but why the citizens' chief magistrate would find a lobbyist's sales pitch irresistible the reviewer did not explain, which is to say, he explained nothing. Apparently a $150,000 lobbyist exerts automatic power over Presidents, which is simply saying that "money is power" because money is power. In fact Presidents do not find high-paid lobbyists irresistible at all. As a result, perpetually nervous business interests, never knowing at any moment whom the oligarchs will capriciously choose to favor, are perpetually being fleeced by "power brokers," by "five-percenters" and other shady political operators who exact exorbitant fees for nonservice and then retire to the Riviera.

The true relation between the party oligarchs and their special-interest clients is the relation between patron and protégé. Financially speaking, the relation is that between an exacter of tribute and those forced to pay, whether in money or services or both. When the political exaction takes the form of an overt threat, it is a shakedown operation pure and simple. A classic example of the shakedown—and there are many—is the activities of thirty Republican and Democratic bosses of the New York State legislature in the late nineteenth century. Known as the "Black Horse Cavalry," they brought up at every legislative session a slew of bills designed to damage various special interests. As soon as the bagmen delivered the expected bribes from the frightened moneyed interests, they would duly table the bills. This sort of ad hoc shakedown operation is rife not only in state legislatures but in national administrations as well. During his Administration, President Johnson, for example, quashed an antitrust suit pending against a national brewery company in return for large cash contributions to the Democratic party machine. Instituting and quashing antitrust suits, in fact, is one of the most expeditious means of shaking down large corporations. The Nixon Administration did this in 1971 when it quashed an antitrust suit against the International Telephone and Telegraph Corporation for a $400,000 guarantee. That the party oligarchs have been subverting the antitrust laws since 1890 did not prompt the objects of the shakedown to resist payment. The recipients of corrupt privilege do not refuse to pay, because they cannot afford to take chances; they never know when the oligarchs just might decide to serve the common interest at their expense.

When the threat is implied and the payment regular, the tribute can be described as an informal tax, a tithe of the client's ill-gotten gains. It is understood by those who depend on corrupt privilege—whether oil magnates or numbers runners—that the dispensers of favor expect payment in return, since what they dispense they can always withhold, or dispense to a rival. That is the tacit threat and there is exceedingly little that the threatened interest can do except pay. To fight against the party oligarchs is impossible for a privileged interest, for who else but the party oligarchs can protect corrupt privilege at all?

The politics of special privilege is also a policy of maximum corruption, for the more corrupt a privilege is, the more dependent on corrupt power are its recipients, the more readily cooperative they are. In consequence, when two privileged interests conflict—as special interests will inevitably do—the one which the oligarchs prefer to favor is the more corruptly privileged one. A good case in point concerns the oil import quotas established by the Eisenhower Administration in 1959 for the alleged sake of "national security." By restricting the import of cheap foreign oil, the quotas cost the American people from $5 billion to $7 billion in unjust annual expense while they provide an estimated $2 billion of the $6 billion yearly profits of the oil industry, which already enjoys the windfall privilege of the oil depletion allowance. The oil import quota system, however, runs counter to the interests of those allegedly mighty petrochemical baronies, Dow, Monsanto, Du Pont, Olin Mathieson, because it hurts them in international competition. Since privileged interests rarely oppose in public any policy which the oligarchs favor, the mighty petrochemical baronies suffered in silence for ten years. In 1969, Senator Philip Hart of Michigan, in the course of investigating the quotas, virtually forced the petrochemical giants to testify in their own behalf, although they did so "sheepishly" according to *The New Republic.* That year, a cabinet-level task force appointed by President Nixon recommended that the quotas be lifted, but Nixon ignored the recommendations. According to conventional political commentators, *The New York Times,* for example, Nixon had "bowed" to the power of the oil industry. If so, what had happened to the power of the mighty petrochemical giants? Apparently their great power had disappeared and disappeared, moreover, just when their particular interest coincided with the common interest in seeing the quotas lifted. Actually, the mythical power of vested interests had nothing to do with Nixon's decision. The oil industry was favored because oil profits are poised precariously on two conspicuously corrupt dispensations—the quotas and the depletion allowances. Oil money, in consequence, is preeminently available political money, readily siphoned off in unparalleled abundance by the party organizations in every state. On the other hand, had Nixon favored the petrochemical companies, he would have reduced corrupt privilege for one interest without even dispensing corrupt privilege to another because the petrochemical companies' interest was the common interest. There was nothing corrupt about favoring them, consequently they were disfavored. Doubtless the oligarchs will contrive some way to protect Du Pont et al. from overseas competition, but it will be a corrupt way, which is to say, it will be done by means of corrupt privilege.

The momentary coincidence of a particular privileged interest and the common interest occurs quite often, but the fact is little regarded. Those who attribute political power to special interests whenever the party oligarchs favor them at the common expense never explain the temporary loss of that power when the oligarchs disfavor them at the common expense. Inadequate urban housing, for example, is often attributed to the power of the real-estate interests, yet the same real-estate interests, given inside information, can profit enormously from construction of urban subways, far more than they allegedly stand to lose from adequate public housing. Despite the alleged power of the real-estate speculators, however, urban mass transport is notoriously ill funded. Why then attribute poor housing to the power of the real-estate interests? If they are powerless to serve their interests in the one case, why should they be considered powerful enough to do so in the other? Why should we believe that special interests hold elected officials in thrall when their interests conflict with everybody's if the same elected officials can disfavor them when their interests coincide with everybody's? No reason whatever; the ideology of economic power, so compelling when discussed in the abstract, crumbles into absurdity whenever it is confronted with the actual deeds of men.

Because the politics of special privilege is a policy of active, maximum corruption, it can only be carried out by means of two-party collusion. There is no way for one party syndicate to dispense corrupt privilege unless the other party syndicate agrees to connive at it. Since the politics of special privilege helps usurpation in general, the collusion, as always, springs up automatically between the party hierarchies. Only intense public pressure or the most glaring public scandal will prod one party oligarchy into reluctantly attacking its partner. Historically, nothing reveals the necessity for two-party collusion more graphically than the swift ruin of Hamilton's grand design for oligarchy. Lacking a fake opposition party organization to connive at his bestowal of corrupt privilege, Hamilton had to face a large number of free men hurt by and opposed to his policies. When a free coalition against him was organized by Madison and Jefferson, the Hamilton oligarchy crumbled forever. A durable one-party national oligarchy is impossible in the American Republic. It takes two collusive party syndicates to manage the inveterate abuse of power which the usurpation of power requires.

In our own time, collusion in respect to special privilege is graphically attested to by Ralph Nader's one-man crusade against it. What Nader has done, quite simply, is fill the vacuum of silence created by elected officials in thrall to collusive party oligarchies. There is nothing to stop a Senator from doing what Nader has done—and far more effectively—except everything I have been saying thus far about the power and the interests of the party organizations. To avoid the suspicion of fundamental collusion, the party oligarchs like to pretend, for example, that the Democrats favor the trade unions while the Republicans favor the corporations. Actually both parties favor and protect both giant special interests. That the corporations are more likely to finance the Republican hierarchy and the trade unions the Democratic machine signifies nothing except a fair splitting of the loot; neither party organization stands to gain if the other party organization is impoverished. Before the trade unions became wealthy on a national scale, privileged trusts and banking interests had the burden of financing both party syndicates.

As a policy of active corruption, the politics of special privilege also involves the continuous effort to corrupt with privilege every new source of wealth that arises, often through technological change. This explains certain public actions which the ideology of economic power would be hard put to explain away, namely the favoring of hitherto unprivileged interests—ostensibly powerless by ideological notions—at the expense of a heavily privileged interest—ostensibly a wielder of great power. A good example of this was the disfavoring of the railways in favor of the trucking industry. After several decades of using the railways as their chief instrument of corrupt politics, the party oligarchs in 1935 brought the truckers under regulation in a way that ensured them large profits at the expense of the nation's rails. They did this, first, by allowing certain truckmen, as an exception to regulation, to set their own rates for hauling farm produce. Since the railway rates for farm haulage were fixed by the Interstate Commerce Commission, the truckers were vested with the permanent privilege of undercutting them. To make sure the truckers got their windfall profits—for otherwise the new dispensation would have been useless—the ICC, through its licensing power, has protected the major truckers from untoward competition from new trucking firms. By shifting privilege to the truckers, the party oligarchs corrupted a new source of wealth at its source and, in doing so, created a new body of clients dependent on corrupt rule.

This continuing policy of active corruption, however, is not carried out by the party oligarchs through simple preference. Such an active and continuing policy is absolutely necessary to oligarchic power. The wielders of usurped party power must entangle all the major sources of wealth in corrupt privilege and corrupt every new source of wealth with new corrupt privilege, for otherwise the politics of special privilege would be futile. It does little good for the party oligarchs to command a large quantity of private wealth and influence if a great deal of wealth and influence is not under their command. In that case, they would have their auxiliary supports, but so would those who oppose them. They would have wealth at their disposal but they could not withhold it from free politics. They would have social influence on their side, but many channels of influence would not be so disposed, and if influence is not uniform it is no influence at all. It is merely the clash of articulated opinion and the public arena would remain free. It would shed light without color, so to speak.

There is in modern times, however, only one way to make all wealth-producing activity dependent on corrupt privilege and beholden to corrupt power. That is to turn all wealth-producing activity into monopoly enterprise. And that is the reason we have a monopoly system today. It is the economy deliberately created by the party oligarchs in the interests of oligarchic power.

9.

The Monopoly Economy

Politically speaking, the essential difference between competition in any industry and monopoly in that industry—whether it is a pure monopoly or the shared monopoly of a few price-fixing firms—is precisely the difference between unprivileged and privileged wealth. To the party oligarchs that is the difference that matters.

In an industry where wealth-producing activity is carried out by a large number of competing firms, the success of each depends largely on the acumen, efficiency and good fortune of the individual owners. The wealth of each is largely independent of specific special privilege and thus largely independent of corrupt power. Very likely, too, the individual wealth of each will be relatively modest; no great American fortune, to my knowledge, ever derived from ownership of an unprivileged, competitive enterprise. When railway promoters were making tens of millions of dollars overnight on the strength of a favorable vote in a state legislature, few competitive factory owners, according to Gustavus Myers' *History of the Great American Fortunes*, were likely to possess, after a lifetime's effort, as much as a quarter of a million dollars. What is more, most competitive industries do not readily form a unified special interest receptive to special privilege; it is difficult to favor a competitive industry as a whole without favoring a few companies within that industry at the expense of the others. The protective tariff on steel, for example, favored Andrew Carnegie at the expense of his rivals; protective tariffs in general tended to hurt most competitors by fostering the dominance of a few. An industry composed of many competing firms, in short, is one whose wealth and influence are not readily at the disposal of corrupt power because its constituent members have no permanent stake in corrupt rule. To the overwhelming majority of nineteenth-century Americans—the farmers, the businessmen, the insurgent workers joined together in groups like the Knights of Labor—this was the salient virtue of the nonmonopoly system. It was seen as the economic arrangement preeminently suited to republican self-government.

Should an industry be monopolized by a single firm or a few collusive firms—the typical condition today—the situation is radically altered, for the most important single fact about monopoly is that it depends absolutely on massive government support and protection. What the government must protect a monopoly from is competition. It must be protected from the incursion of new firms into its field; it must be protected from outbreaks of price competition within its field; it must be protected from competition engendered by technical advances—as Kennedy protected AT&T's overseas communication monopoly by giving it control of the communications satellite system developed by the government at public expense. Every monopoly, for its survival as a monopoly, depends on an enormous range of special privileges, privileges involving corporation law, patent law, government regulation, tax policy, monetary policy, tariff policy, antitrust policy and so forth. All wealth derived from monopoly—and today there is no great fortune which does not derive from monopoly enterprise—is absolutely privileged wealth, for the market worth of any monopoly, the value of its stocks and bonds, consists largely of the expectation that it will remain a monopoly. This assurance only an irresponsible, privilege-dispensing government can give.

To protect monopoly, the government, for example, uses its banking and other laws to lodge the nation's credit in the hands of men themselves committed to existing monopolies, for in that case they can deny capital to new competing firms, as J. P. Morgan protected AT&T's monopoly by denying capital to rival companies which sprang up when the company's patents temporarily ran out. To hinder competition from small firms, the party oligarchs have arranged their tax policies so that interstate businesses bear a lighter tax burden than intrastate businesses. To prevent competition from breaking out within a monopolized industry due to competition within a related industry, the oligarchs make sure that the basic industries—power and transport—on which the monopolists depend are themselves organized monopolistically. This task the oligarchs accomplish through the Federal regulatory agencies, which have become, contrary to their professed purpose, "protectors of industry against the rigors of competition, particularly price competition," to quote Louis Kohlmeier, author of *The Regulators*. Further examples of monopoly-protecting arrangements could be extended to book length, since virtually all present-day economic policies are adopted to protect the monopoly system. As Paul Baran and Paul Sweezy note in their useful treatise *Monopoly Capital*, "The effect of government intervention into the market mechanism of the economy, whatever its ostensible purpose, is to make the system work more, not less, like one made up exclusively of great corporations." The innumerable favors which big business is said to exact by its economic power are simply the privileges on which monopoly enterprise depends for survival, for the prosperity of a monopoly and its survival are one and the same thing.

This is the heart of the matter. It is just because monopoly is absolutely dependent on special privilege that the party oligarchs first created and today sustain monopoly, for all the wealth in the country that derives from monopoly wealth is privileged wealth, wealth allied to those who can dispense and protect special privilege. This is the reason Theodore Roosevelt saved the U.S. Steel Corporation from financial ruin in 1907 by secretly helping it to buy out a competitor; this is the reason the party oligarchs saved the Standard Oil monopoly from independent rivals by passing oil legislation in the 1930s that "amounted," according to Baran and Sweezy, "to government enforcement of monopoly prices." This is the reason Franklin Roosevelt set up the NRA to enforce price-fixing when the panic-stricken monopolists were crumbling under the pressure of their perennial nemesis—price competition among themselves.

By supporting policies that destroy competition and foster

monopoly, the party oligarchs not only transform wealth into privileged wealth, they accomplish at the same time another fundamental goal of oligarchic politics: the creation of private power, hidden from and unaccountable to the citizenry. A competitive firm has little decision-making power, since it is subject to the discipline of the marketplace. A monopoly, by definition, has discretionary power. It can control to a great extent its own prices, decide how much to produce, decide the kind and amount of its investments, decide freely even where to locate its plants. In doing so the giant monopoly enterprises make far-reaching public decisions which determine, in large part, how the nation's wealth and credit will be disposed. Yet because these decisions are privately made, the political leaders can disclaim all responsibility for them. Although they affect the lives of every citizen, they are effectively removed from the political arena, which, as will be seen, is precisely what oligarchic politics requires, for the less the oligarchs appear to do, the safer their power is. Such economic power, be it noted, is delegated power, power which the party oligarchs have deliberately bestowed on their client-monopolists, since by their very existence they form a layer of irresponsible control between the party oligarchs and the citizenry.

It is obvious, therefore, that those who wield party power, or would consolidate party power, have compelling political reasons of their own to foster monopoly and no political reason of their own to sustain an economy of small competing producers. We should expect to find in the history of monopoly capitalism the oligarchs' determined effort to engender monopoly and destroy competition—and that is what we do find. We should expect to find that effort strenuously opposed by the great majority of Americans—and that too we find. What we will not find is what conventional history tells us to look for, namely the "triumph of laissez-faire," for the history of the formation of monopoly capitalism is a history of deliberate government intervention to further monopoly. Nor will we find great monopolies creating themselves by beating out competitors in free and unprivileged competition, for, as Ida Tarbell wrote in 1936 in *The Nationalizing of Business,* the "consolidators . . . based their operations usually on exclusive privileges which competitors in the same field were unable to get." These privileges were granted or safeguarded by those controlling the government, for they deliberately supplied would-be monopolists with every legal and financial dispensation required to facilitate monopoly, either directly through law or indirectly through the subversion of law carried out by courts corrupted by the party oligarchs themselves. We will find, in short, what the majority of Americans once clearly understood—that behind every monopoly stands the government and, by extension, the party bosses. The notion that the monopoly system developed through autonomous economic processes is an ideological myth.

The *political* history of monopoly capitalism is a complicated one, and since it has not yet been written systematically, I can do little more here than make a few salient observations to demonstrate the decisive role of oligarchic power in the formation of the monopoly system.

In microcosm that role can be clearly seen in the very means by which the majority of great American corporations were formed. That means, it is essential to emphasize, did not consist in a single "efficient" firm "growing" at the expense of rivals in unprivileged competition. The majority of large American corporations did not grow; they were created by outside promoters—J. P. Morgan preeminently—through consolidation. Though varying greatly in detail, the basic operation consisted of a promoter financing a new corporation—a trust or holding company—through which he would buy several competing firms and place them under central financial control. The U.S. Steel Corporation, which consolidated more than one hundred steel firms, is a classic example of combination. The promoter gained control of the individual companies by buying their stock with the new company's stock, whose face value far exceeded the value of the seller's stock. The promoter could do this because he had issued stock in the new company far in excess of the combined worth of the individual companies he sought to control. U.S. Steel, for example, was capitalized at $1.4 billion, although the combined assets of the consolidated firms was only $682 million. The rest, in the jargon of Wall Street, was "water"—the difference between the real assets of the constituent companies and the value put on the stock of the controlling company. In selling their companies, the owners accepted a profit which consisted largely of "water." In buying the stock of the new company, investors were investing in "water." There was only one reason the sellers sold and the investors invested: the assurance that the new company would make good the "water," would one day be worth its overcapitalization. That assurance, however, is based on a single expectation, that the new company will reap *monopoly* profits in the future. Without that secure expectation, the operation of combination—an exceedingly intricate promotion—could not be carried off. Sellers would not sell, investors would not buy, a process which brings enormous immediate profit to the promoter through the sale of watered stock would bring no profit whatever.

There is, however, only one agency that can assure future monopoly profits, namely the wielders of usurped political power, for every monopoly is absolutely dependent on corrupt privilege for survival. The act of combination cannot take place, ten J. P. Morgans could not make it take place, unless all parties concerned were convinced that the wielders of political power would guarantee that monopoly by every possible means, including, needless to say, nonenforcement of the 1890 Sherman Antitrust Act outlawing "combinations in restraint of trade." Those who bought U.S. Steel stock in 1901 had to know, as it were, that in a financial crisis such as that of 1907 a national administration would save U.S. Steel from competition—competition that the company could not meet because it had to charge high prices in order to reap the profits needed to pay dividends on the watered stock required to form it in the first place.

If the political powers wanted to block a particular combination, no major public action would have been required. The mere whisper of their antipathy to that combination need only pass along Wall Street and the combination could not be effected; sellers would not sell, investors would not invest. The financial "colossi" of Wall Street could no more combine an industry in defiance of the government than water can flow uphill by itself. In 1889, to take a revealing example supplied by Gustavus Myers, the railway magnates desperately wanted to combine their roads to stave off financial ruin. Yet these alleged economic powers, the richest men in the country, were literally afraid to lift a finger to save themselves. Passage of the Interstate Commerce Act in 1887 and the rising demand for an antitrust act had convinced them—erroneously as it turned out—that the citizenry had regained sufficient control of their government to make railway consolidation dangerous. This timorous conduct of the railway magnates severely strained the ideological resources of Myers, a firm believer in the ideology of economic power. He lamely attributes their timidity to a certain personal cowardice that had set in among them as a result of "moral degeneracy." The truth is, the railway magnates, not being economic ideologues, knew full well that they prospered by "government edict"—to use Myers' phrase—not because they controlled the government but because the party oligarchs controlled the government. What frightened them was the imminent prospect of the oligarchs' losing their control. The notion that the monopolists created themselves in defiance of the ruling powers is formed by combining one fact with the usual mythology: the fact that the great majority of Americans opposed monopoly; the myth that their elected representatives were trying to represent them. From which it follows that imperious "economic processes" and "dominant" economic interests thwarted the politicians' intentions. This is how apologist history is written.

So far from occurring in defiance of the ruling powers or even independently of them, economic combination would not have come about if, among other measures, the ruling oligarchs had not deliberately altered the corporation laws to facilitate combination. In both the common law and early Supreme Court decisions, a corporation was essentially an association created and authorized by the state for the purpose of accomplishing some public good—the building of a road, a canal and the like. Legalizing a holding corporation meant chartering corporate entities whose sole purpose was to gain financial control over other corporations. This is not only not a public good— the antitrust law virtually defined it as a public evil—it does not serve a public purpose. Combination, however, was the purpose of the oligarchs, which is why they altered state corporation laws to help achieve it.

Even where consolidation was not the basis of monopoly, the role of corrupt government was indispensable since most noncombination monopolies were monopolies based on the oligarchs' corruption of patent law. A temporary patent monopoly is granted by constitutional provision to encourage the application and diffusion of new knowledge—a temporary privilege for the common good. In a series of decisions after 1896, a corrupt judiciary completely subverted this constitutional purpose and began transforming a temporary privilege into a virtual property right and consequently the basis of a permanent corporate monopoly. In 1908, when the Supreme Court upheld the right of a patent holder to suppress a particular patent, all links with the Constitution were severed; a provision set down to encourage invention had virtually become a private right to bury one. Finding judges with that kind of brazen effrontery is one of the abiding tasks of the party oligarchs.

According to Arthur Burns, author of the classic 1936 treatise *The Decline of Competition,* the new corporation laws and the corrupted patent laws were two of the three main factors in the creation of monopoly capitalism. The third factor, according to Burns, was the oligarchs' use of the antitrust laws, not to break up combinations in restraint of trade but to prevent small firms from trying to break monopoly combinations, which suggests in itself the lawless lengths to which the party oligarchs have gone to further monopolization. None of Burns' three major factors are economic; each was a political act intended to produce an economic result, namely monopolization. The chief role which "laissez-faire" played in all this was that when the citizenry demanded government intervention to undo the results of the oligarchs' intervention, they were met with laissez-faire arguments about the impropriety of intervention.

Another political factor in the formation of monopoly was the raising of protective tariff barriers, which had the effect of fostering monopoly in competitive industries. This economic effect of protection was not widely recognized by politicians until the 1880s, a decade when American industry as a whole no longer needed protection from foreign competition. At that very moment, the Republican party oligarchs raised the now unnecessary tariffs higher than ever before and kept them that way for forty years, helped by the traditional low-tariff Democrats, who soon began to ease their opposition to protection. By 1913, when they controlled the central government under Wilson, the Democrats made only pro forma efforts to eliminate the protective system. High tariffs, a partisan issue when it reflected sectional interests, became effectively bipartisan when its monopoly-fostering effects made it useful to both party hierarchies.

It was the same Wilson Administration which instituted yet another device to foster monopoly and damage competition. This was Wilson's extraordinary effort, made under cover of wartime mobilization, to standardize thousands of American products, including even bricks and bedsprings. Carried out ostensibly for wartime efficiency, Wilson did this in order to make as many buyers as possible dependent on standardized products in their businesses. This makes it doubly difficult for a new competing firm to enter a field with a better product and that much easier for "rival" manufacturers to fix prices among themselves. The detrimental effect on competition is obvious, and "efficiency" had little to do with it; most American products are standardized at the level of shoddy.

Behind all the many acts of government designed to foster monopoly was the essential precondition for consolidation and monopoly: the concentration of surplus wealth in the hands of a few speculators and promoters. This, too, did not come about through any autonomous economic process. For the most part, it was deliberately and swiftly accomplished by sweeping government edict, through the chartering of railway corporations. The story of the railways is familiar by now. The government, state or Federal, would give a corporation gotten up by a railway promoter a charter to build a road. Along with the charter, the lawmakers would give the promoter enormous tracts of public land, large grants of public money and guarantees of additional help. With these extraordinary bonanzas in hand—the original corporation usually having no assets of its own except bribe money for the legislature—the promoters would then sell millions of dollars' worth of stock to investors, thus converting public wealth into private wealth, much of it lodged in their hands. Overnight, the railway promoters became richer than Americans had previously dreamed possible. As Myers rightly observed, "in contrast to the slow, almost creeping pace of the factory owners in the race for wealth, the railroad owners sprang up at once into the lists of the mighty wealth possessors, armed with the most comprehensive and puissant powers and privileges . . . besides which those of the petty industrial bosses were puny."

To Baran and Sweezy, the construction of the railways, by its sheer financial scope, forms a unique event in the history of American capitalism; between the Civil War and World War I, half the wealth invested in American industry was invested in the railways. More significantly, it was a political act of bestowing special privilege and of concentrating wealth by means of corrupt privilege that probably has no parallel in history. It was largely by dispensing windfall privilege on such a lavish scale (and "taxing" the recipients in money and services) that party organizations in state after state gained ascendancy over state parties and politics. That would-be party bosses could dispense such corrupting privilege *before* securing corrupt power was due to one essential fact—railway building, initially, was universally popular. By the time Americans realized what had been done—it took only a few years—party regulars had already gained ascendancy.

Significantly, the recipients of these unprecedented bonanzas were not established capitalists and banking interests, allegedly using their existing economic power to extract further privilege from servile legislators. Those whom the lawmakers usually chose to favor—perhaps because it looked more democratic—were for the most part obscure adventurers, "new men" from the lower ranks who beat out their rival adventurers through superior knowledge of whom to bribe in a legislature. Much of the "cutthroat competition" of the post–Civil War period was not economic competition at all, but rather the competition for legislative privilege, the competition of courtiers, not of entrepreneurs. That the enormous bribes involved were far smaller than the financial worth of the privileges dispensed has led many historians to suppose that the legislative bosses were merely fed crumbs by their economic masters. This is a shallow and bourgeois notion of human conduct, however, one which supposes that the infinite desire for useless riches is natural and the limited desire for usable wealth a limit imposed by the power of others. For the various political bosses, money was essentially the means to determinate political ends, chiefly to consolidate their control of state parties. For that they took what they needed. Compared to the infinite greed of their clients, men with no recognizable human goal except endless accumulation, the motives of the party bosses are becomingly human; at least they want what the noblest men in history have also wanted, namely the exercise of political power. (The party boss differs from such noble men because the latter seek power—the capacity to act in public concerns—in order to distinguish themselves among these fellows and win lasting glory. The party boss has no such nobility of purpose. He cannot win public glory and distinction with his power, for he must exercise it in the shadows in order to have it at all.)

The effect on monopoly of this government-created concentration of wealth through the railway corporations is complex and intricate. The main point, however, is that those who now commanded scores of millions of dollars by government edict did not seek to invest in competitive enterprises. They sought to create—and manipulate the stocks of—monopolies, and they used their disproportionate economic influence to do so. When Western Union tried to effect a monopoly, it was the railway adventurer Jay Gould who not only financed the effort but gave Western Union free rail service to help it drive its competitors to the wall. By their control of the railways, those speculating in monopoly enterprise frequently supplied chosen companies with secret rebates to help them destroy their competitors. As a Senate committee reported in 1886, railways were being used by their owners "to foster monopoly, to enrich favored shippers, and to prevent free competition," through "an elaborate system of secret special rates, rebates, drawbacks, and concessions." In general, the government-created promoters were Gullivers in a Lilliputian economy, and much of the well-noted instability of the late-nineteenth-century economy was due not so much to competition per se but to the frights, alarms and distortions engendered by these oligarchy-created raiders. They were like tinhorns muscling in on a penny-ante poker game.

Having concentrated wealth by edict, the party oligarchs did not try to counteract its monopoly-creating potential. On the contrary, they never relented in their effort to keep surplus wealth concentrated in the hands of a privileged few. The prevailing "tight-money" policy of the time was upheld chiefly to protect that concentration, which is why the majority of Americans demanded—in vain—an easier and more equitable credit system. Where possible, too, government bond issues and other Treasury operations were put in the hands of a tiny handful of privileged private bankers, who made millions overnight by serving, in Myers' words, "as licensed speculative middlemen for a Government which could have disposed of the bonds without intermediaries." The oligarchs' determination to concentrate control of surplus capital in the fewest hands shaped the entire career of J. P. Morgan, who was, essentially, the licensed banker and monopolist of the national Republican oligarchy. It was this privileged position more than anything else which made Morgan so influential an international banker and so successful a monopoly builder. When Morgan sought to effect a combination, interested parties knew that his assurance of government protection was not the empty promise of the average Wall Street swindler. Interestingly enough, Morgan held his position by inheritance. His father before him had been a Republican financial agent, the elder Morgan serving as the government's financial representative to England during the Civil War, where he made a small fortune fiddling on his own.

Morgan's privileged relation to the Republican oligarchy, however, was unique only in its intimacy, for corrupt government stands behind every American monopoly and every great American fortune. Without the intervention and encouragement of the party oligarchs, monopolization could not have taken place; without the protection of oligarchic power, no monopoly would survive even today. For all its far-reaching consequences, the monopoly system is no more, essentially, than the monumental culmination of the politics of special privilege.

The history of monopoly capitalism is preeminently a *political* history, with the party oligarchs as the central actors. Unfortunately, this is not the kind of history we are customarily taught. An economy created through the oligarchs' active efforts to destroy competition is described by historians as the inevitable consequence of competitive capitalism itself. A history marked by that intervention is described as the "era of laissez-faire"—the era of the nonexistent, for nonintervention was the policy of neither the party oligarchs nor the majority of Americans who opposed them. Yet even historians who recognize the role which government privilege played in creating monopoly capitalism adhere to the basic axiom of the self-created economy. By a sort of lemma of that axiom, they argue that the political privileges granted to the future monopolists were extracted by the future monopolists, who apparently used their economic power over politicians to gain the privileges that brought them the very wealth that gives them their economic power. This is tantamount to believing that effects create their own causes, that the newborn baby compelled its parents to conceive it. It is tantamount to believing that when Congress put a Maecenean fortune into the hands of Leland Stanford, Collis P. Huntington, Charles Crocker and Mark Hopkins by authorizing them to build the Southern Pacific Railway, three California shopkeepers and an obscure lawyer controlled the Congress of the United States. When the sequence of events is ignored so blatantly, when common sense is violated so grossly, it is fairly certain that ideological thinking lies at the root. In the case of monopoly capitalism, the ideology involved is particularly pervasive because it is at one and the same time a theory elaborated by "radical" Marxian critics and a justification utilized by the party oligarchs themselves.

According to Karl Marx and Theodore Roosevelt, big business was the "result," in Roosevelt's words, "of imperative economic law," or what Marx called "the laws of motion" of a capitalist society. The usefulness of this doctrine to Roosevelt—he faced resurgent anti-monopoly sentiment at the time—is obvious enough. To attribute the results of political action to immanent "laws" is a corrupt politician's first line of defense, a way of evading political responsibility for what he actually did. A citizenry which grasps the truth that corrupt, self-serving power created the monopoly system forms a dangerous republican opposition—and did; a citizenry persuaded that monopoly capitalism created itself does not form an opposition at all. It prepares to endure what cannot, ostensibly, be cured. This, of course, was quite clear to Roosevelt, who secretly saved U.S. Steel in order to maintain the fiction of "imperative economic law," a "law" which allegedly made the economic triumph of U.S. Steel inevitable—so inevitable that it was falling apart.

Marx's reasoning is more intellectually interesting, at any rate, than Roosevelt's self-serving because it goes to the heart of his class analysis of modern economic history. Marx tried to show that capitalist competition under conditions of laissez-faire would lead to a concentration of competition among fewer and fewer firms. The prediction itself is inaccurate since, while there is surely concentration, there is no serious competition. Marx, in a word, did not predict monopoly nor, as Baran and Sweezy note, although they themselves are Marxists, did he grasp its future significance. He did not because he fully agreed with the central point I have made, namely that every monopoly is the creation and ward of government. For this very reason Marx looked upon monopoly as a relic of precapitalist political economies. He took for granted that the capitalist state would not create monopoly or deliberately deform competition with special privilege or intervene in economic matters at all. Marx apparently assumed that the state under capitalism would be committed to competition and to laissez-faire. The American "state," in the form of the ruling party oligarchs, however, actively dispensed monopoly-fostering privilege. Why then did Marx accept as "given" a public policy that surely did not exist in America? His reason, it seems to me, stems directly from his class analysis of politics and history. Marx considered laissez-faire economics the ideology of the bourgeois class, which it was to a great extent in England. He also laid down in a famous dictum that the "state is simply a committee for managing the common affairs of the entire bourgeois class." Hence, as the new ruling class it would make "the state" translate its ideology into reality and protect the competitive system. In America this did not happen. The very opposite did. This is because the "bourgeois class" did not rule America. If it did, it surely manifested its power in a manner indistinguishable from impotence—by losing, and losing absolutely, to the oligarchs in the long decisive struggle over monopoly and special privilege. This is a fact of American history and no amount of special pleading will change it one iota. To describe that decisive struggle as a mere conflict within the "ruling class" between a handful of privileged capitalists and everyone else in that "class," including the great mass of farmers, is a common dodge of ideologues. However, it will not save the class analysis of American politics; it merely demonstrates its inadequacy.*

Power in America for the past hundred years has not been in the hands of a class, it has been largely in the hands of the party oligarchs. They created the monopoly system of special privilege in the interests of enhancing their power—which it has certainly done. The political superstructure created its economic base, reversing in the realm of action an essential dictum of economic ideology. Because that ideology holds that the present-day American economy created itself by its own laws of "motion" or "power," it has served as the oligarchs' most

---

*The political distortions engendered by class analysis is well illustrated in a common ideological treatment of America's small farmers. Since they, like small businessmen, were antimonopoly, they have often been categorized as "capitalists." One result of this is that the great Populist revolt against the party machines is often described as "essentially conservative." This is because "small capitalists," by ideological definition, are in the backwash of history trying to "hold back social change," a mealymouthed way of saying that the oligarchs were trying to get rid of them. This empty class analysis was used by the head of the American Federation of Labor, Samuel Gompers, to justify his refusal to help the Populists in 1896. According to Gompers, the "working class" had no interests in common with Populism's rural "capitalists," implying, of course, that the overthrow of the party oligarchs could not possibly help wage earners. The truth, as will be seen, is that it would not have helped trade-union bosses. While self-serving ideologues like Gompers were calling desperate farmers "capitalists," the party oligarchs were undertaking a massive propaganda campaign to persuade farmers to think of themselves as capitalists, for one of the chief problems the party oligarchs faced was that American farmers wanted to remain farmers, not because farming was a good "business" but because it was a way of life. Ideological categories always describe as natural, inevitable or inherent what the wielders of corrupt power are actively trying to accomplish.

important apologia next to the central myth of two-party competition. By virtue of economic ideology, the party oligarchs today are able to pretend that every giant corporation was the fair victor in a free competitive struggle, whereas in fact they would crumble tomorrow if their corrupt privileges were taken away. By virtue of economic ideology, apologist historians can rewrite American history so that the politicians who built the trusts in defiance of the people are portrayed as servants of the people defied by powerful trust-builders. By virtue of that economic ideology, the decisive political struggle over monopoly has been reduced to an essentially insignificant squabble between "big" and "little" capitalists, a doctrine which obscures, conveniently for the party oligarchs, the very nature of the political issue involved, namely the difference between an unprivileged economy suited to self-government and an economy bound by corrupt privilege to the usurpers who created it.

In fostering the system of monopoly capitalism, the party oligarchs were chiefly, if not exclusively, concerned with its political import. They knew the political difference between privileged and unprivileged wealth and acted accordingly, as circumstance and opportunity allowed. It would be a mistake to suppose that they had any clear economic blueprint in mind, or all but the vaguest idea in any given year what the economy would look like ten years hence. The self-serving of the American party oligarchs is persistent, not planful. What kind of economic system they were creating, how it would work, whether it would work, they give little evidence of understanding for some time. That monopoly capitalism, for all its enormous advantages to oligarchic power, would create problems for it, political leaders did not really recognize until the Great Depression began demonstrating that the new system, if left to itself, would destroy both itself and party power as well. Since that time, one of the chief burdens of the party oligarchs has been to solve the problems created by monopoly capitalism in a manner satisfactory to oligarchic rule.

The essential problems can be reduced to three, which I will take up in the following chapters. The first was the need to control the workers employed by the monopoly industries, since the monopolists could not be trusted to control them. The solution to this problem was the legalization of the trade unions and the government creation of "industrial" unions in the great monopoly industries. The second was the need to protect the monopoly system by autonomous means largely hidden from public view and so re-create the facade of a politically independent, unprivileged economy which the oligarchs had already destroyed. The solution to this was the "independent" regulatory agencies and bureaucratic government in general. The third problem arose from the fact that the monopoly economy cannot generate sufficient demand to prevent its falling into stagnation and depression and therefore needs vast yearly infusions of public money. The political problem of how to spend billions of dollars yearly on public purposes without endangering the party oligarchies was solved after World War II with the permanent war economy.

As for the nonmonopoly economy long since destroyed, a great deal has been said against it and justly. There is much that is brutish, ugly and demoralizing about an economy based on private profiteering. There is no blinking that fact, although at a time when socialists themselves are trying to give socialism "a human face," the spiritual failings of the nonmonopoly economy do not appear as decisive as they once did. The best argument for that economy, in truth, is the determination of the party oligarchs to destroy it. Perhaps that is the only argument for it, but it is an extremely important one—except to those who implicitly deny that oligarchic political power exists: political apologists on the one hand and economic ideologues on the other.

10.
The Myth of Trade Unionism

About the trade unions a great deal has been written, most of it ideological humbug couched in widely used clichés. Trade unions, for example, are conventionally referred to as "the trade-union movement," implying that they represent a genuine self-generated force, whereas they have always been the wards of government. The actions of the AFL-CIO chiefs are invariably imputed to "organized labor," as if the interests of union bosses and union members were invariably identical, which surely begs an important question, or, more precisely, pretends that no question arises. To discuss trade unions in terms of their fictions, however, would be as futile as running around a circle in search of its starting point.

What breaks the circle is a fundamental political fact about unions and the implications of that fact. It is this: with only occasional and inconsequential exceptions, the trade-union organizations put their enormous wealth and influence at the service of Democratic machine politics, of local, state and national Democratic bosses, and hence of the party oligarchy as a whole. Whatever issues the Democratic syndicate cares to raise, the unions obligingly propound. Whatever issues it wishes to bury, the unions fail to mention. There is no oligarchic abuse of power too gross for the union chiefs to support. When the party oligarchs instituted Jim Crow in the South, Southern trade unions promptly raised the color bar and kept it raised until the oligarchs themselves were forced to relent. Whenever the party bosses decide upon war—from World War I to Vietnam—the union chiefs invariably shout the loudest war cries.

In almost every Democratic primary, the AFL-CIO chiefs pour their abundant supplies of money and manpower into the hands of machine candidates while insurgents dangerous to machine power get nothing. When the insurgent followers of Eugene McCarthy tried to defeat a Massachusetts Congressional hack named Philip Philbin in 1970, for example, the state AFL-CIO worked zealously to secure his renomination. Wherever the twists and turns of collusion lead, the union chiefs faithfully follow. Where the Democratic machine does not want to win, the unions sit out the general elections regardless of how industrialized the area may be. Where an incumbent machine hack is too grossly reactionary for union chiefs to support openly, they oblige the party bosses by not supporting a reform challenger. In heavily unionized West Virginia, for example, the state AFL-CIO found it awkward to endorse the reactionary Senator Robert C. Byrd in 1970, but it denied support to his primary challenger, who had to run a penniless campaign. When Byrd's reputation was less well known and hence less embarrassing to the state AFL-CIO, the union chiefs had supported him outright.

The only thing that complicates the union record of subservience to machine politics is the occasional need to keep up appearances. In Texas, for example, the state union chiefs stand in the liberal wing of the Democratic party but manage to desert it when it seriously threatens the Old Guard, giving the unions "a reputation for treachery in Texas politics," according to Robert Sherrill, "that it is still trying to live down." In the South, where many unions cannot readily support Bourbon candidates, they oblige the Bourbon rulers by rendering themselves politically "ineffectual," to quote V. O. Key. This self-induced ineffectuality in the South is sometimes attributed to the Federal prohibition against union support of candidates for Federal office. This, however, is a transparently fake alibi. The union chiefs honor the law where it serves the Democratic machine to do so and break it with impunity (itself a perfect example of two-party collusion) where it serves the machine's interests to do so, notably in Northern cities, where the trade-union chiefs have a record of consistent support for local machines and antagonism to local insurgent politics that reaches back to the 1880s, when the AFL got started.

The trade-union leaders are so obliging a tool of machine politics that they will even forgo appearances when the Democratic oligarchy requires it. When the national party was trying desperately in 1965 to restore the crumbling Byrd machine of Virginia, the state AFL-CIO threw its support to a union-baiting Byrd lieutenant in the crucial primary race for governor. Unions are so pliant a tool of machine politics they can be used even in the more devious machine stratagems, such as packing national party committees with machine hacks, as they did in 1971, and joining the regulars to thwart party reform. When the Democratic oligarchy tried to block Morris Udall's bid for a Congressional leadership post in 1971, the AFL-CIO fell in with the scheme of splitting the liberal vote by strenuously lobbying for Congressman James O'Hara of Michigan. When O'Hara was eliminated in the runoff, the AFL-CIO obliged the oligarchy again by not giving its support to Udall, thus ensuring victory to the oligarchs' choice. So routinely subservient are the trade-union chiefs that their nonsupport of a major Democratic candidate in a general election is a fairly sure sign that the Democrats are dumping the election. When the New York Democrats determined to defeat Arthur Goldberg—a "labor hero"—in the 1970 governorship race, the state AFL-CIO did its share by endorsing Governor Rockefeller. When the national Democratic syndicate decided to defeat George McGovern in 1972, the national AFL-CIO conveniently refused to endorse him.

Proof of the trade unions' subservience to the Democratic machine does not rest, however, on these random illustrations but on the overall effect of that subservience. If the great wealth and influence of the trade-union organizations were *not* at the disposal of machine politics, if they were ranged instead behind the opponents of usurped party power, there would be no Democratic machine.

In the official trade-union ideology this political subservience is implicitly denied—that is what ideology is for. Union support of the oligarchs' policies and candidates is said to be determined exclusively by the "bread-and-butter" interests of union members. The trade-union chiefs, in this view, support only those men and policies which bring immediate profit to the membership. Nowadays there is much handwringing over the trade unions' selfish outlook, but nobody denies that such is their outlook. Even antiwar politicians have attributed the AFL-CIO's vehement support of the Vietnam War, for example, to "labor" interest in securing wartime jobs. The obvious fact that the war-induced inflation has been hurting union members since 1967, the equally obvious fact that the Federal Government could create far more union jobs if it spent its money at home rather than in Saigon, never seems to give the lie to the official explanation.

The same holds true when it comes to explaining away the unions' role in electoral politics. According to Alexander Heard, a student of campaign financing, "Labor interest in all candidates and parties is solely utilitarian: can they help in achieving labor's social, economic, and political goals?" According to *The New York Times*, "Service to labor is usually the criterion" for trade-union support of a candidate. This is the official line but it cannot explain anything the unions actually do in politics.

It surely cannot explain the examples I just gave of union support for antiunion and antireform candidates. It does not explain union refusal to put forward primary challengers to reactionary incumbent machine hacks. What is more, it does not explain the AFL-CIO's real relation to those who stand openly opposed to all the trade unions' professed "social, economic and political goals," namely the Southern Bourbons. Does the union hierarchy use its wealth and influence to undermine the power of the Bourbons? It does not. In the South the union chiefs support the Bourbons by not seriously supporting anti-Bourbon Democrats. In Congress they support the Bourbons by supporting all those machine hacks with "good labor records" who biennially restore the Bourbons to the seats of legislative power. There is no talking this away. To support the means is to espouse the ends. The relation between the AFL-CIO and the Southern Bourbons is all-out support for the enemies of the union's professed goals. What "utilitarian" political standard accounts for that? When union lobbyists threw their weight behind Congressman O'Hara because of his alleged "labor record," by what "criterion of service" to labor did they help the Congressional oligarchy stop Udall when that same oligarchy stocks key committees with Bourbons? By no criterion of "service" which the union chiefs would care to admit.

Consider, too, the union chiefs' overwhelming support in the 1968 Presidential nominations for the machine candidate, Hubert Humphrey, and their bitter opposition to his insurgent rival, Eugene McCarthy. According to the official line, the unions' action was dictated by Humphrey's superior record of service to "labor." Unfortunately for the official line—if anyone cared to examine it—when the same Hubert Humphrey had made his 1960 bid for the Democratic nomination against John Kennedy, the AFL-CIO had given him no support. As a result he ran a shoestring campaign despite a labor record far superior to Kennedy's. Indeed, in Humphrey's decisive defeat in the West Virginia primary, the state AFL-CIO adhered to the criterion of service to labor by tying up the state for Kennedy. Why did the AFL-CIO support labor hero Humphrey in 1968 but not labor hero Humphrey in 1960? Because in 1968 Humphrey was the machine candidate and in 1960 he was not. What the Democratic machine orders, the AFL-CIO carries out. That is the only criterion which the trade unions follow in politics.

For such continuous subservience to corrupt power there is only one political explanation: the trade-union organizations must be deeply and utterly dependent on some form of corrupt privilege. The real interests of the trade-union chiefs must be such that only corrupt power will further them. Yet whatever those interests are, they cannot be identical with the broad interests of some twenty million organized workers; union members suffer as much as anyone else from the actions and omissions of self-serving power—from grossly unjust tax laws, from waste of the public wealth, from rotting public services, from costly health care, war-induced inflation, real-estate speculators, polluted environments, the killing and maiming of their kinsmen in dubious foreign battle. Nor can that special interest be the narrower rank-and-file interest in fair wages, ample leisure, fair treatment and economic security. These are the interests of all who work for wages, and no interest common to the great majority of the people depends on corrupt power for its fulfillment. If service to the interests of organized workers were truly the criterion of union political activity, the union chiefs would not be subservient to corrupt power. Yet they are.

What the true interests of the union chiefs are will never be discovered in the ideology of trade unionism, whose central tenet is the absolute identity between the interests of the union and those of its membership. A trade union, according to trade-union ideology, is an economic organization of workers who enjoy, by that very organization, through its wealth and solidarity, a degree of economic power which the union exerts in collective bargaining with employers. Whatever strengthens the organization increases the economic power of the members and thus their ability to serve their own interests. Trade-union organizations cannot, by ideological definition, be self-serving. By that same ideological definition, however, they should not be politically servile. Since economic power allegedly flows from the union organization itself, that power should be entirely independent, and trade unionists insist that it is. They often go further, claiming that union economic power is the only real power America's workers can expect to enjoy. If this were true, however, the political subservience of the trade unions would be entirely inexplicable. Why should those who wield independent power take orders from party machines?

It can be justly argued that trade-union organizations need a certain structure of law to put their economic power on a firm foundation, laws such as those guaranteeing the right of workers to organize, laws compelling employers to "bargain in good faith" and the like. Without such laws, and the political backing implied, no trade union was ever able to organize a major industry against its will. Without such laws, no trade union even today could compel a giant corporation to bargain in good faith. Without the support of the political authorities, remarkably few major strikes have ever succeeded. The legal foundation of trade unionism, however, has been established, essentially, since 1947. That year, the Taft-Hartley Act reiterated word for word all the fundamental pro-union provisions of the 1935 Wagner Act, including the "duty" of employers to bargain collectively, one of the most important provisions of all. By reiterating the Wagner Act provisions, however, the Taft-Hartley Act went beyond them because all the key terms—the "duty" to bargain, for example—had already been defined in thousands of pro-union decisions of the National Labor Relations Board, which the Wagner Act created. The Taft-Hartley Act gave statutory legal status to these administrative decisions and thereby made it compulsory for employers to bargain collectively with unions to a satisfactory conclusion. With that, the legal foundation of trade unionism was essentially complete, a Republican Congress having established by general law all that an earlier generation of trade unionists had hoped to win piecemeal through individual union-management contracts. Compared to its pro-union features, the anti-union provisions of the Taft-Hartley Act are trifles, the prohibition against closed shops, for example, being virtually inconsequential. Since 1947, however, the trade-union chiefs have been, if anything, even more subservient to the party oligarchs than ever. This the ideology cannot explain.

That political subservience is a fact that will not go away. It follows, therefore, that trade-union economic power must be a *fiction*, that trade unions cannot win benefits for their members by exerting independent power in collective bargaining, that trade unions have no such power to exert. Such, in fact, is the case, although it is obscured by the sound and fury of collective bargaining, by liberal Democrats extolling union power and by conservative Republicans deploring it. As the economists Baran and Sweezy rightly observe, if unions really wielded economic power "one would rather expect them to capture a steadily increasing share [of total income] for the workers." Yet unions have not done this and what is more do not even try to do this. In the economic history of every industrial country, the organization of industrial workers has made no change in the essential relation of wages and prices and thus in the share-out of total income. The relation, in essence, is this: as the unit cost of labor increases, the price of a commodity increases. When an increase in real wages occurs, it is usually because the wage increase given is proportional to an increase in the workers' productivity. In that case, due to increased productivity, the unit cost and the price remain the same despite the wage increase. In short, increased productivity, not union power, is the chief source of a real rise in workers' wages. All that the industrial unions try to do is win for their members a due share of that increased productivity as well as wage increases proportioned to a rise in living costs. This is a "policy," as Baran and Sweezy rightly point out, "of merely preventing capitalists from appropriating a larger share of total income." Yet even this modest, status-quo-preserving policy provides no evidence of union economic power, because that policy is not the independent policy of the unions and its achievement is not an independent union achievement.

The policy of preventing the industrial monopolists from hogging more and more of the total income is the policy of the central government itself. Securing for industrial workers a share in increased productivity as well as wage increases proportional to rising living costs is the policy of the party oligarchs. It has been their policy ever since they came to realize that if the industrial monopolists were allowed to determine wages, they would reduce effective demand in the country and bring on depressions and consequent ruin to themselves as well as to party power. In organizing the industrial unions after 1936, what Roosevelt did was create a hidden governmental arm—the "independent" trade unions—to administer a government wage policy which had to be implemented whether industrial workers were in unions or not, a policy of preventing the monopolists "from appropriating a larger share of total income." The wage settlements which comprise that policy are not won by the industrial unions, they are merely funneled through the industrial unions.

The machinery for setting the nation's industrial wages works essentially as follows: by common agreement among the oligarchs, the industrial unions and the major industrial corporations, one industrial union is allowed to be the wage leader, just as in setting prices for a monopoly industry one company, by common consent, is usually allowed to be the price leader. The contracts negotiated by the wage leader are then heralded as the standard to which other unions and nonunion workers are supposed to aspire. In practice, wage leadership was given to the United Automobile Workers, the largest industrial union, in collaboration with General Motors, the largest industrial corporation. In 1948, the UAW and GM actually drew up a basic contract which explicitly embodies the government's wage policy: wage increases, according to that contract, were to be determined by the annual increase in productivity—an estimated 3 percent—and increases in the cost of living. The government, for its part, was supposed to ensure stable prices, which it did until the Vietnam War. To help convince union members—the only people not party to the agreement—that the UAW was a worthy wage leader, the union's late president, Walter Reuther, was built up as the one truly unblemished hero of trade unionism. So precious a commodity was Reuther's reputation as an independent man that the oligarchs even allowed him not to endorse the Vietnam War, although the UAW never supported the peace movement either. It just went into limbo for a few years, splitting with the war-hawk AFL-CIO in 1968 in order to do so. The part which union economic power plays in all this is nil, like that power itself.

In denying that trade unions exercise economic power, I seem to be ignoring the notorious power of the craft unions and particularly that of the two dozen unions comprising the building trades. In many ways the craft unions *are* different from the newer industrial unions. They are not, for one thing, essential parts of the monopoly economy. Whereas four corporations employ almost all the nation's automobile workers, literally thousands of building contractors employ the members of the construction unions. Yet even these unions do not wield independent economic power. The high hourly wages which construction workers earn (when they work) are not due to union power but to the scarcity of employable workers. This scarcity, however, is entirely the result of state and municipal ordinances. By means of building codes, apprenticeship laws, licensing laws and other measures, corrupt local governments secured for the craft unions the power to control and restrict the number of skilled workers in the field. Corrupt local governments, for example, compel contractors to hire only union help by prohibiting any but licensed workers to take part in construction while giving the licensing power to the union bosses. To protect craft-union control of the skilled labor force further, the same municipal governments award huge city building contracts only to companies that hire union members, or more precisely, that commission union business agents to do the hiring. The building trades unions—and other craft unions—are simply government-created monopolies. They have privileges but no independent power. The benefits which craft-union members receive from sharing in monopoly privilege they get entirely at government behest. Since it is a corrupt privilege granted at the expense of the many, the craft unions have been serving local political machines for almost a century. The real difference between the craft unions and the later industrial unions is that members of the former derive real benefits from union membership (they often pay huge entry fees for the right to share in monopoly privilege), whereas industrial union members only get what they would have to be given anyway in order to maintain the monopoly economy.

It is obvious, therefore, why trade-union organizations are subservient to corrupt power. Without the constant connivance of the party oligarchs, union members would have little reason to belong to trade unions. Only corrupt monopoly privilege keeps craft unionists in craft unions. Only the oligarchs' connivance at a momentous fiction—the fiction that industrial unions win benefits for workers by their independent economic power—keeps industrial workers in industrial unions. The ultimate special privilege which trade-union leaders receive from the party oligarchs is the privilege of being trade-union leaders; the standing debt which the AFL-CIO owes to the party bosses is payment for its very existence.

Politically speaking, however, the crucial question is why the oligarchs have found it so useful to put millions of workers in trade unions (including, since 1960, government-created government employees unions). In what way, that is, does the existence of trade unions serve the interests of oligarchic power? The answer is—in every way possible.

Aside from political money and support, the primary service which the industrial unions render to oligarchic power is to *disguise* the political determination of industrial wages. The oligarchs' need to disguise this is readily apparent. If industrial workers were to recognize the political basis of their weekly paychecks, they would press, they could not help but press, their demands directly upon government itself. Organization control of elected officials cannot withstand an electorate whose interests are so visibly affected by public decisions. Party power cannot bear too many real issues appearing in the public arena, such issues as the share-out of total income between workers and corporations. By siphoning wage settlements (and other benefits) through industrial unions, the oligarchs at once remove both the issues and the political pressure. Workers, persuaded that their interests are served not through politics but through "collective bargaining," not through the exercise of their political power as citizens but through the economic power of an economic organization, are to that extent shunted out of politics, like trains switched from one track to another. The willingness of millions of citizens to act for themselves becomes sharply impaired, for men do not take readily to politics when politics appears irrelevant to their most immediate concerns. This is the primary function of industrial unions—to make politics appear irrelevant to millions of citizens.

This function of political disguise explains why the oligarchs formed industrial unions when they did, namely after 1936. Until then the oligarchs had not needed a disguise for wages. They expected the monopolists to determine wages. This, however, had twice proven a failure, first in the 1920s and then, more decisively, under the NRA. Recovering their monopoly positions in 1933, the industrial corporations raised prices and slashed payrolls so eagerly that in 1934, a Depression year, their profits were greater than they had been in 1926, a year of relative prosperity. Given the economic propensities of the monopolists, industrial wages had to become a direct responsibility of government. For millions of industrial workers in 1936 the necessity of political action was about to become clearer than ever, and given the huge Democratic majorities, hope of political success in the form of general labor laws would shortly rise higher than ever. Moreover, by

1936, and certainly by early 1937, the right of Congress to legislate upon terms and conditions of labor under the Constitution's commerce clause had been substantially upheld, a point Justice Harlan Stone made to Roosevelt in a friendly effort to persuade him to call off the court fight. Little, therefore, stood in the way of establishing a public industrial wage policy mandated by law, with provisions for minimum wages, maximum hours, cost of living and productivity raises and security of job tenure.* At precisely that perilous moment, Roosevelt called on three faithful trade unionists, John L. Lewis, Sidney Hillman and David Dubinsky, to put workers into industrial unions and shunt them out of politics. The three union leaders put their newly formed Committee for Industrial Organization into action in early 1937 and did just that. Under pressure from the Administration, major industries that had resisted unionizing with ease were rapidly organized, often in a matter of weeks. Virtually dead by 1932, the "trade-union movement"—the only "movement" of lackeys known to history—was re-created overnight by the party oligarchs.

Why, it might be asked, did the oligarchs not delegate a degree of economic bargaining power to the industrial unions? The answer is that if industrial unions had independent economic power, it would defeat the whole purpose of industrial unions. Unlike the craft organizations, industrial unions impinge directly on the monopoly system itself. If they had economic power, they would have the power to alter the share-out of total income, determine the level of prices and profits and thus the entire structure of investments. They would be making, or fighting to make, sweeping public decisions without the shred of right or authority to do so. The government—any government—would have to intervene to halt such lawless proceedings. For the party oligarchs, however, such intervention would be self-defeating. If

*It is sometimes said in objection that the giant corporations would defy such laws without the "countervailing" power of unions. This assumes that the giant corporations can defy the government but cannot defy a government-created trade union. In fact corporations could crush industrial unions if federal law did not prevent them from doing so. To say that the party oligarchs had to enact and enforce union-creating laws because they could enforce no other kind of labor legislation is patently absurd.

they stripped the industrial unions of their delegated power, union members would begin to abandon their unions for politics. If they made permanent industrial settlements by means of general law, union members would also turn to politics in order to win more favorable laws. If industrial unions had economic power, the very exercise of economic power would destroy them, since the effect of using it would be to push all economic issues—and workers—back into the political arena, which is exactly what industrial unions were created to avoid.

Not only do trade unions lack independent economic bargaining power, union leaders do not want it. They know full well that its exercise (and the rank and file would demand its exercise) would put an end to trade unionism. This is the reason union chiefs have willingly allowed what few economic weapons they had to be taken from their hands. Railway strikes were a fairly potent economic weapon, so the union chiefs willingly surrendered it at the turn of the century in exchange for Federal legalization of the railway unions, whose economic power is small but whose control over railway workers is singularly strict. Sit-down strikes and secondary boycotts were also relatively effective; the first was taken from the trade unions by New Deal legislation, the second by the Taft-Hartley Act. The trade-union chiefs scarcely even pretend to want these weapons back. As for trade unionism's ultimate weapon, the strike, it is essentially a ritual act carried out not to impress the corporations—they can outsit any strike—but to impress union members with the unions' determination in their behalf. Industrial unions had to be a total fraud, and this is why the AFL chiefs did not in fact want to organize them. Their refusal, conventionally attributed to craft-union conservatism, was due to an understandable reluctance to perpetrate a fraud that might well explode in their faces. The AFL chiefs did not come around until Roosevelt created the CIO and presented them with a pointed threat: if they did not start forming industrial unions, the upstart CIO would dominate the "House of Labor."

In creating industrial unions, the oligarchs not only shunted their members out of politics, they served their own interests in another way. They transformed millions of citizens at one stroke into the dependent wards of their own dependents. This was the direct result of securing benefits to workers through unions rather than directly through general law and public policy. The benefits a citizen receives by law he holds in his own person as an individual right which law itself creates. Those entitled to an old-age pension under the Social Security Act depend on no one to make good their claim. Only that extreme rarity, an openly criminal regime, could deny them their rightful claim. Similarly, laws protecting wage earners from economic exploitation and arbitrary treatment protect them as individuals because the laws create rights which they hold as individuals. Every just law of this kind secures benefits for citizens without sacrificing their independence; indeed it probably enhances their independence. (The right-wing line that general welfare laws make people dependent on government is precisely untrue. No general privilege renders the citizenry dependent on the prevailing powers; only special privilege can do that. The Right never attacks special privilege since it is merely the right corner of the party oligarchy's one mouth.) The oligarchs thus have no interest whatever in enhancing the personal independence of the citizenry, since such independence is an elementary condition of republican self-government.

The contrast between beneficial laws and trade unionism is fundamental and decisive. A wage earner who receives his economic benefits through a trade union has no individual rights to those benefits and no independence whatever. His sole substantial right is the right to join a trade union; it is the union chiefs who enjoy the right to speak in his name and he must depend on their goodwill and good offices. A union member, for example, has no right to fair treatment even when it is stipulated in the union contract. If mistreated, all he can do, essentially, is complain to his union officials, since it is they who hold the right to defend him—and the implied discretion of not doing so. This discretion is itself an instrument of control over union members. It is as if American citizens had no constitutional rights except the right to join the American Civil Liberties Union, which alone was authorized to defend their liberties at its own discretion.

Yet an individual union member cannot readily compel union officials to act in his behalf, since union members have no rights within their unions vis-à-vis the union organization (recent court decisions have amended this somewhat). When Senator John McClellan of Arkansas proposed a "bill of rights" for union members in 1959, a combination of organized labor and Southern Bourbons defeated it, as Evans and Novak relate in their biography of Lyndon Johnson. The trade-union ideology, it is worth noting, completely justifies the union chiefs' opposition to rights for union members. According to that doctrine, individual rights within unions are unnecessary, since the interests of the organization and those of the rank and file are identical. Moreover, according to that ideology, such rights would be positively harmful to union power, since any rupture, or, indeed, any formal distinction between the members and the organization threatens the solidarity from which union economic power ostensibly flows. By the strict inner logic of trade unionism, a union can only represent its members when they submit to the union leadership.

Although trade unions now and then talk about "trade-union democracy," the ability of union members to control union officials is virtually nil. This is because every condition that makes self-rule possible, let alone a reality, is lacking within most trade unions. The essential condition of self-rule, in a trade union as well as a political community, is that members can act together independently of their temporary rulers. For such acting together, however, the unions provide no mechanisms, no forums, no necessary conditions. It is the leaders, not the members, who control the money, the patronage, the union jobs, the union meetings, the union press and all sources of information about union affairs. It is they who control the union's electoral machinery and in many unions actually appoint the committees that nominate candidates for union office. The union chiefs, in short, have everything an elective despot needs to secure his despotism, including an ideology which makes opposition itself anathema, since any serious opposition can be readily denounced as disruptive of solidarity, injurious to union power and treachery in the face of the enemy (the management is always vehemently "antiunion" in trade-union propaganda). The ability of trade-union members to control trade-union officials goes counter to everything in the trade-union creed and runs athwart everything in the trade-union structure.

This is why "trade-union democracy" is so transparent a farce, why most union chiefs reign uncontested for decades and readily pick their own successors. Of all the self-perpetuating oligarchies in the world, none can so easily perpetuate themselves as the chiefs of the trade-union organizations. In taking industrial workers out of the hands of the monopoly capitalists and putting them into the hands of the union chiefs, the party oligarchs merely shifted them from one system of indirect political control that failed to another system of control that thus far has succeeded. That, in essence, was the "New Deal for Labor."

The trade unions' usefulness to corrupt power does not end there, however. By putting millions of citizens into an empty economic bag, the oligarchs not only shunted them out of politics, they put them under the control of organizations with every interest of their own in keeping them out of politics. Thwarting the free political activity of union members has been the central policy of trade-union leaders since the emergence of trade unions. This policy the trade unionists once practiced quite openly, since it is absolutely justified by the trade-union creed. Political activity, as the old AFL leaders rightly insisted, was injurious to trade-union organizations. The divisive clash of political opinions weakened union solidarity; political action weakened loyalty to the union; political hope distracted members from the "real" issues of trade unionism—the effort to secure better wages and other benefits through collective bargaining at the workplace. What a strong union requires is members who are politically apathetic, who do not hanker after beneficial laws, who seek only improved contracts for themselves, who are imbued, in the argot of trade unionism, with "wage consciousness." Although the union chiefs themselves were neck deep in machine politics, the rank and file were exhorted to mind only union business. This is known in trade-union argot as "organization consciousness." From the point of view of trade unionism, whatever impairs the ability and willingness of union members to act politically is a contribution to trade unionism; whatever enhances that ability and willingness imperils the "House of Labor."

Since the 1890s, trade-union leaders have been drumming it into the heads of union members that politics and political action are essentially futile, that in unions lie their only hope for betterment. Around the turn of the century this propaganda line often took the form of quasi-Marxist propositions about the inherent sham of democracy in a capitalist country. Alternatively, union chiefs argued that democracy itself was useless to workers, since the majority of Americans were antilabor. Since the unions are now open affiliates of the national Democratic hierarchy, the unions' antipolitical line of necessity has become somewhat more subtle, but remains nonetheless effective. Union members, for example, are constantly exhorted to look on the world outside their unions as a place full of snares, pitfalls and enemies of labor. As a *Nation* editorial complained in 1968, the trade-union chiefs were still telling their members that the AFL-CIO is a "garrison holding off hostiles at gunpoint." This is, of course, blatantly untrue, but it is an honest trade-union untruth. Unless union members are kept in a state of fright, unless they are constantly told that every politician out of the ordinary, every grass-roots political activity, even their neighbors next door are potential enemies of labor, how can the union chiefs keep them free from politics and so keep their unions strong?

To further hamper and discourage free politics among union members, the union chiefs constantly endeavor to persuade union members that they are not citizens but "workers." As Samuel Gompers himself complained, the refusal of American wage earners to see themselves merely as workers laid a heavy handicap on American trade unionism. Seeing themselves as citizens, they were inclined to take an all-too-keen interest in politics, particularly at the local and municipal level. Seeing themselves as citizens, they were inclined to believe that representative government was both possible and desirable. To help counteract such antiunion tendencies, the AFL was among the very first to endorse—in 1908—the new system of vocational and industrial education then being concocted by public school "educators" for the sons of urban immigrants. At first the AFL chiefs were wary of this "new idea," as it was called, suspecting a sinister plot to crimp craft-union privileges. When they realized that vocational education was not even meant to teach boys a trade but merely to prevent them from learning what free citizens should learn (see next chapter), the AFL gave it its wholehearted approval and still does. It was a genuine windfall: a system of public miseducation designed to teach the children of factory workers what the trade unionists were trying to teach their fathers, namely that a citizen who labors is a laborer.

The contrast between the trade unions' view of education and that of a much earlier generation of organized American workers could not be more glaring or more instructive. The insurgent republican workingmen of the 1830s period—members, for example, of the Working Men's Party—demanded as their first political goal—they were not "wage-conscious" trade unionists—the establishment of free public schools that would teach their children "to be jealous of naught save the republican character of their country." That is just what the trade unions do not want America's children taught.

Because ample leisure, too, is a prerequisite of political liberty, the trade-union chiefs' efforts to secure increased leisure for their members have been largely negligible and pro forma. The forty-hour, five-day factory week was achieved by the end of the 1930s. After three decades of trade-union "leadership," the work week for factory workers has remained exactly the same, while the new movement for a four-day week has arisen, significantly, among unorganized workers who do not have "powerful" trade unions to speak for them. Here, too, the contrast between the trade unions and the republican workingmen of 1830 is instructive. The insurgent workingmen made the securing of ample leisure the second major goal of their political activity, and precisely because it was the prerequisite of political liberty.

Intent on thwarting the independent political activity of union members, the trade-union chiefs have also taken practical steps to prevent it from breaking out within unions—by destroying the autonomy of union locals, for one thing, by drastically centralizing control of union political funds for another. According to Alexander Heard, virtually all AFL-CIO political money is controlled by the central bureaucracy through its political arm, the Committee on Political

Education, and is siphoned into machine coffers. The union chiefs hamper free politics, too, by their persistent efforts to keep union members within every political community divided from each other along craft and industrial union lines. The implicit goal of a national craft union, for example, is to persuade a union member in Utica, New York, that he has more in common with a colleague in Spokane, Washington, than he does with his next-door neighbor. Keeping union members perpetually divided and so unable to act together is the real purpose of "organization consciousness."

Where *local* labor associations have sprung up across the national trade-union lines, the trade-union chiefs always endeavor to pack them with union loyalists, men, that is, who will work to prevent the association from taking or encouraging independent, local political action. Whenever local labor councils incline toward independent politics, the union chiefs move in to crush the dissidents, often with the help of the local political machine. When one such dissident local council in New York City convened during World War I to launch a local third party, the state AFL chiefs packed its meeting with armed thugs who forcibly kept the real delegates from adjourning and then voted down their resolution to enter politics. Whether a labor council takes part or not, the very existence of nonmachine politics in a community is dangerous to trade unions, since it cannot fail to arouse political interest among union members. This is the chief reason the trade unions have had so little interest in organizing workers in the South and West, where party organizations are either nonexistent or relatively weak. The more open politics is, the more likely union members will turn their union locals into centers of political activity, something neither the union chiefs nor the party oligarchs want. The same fear of independent political sentiment explains the AFL-CIO's massive effort to discredit George Wallace in the 1968 Presidential elections. That Wallace was a racist had nothing to do with the matter, since the unions support racists all the time, including their ancient benefactor, Woodrow Wilson.

This antipolitical policy of the trade unions—no politics for the members, corrupt politics for the union—culminates in the trade unions' long-standing opposition to general welfare legislation. Every such law, as I have said, arouses political hope and undoes overnight years of union efforts to inculcate political apathy and narrow wage consciousness. More importantly, every beneficial law renders union members that much more independent of their trade-union organizations, which can only hold on to their members if they appear to be the sole source of economic benefits. As a union leader said at the 1932 AFL convention in opposition to Federal unemployment insurance: "The only way to get wage-earners interested in the trade-union movement and make it a driving force is to convince them that . . . it is only through the strength, the fighting strength of that economic organization that you are going to get higher wages and shorter hours." This is quite true, and before the 1930s, trade-union leaders openly opposed beneficial labor laws—maximum hours legislation, for example. Such legislation, as they rightly pointed out, was a "union-busting" device. That such laws might benefit workers is of no concern to a trade unionist, since, by the central tenet of trade unionism, nothing that injures trade unions can possibly be good for workers. From this point of view, it is a great advantage to labor that American citizens receive grossly inadequate old-age pensions because this makes union members dependent upon, and grateful for, union pension plans, many of which are outrageously corrupt.

As official members of the liberal wing of the Democratic machine, however, trade unions cannot openly oppose welfare legislation any longer, but such legislation remains, unalterably, a union-busting device. The union's secret opposition to reform, therefore, parallels that of machine liberals in the Democratic party. They protect the power of the Southern Bourbons who defeat the measures the unions must now pretend to favor. In a strict sense, therefore, trade-union support of the Bourbons is indeed utilitarian. The criterion which the union chiefs employ is indeed service to labor, meaning, however, themselves.

It should be glaringly obvious why the party oligarchs created and now sustain the "trade-union movement." Here is a vast and wealthy organization whose interests are absolutely identical with those of the party oligarchs. Like the oligarchs, the unions are determined to control and degrade free citizens, to render them politically inert, divided and ignorant, to disguise from them in every way the relevance of politics to their lives, to cripple their capacity and willingness to act in their own behalf, to see them—and all citizens—bereft of protective and beneficial laws and of the very hope of winning them. Here is an organization whose leaders are so absolutely dependent on corrupt power that they will scruple at no act of political corruption. Yet they will serve corrupt power with a clear conscience—as faithful servants of the trade-union creed. From the point of view of republican self-government, a trade-union chief is absolutely corrupt; from the point of view of trade unionism, he is absolutely honest. This is why, at bottom, the party oligarchs created trade unions—political liberty is the enemy of both.

At this point a question properly arises. If the trade unions are so eminently useful to the party oligarchs, why were the latter so long reluctant to organize the major industries? Why did they wait until necessity forced their hand? The reason for this lies in the very fact that industrial unions *are* a fraud upon millions of citizens. The risks involved in perpetrating such a fraud were—and still are—considerable. If the fraud ever failed, the oligarchs would be worse off than ever. They would have encouraged industrial workers to organize; they would have taught them the habits of cooperation; they would have provided them with a mechanism—dues—for amassing large sums of money. Should union members ever clearly realize that their unions are worse than useless, they would have no alternative but free politics, and they could turn to it with considerable advantages—their money, their organizations, their local union forums. This is the last thing the party oligarchs would want. They had every reason to be reluctant and to act as they did only when it became necessary, that is, when they had to take responsibility for industrial wages. As long as the oligarchs entrusted the monopolists to determine wages, they opposed industrial unions (company unions excepted). As long as they did so, no industry could be organized, trade unions having no power to organize a major industry against the wishes of the political powers.

Since trade unionism is a fraud, the essential labor policy of the party oligarchs is aimed at keeping union members from realizing it. This effort consists in giving support and credence to all the fraudulent claims and pretensions of the trade-union ideology. The oligarchs do this in great part just by serving their own interests, which are identical with the unions. Trade unionism claims that citizens who labor have no hope save in unions; the oligarchs make good the claim by their constant endeavor to blast public hope. Trade unionism claims that workers can only win benefits through unions; the party oligarchs prove this by constantly trying to thwart general reform. Trade unionism claims that politics is largely futile; the oligarchs constantly try to make politics appear futile. However, the oligarchs must take more active steps to maintain the "trade-union movement."

The essential fiction—the fiction of union economic power—the oligarchs perpetuate by the universal pretense that it exists. Wage benefits are funneled through industrial unions. The unions' claim that they win these benefits is simply never contested by anyone in public life. It is the perfect bipartisan lie: conservative Republicans deplore union power, liberal Democrats extol it. It is nonexistent, like the difference between a conservative and a liberal machine politician. To convince workers further that the unions wield economic power, the major corporations, at the oligarchs' behest, also play their indispensable part. While collective bargaining goes on behind closed doors, labor and management try their best to contrive the appearance of a genuine tug-of-war, a real pitting of strength against strength. Given that charade of struggle, management's ultimate "concession" to union "demands"—which almost always matches the government's wage policy—becomes the trophy of victory which the union chiefs bring back to their rank and file, whose only influence in all this consists of the genuine fear of the oligarchs, the unions and the corporations that they will get fed up with their unions. This fear occasionally brings industrial union members a slightly larger wage increase than the wage policy calls for. Disgust with their unions is the only power union members have and it is based entirely on the oligarchs' fear of their unused power as citizens. On the other hand, union solidarity makes the rank and file totally powerless, exactly the reverse of the trade-union creed.

It is entirely in line with the official fiction of union economic power that the Vietnam War–induced inflation was universally attributed to that fictive union ability to push up wages. The truth of the matter is that industrial union members, despite huge wage increases, could barely keep up with rising living costs. Between 1968 and 1970 their real wages actually fell slightly. It was soaring prices, particularly in the service sector of the economy, which forced union members to demand large wage increases, not the reverse. All the unions seemingly did was keep wages more or less in line with living costs, but they did not even do this, the party oligarchs did. To do so is their general wage policy. So was the Vietnam War, and the two policies, wages and war, came into significant collision. Given the oligarchs' wage policy and their reluctance to levy a war tax to pay for an unpopular war, inflation was the result—union economic power had nothing to do with it. Given that unpopular war, on the other hand, the oligarchs had to keep wages in line with living costs, otherwise industrial workers would have been paying for the war, which would only have made it even more unpopular. In other words, the oligarchs kept up union wages, not because of unions, but because union members are citizens who can vote. Since the giant monopolies are the servants of the oligarchs, they had to give huge wage increases to these same voters even though it cut into their profits. By the time President Nixon launched his "new economic policy" in 1971, all that the prolonged war inflation was demonstrating to increasingly restless union members was the irrelevance of their unions to their immediate concerns. Worse: their unions, after all, are the war's chief supporters, a fact which was making it a little too obvious that the bread-and-butter interests of union members do not determine the policies of union leaders.

To help keep union members convinced that their unions are their best representatives, the oligarchs also help sustain a second major trade-union pretense, that the unions actually wield independent political power. Since it is impossible to render twenty million Americans totally apathetic politically, the fiction of union political power is the perfect way of diverting them from acting on their own. Every four years organized labor submits a list of reforms to the Democratic national convention, which duly incorporates these "demands" in the party platform, thus demonstrating the power of the unions in the councils of the Democratic party. Trade-union leaders are cosseted and pampered, their influence at the White House constantly paraded before the membership. The AFL-CIO's rubber-stamp conventions are invariably addressed by exalted officials. The most blatant union truckling to the Democratic machine is invariably described as the Democrats' truckling to unions. This is yet another perfect bipartisan lie: liberal Democrats extol this nonexistent union influence, conservative Republicans deplore it.

The third major trade-union fiction which the oligarchs perpetuate is the pretense that unions are independent, politically nonpartisan bodies which only support those candidates who serve the interests of labor. Perpetuating this fiction is complicated by the fact that the trade unions must be overwhelmingly partisan. If the trade-union chiefs actually switched back and forth between parties, they would seriously endanger the whole system of collusion. In any Democratic machine city, for example, the unions would often be forced to support local independent Republicans against both the machine's candidates and the Republican hierarchy's determination to lose. The only safe way to avoid this, while keeping up the pretense of nonpartisanship, is for the oligarchs to give the union chiefs some relatively durable pretext for declaring one party the true friend of labor and the other its inveterate foe. In this case, the unions can support the most egregious machine Democrat—such as Philadelphia's Mayor Frank Rizzo—against the most plausible Republican without too many questions arising.

Just how spurious such a pretext can be is well illustrated by the performance put on by Samuel Gompers and Woodrow Wilson in 1914 when the AFL leader decided to bring the federation into the national Democratic party—previously union-machine alliances were local ones. To square this with the creed of "nonpartisanship," Gompers demanded that the Democrats show public concern for the interests of union members. This Wilson promised to do in a provision of the forthcoming Clayton Antitrust Act. When the Clayton Act was passed, its labor provision proved to be empty verbiage. Gompers proclaimed it "The Magna Carta" of labor and led the AFL into the national party as a reward for its friendship to unions.

In our own time the essential pretext for union adherence to the Democratic party has been built on the Taft-Hartley Act and is equally spurious. Since the Taft-Hartley Act effectively compels employers to bargain in good faith according to the definition of good faith laid down in thousands of administrative decisions of the National Labor Relations Board, it is, as I said, the culminating victory for trade unionism, its true Magna Carta. The union chiefs have been attacking it ever since; indeed they had to, the allegedly "crippling" effects of the measure being their basic alibi for economic impotence. They could scarcely admit that Taft-Hartley gave them everything when the result is that they are nothing. Since the "Slave Labor Act," as the unions called their Magna Carta, was enacted by a Republican Congress and since the Democrats have promised ever since to repeal it, unions have had a durable pretext for nonpartisan adherence to the Democratic party, which could not have passed such a legislative victory for the trade unions precisely because the unions had to attack any such measure, which would have left them without a party to support nonpartisanly. To underscore Democratic opposition to Taft-Hartley, President Truman vetoed the bill, but it was overridden, as he doubtless expected, by the overwhelming vote of 331 to 83 in the House without a word of debate, and by 68 to 25 in the Senate.

Appearances must be kept up, though barely. In 1965 the heavily Democratic House voted to repeal one provision of the Taft-Hartley Act, the hated, though quite inconsequential, section 14(b), which authorizes states to pass right-to-work laws. Since the Democrats had no intention of repealing that provision (it serves as the unions' excuse for not organizing in the West and the South), they conveniently killed the repeal measure in the Senate. This was done by allowing Senator Everett Dirksen to play the indispensable Republican enemy and filibuster it to death. Though the filibuster could have been broken easily by round-the-clock Senate sessions, Democratic Majority Leader Mike Mansfield refused to call any as a matter of "principle." Vehement efforts by the trade unions to punish Mansfield, the Senate Democratic leadership, the Bourbon opponents of repeal and machine Democrats who support Southern Bourbons are, of course, nowhere in evidence. Repeal of Taft-Hartley would be a disaster for the trade unions. On the other hand, Western Democratic Congressmen who vote against repeal of 14(b) are mercilessly hounded by the unions when the Democratic bosses give the signal. The trade unions support legislators who pretend to oppose a law they have no intention of repealing and attack those who oppose repealing a law which the unions have no wish to see repealed. So much for the trade unions' nonpartisan politics. Like everything else in the trade-union creed, it is absolutely fraudulent.

The success of the trade-union hoax demonstrates as well as anything can the real pervasive power of the party oligarchs. The frauds and fictions of trade unionism are far from impenetrable. Some of them are as frail as gossamer and public recognition of a few jagged facts would tear them apart. That the unions went all out for Hubert Humphrey's nomination in 1968 because of his labor record is exploded by the obvious fact that the unions had refused to support Humphrey just eight years before. Yet what public men who matter called this fact to the public's attention? None, because almost nobody can matter in public who is not approved by the party oligarchs. What they do not wish to see exposed will not be exposed, what they wish to keep dark will remain in darkness.

As children of public darkness, the trade unions are absolutely corrupt, a condition which Lord Acton attributed to absolute power but which in their case is inseparable from absolute impotence. Beginning with the proposition—doubtless sincerely held at first—that free politics in a free Republic is no business of a worker, that self-government is inherently a sham, that real power is always economic, the trade unionists have demonstrated what happens to those who act upon ideological fictions. They become the servants of those who strive to make self-government the very sham which the ideology claims it to be, namely the prevailing wielders of corrupt, usurped power. This is the real lesson of trade unionism. Those who will not fight for political liberty, who do not make the enhancement of liberty and self-government their principle and goal, will end up as the bulwark of the enemies of liberty and of the usurpers of the citizens' constituted power. The trade unions did not become stagnant. They did not betray their early promise. They were born dead, and the only tragedy of trade unionism is the waste of brave men who mistakenly believed in it.

11.
The Rule of Caprice

Political deeds have public consequences. When William McKinley decided to protect the "integrity" of Imperial China, the result was a sharply increased American involvement in Far Eastern affairs. When Franklin Roosevelt supported industrial unionizing, the result was the rapid expansion of unions within the bastions of industry. When a municipal sanitation department cuts back on service, the result is an increasingly dirty city. Yet suppose such political deeds were carried out in secret, completely hidden from public view. The results they produce would be drastically altered in appearance. They would seem to be not the consequence of deeds but that which "just happened." Ignore McKinley's "open door" policy, and America's Far Eastern involvement will appear the consequences of some general trend such as "America's rise to world power." Ignore Roosevelt's role in creating industrial unions and those unions will appear to have grown by themselves. Ignore the sanitation department's curtailment of service, and the rising level of litter will appear, perhaps, as a symptom of social breakdown. Whenever the results of deeds are divorced from the deeds themselves, they lose their political character and appear to be the results of happenstance, of larger social forces and historic trends, or even of the providence of God. Although they are the consequence of political action, they will appear beyond reach of political action, since what men do not appear to have done they appear incapable of undoing.

To those who wield irresponsible political power, the advantage of hiding deeds is obvious and profound. By divorcing deeds from their results, they can produce results which serve their own interests yet bear no responsibility for them, for what appears to just happen, or what appears to issue from social and historical processes, is the specific responsibility of no man. They can produce results which every citizen resents yet risk no political reprisal, since only fools and madmen take arms against the inevitable. By hiding the political determination of public results, the wielders of corrupt power can disengage politics from those results so completely that their very power will appear nonexistent, since to all appearances it plays so little part in what actually happens.

Modern tyrants have always understood this quite well and so, of course, have the "friends to republican government," to borrow James Madison's phrase. In the Soviet Union, the official newspaper *Pravda* prints scant political news and rarely describes the movements and personalities of Politburo members. (*Pravda* is filled with reports about labor and production, presumably a deeper stratum of reality than mere politics, but in practice not even the most rigid economic ideologue actually believes this.) Every Russian knows that the Politburo decides everything, but Russia's despots will never confirm this, knowing full well that when political deeds and actors are hidden, the results of their actions in any case will lose their political character and appear to be what the Soviet rulers claim them to be— "necessary stages" in building pure communism.

Certain modes of political action cannot, by their very nature, mask the political determination of results. One such mode is to bring about results through the enactment and enforcement of general laws which prohibit (or reward) some particular line of conduct. The result of such legal acts will be a sharp decrease in the prohibited (or increase in the rewarded) conduct. Yet nobody would say of the result that happenstance, historic forces or providence had anything to do with it. The links connecting the result to the law to the lawmakers are clear and unbroken. Because they are, the political determination of the result remains obvious to all.

The links remain clear even when lawmakers create by law an

administrative body to carry out some public purpose defined by the lawmakers. This is true insofar as the administrative body, in all its various rulings, is strictly bound by the purpose of the law and cannot choose any means but those which fulfill that purpose—which is, after all, what defines an administrative body. Since the results which the administration brings about are dictated by the law's stated purpose, the political determination of the results still remain clear. When people hear that some multimillionaire pays no income tax, they rightly blame a loophole in the law—an action of the lawmakers—not a loophole in the Internal Revenue Service.

Not every public body which is called an administrative body, however, carries out the express purpose of the law it was established to administer. Such a body may in fact be quite free to ignore the express purpose of the law; it may enjoy discretionary power of various kinds; it may be free to make *ad hoc* decisions which differ in every case and so have no common basis in general law. In a word, it may rule by caprice. If the scope of that caprice is so great that the public body is in no way bound by the general purpose of the law and can bring about results quite different from the law's purpose, it cannot be called an administrative body, whatever its official designation. For such capricious administrative agencies there is a familiar and fitting name—bureaucracy, which can be defined as a pseudo-administrative body which enjoys sufficient scope for caprice to enable it to *not* administer the law. That an administrative body is large, that its organization is "hierarchical" does not make it a bureaucracy. What defines bureaucracy is the capacity to rule capriciously. In this sense, five-man Federal regulatory agencies may be—and in fact are—far more bureaucratic than the giant U.S. Postal Service.

The political consequence of bureaucratic rule—the rule of caprice—provides the key to grasping its political significance. Because a bureaucracy can, through its scope for caprice, produce results which bear no connection to law and lawmakers, the results of bureaucratic rule appear to be the consequence of no political deed and the responsibility of no political actor. They will appear to just happen or to constitute a general trend, reflecting the effect of social forces, historic laws or the providential hand of God. For the wielders of oligarchic power, the advantages of ruling through bureaucracies are clear. By means of bureaucracy they can hide the political determination of every self-serving result they wish to achieve yet evade all responsibility for them. The oligarchs may, for example, enact a law creating an ostensible administrative body to carry out some apparently praiseworthy purpose. Yet by endowing that body with sufficient scope for caprice, they are in a position to evade that purpose and even to carry out a contrary purpose. By putting the bureaucracy in the hands of agents deliberately chosen to carry out their undisclosed purpose, the oligarchs can make sure that the rule of caprice brings about the results they wish—they *embed* their undisclosed purposes in the bureaucracy itself. Since these purposes, achieved through bureaucracy, will bear no relation to the expressed purpose of law, the oligarchs bear no responsibility. If the results are directly contrary to the expressed purpose of the law, it may even seem as if social forces too potent for mere lawmakers had thwarted their praiseworthy aims. By masking deeds through bureaucracy, the wielders of corrupt power can make political actions appear so inconsequential that the citizenry will think politics irrelevant to their lives. Indeed, were a political community ruled exclusively by bureaucratic means, politics itself would disappear, since whatever happened would appear the results of providential processes, a truth wonderfully re-created by Franz Kafka, who, for this reason, gave divinity the attributes of a bureaucracy and bureaucracy the attributes of divinity.

Perhaps the most important example of the politics of bureaucracy is the oligarchs' creation of the major Federal bureaucracies—the regulatory agencies and commissions, the Federal Reserve Board and the like—to sustain and enlarge the monopoly system.

The American people's historic opposition to monopoly is beyond all dispute. Since the birth of the Republic they have registered that opposition in innumerable ways and in major legislation. "The nation's commitment, embodied in the antitrust laws, to competitive pricing," to quote former Chief Justice Earl Warren, means that the oligarchs can only maintain the monopoly system in defiance both of fundamental law and of long-held republican principle. To do this openly is beyond their political capacity. Moreover, to maintain the monopoly system openly would destroy the central myth of Big Business, namely that the economy we have was self-created and, in consequence, is self-sustaining.

Such being the case, virtually every regulatory agency is charged by law not to support monopoly, but, on the contrary, to maintain "fair competition" in the industries they regulate. In practice, however, regulatory agencies work to destroy price competition. As Kohlmeier demonstrates in *The Regulators*, "they are the nemesis of competition as defined by the anti-trust laws and the Department of Justice." The reason the regulatory agencies can defy the law is precisely their scope for caprice, which was deliberately bestowed upon the agencies by the party oligarchs to carry out their monopoly policy. The Congressional oligarchs do this by giving the agencies the authority to carry out the laws' stated purpose while leaving the means to do so unspecified. Claiming that the means are merely technical, Congress gives the agencies full discretionary power to decide the technicalities themselves. To broaden still further the scope of regulatory caprice, the Congressional oligarchs allow the regulatory agencies to make two sorts of rulings. The first is a general ruling covering the agencies' entire field of jurisdiction and requiring public hearings and sworn testimony. Since general rulings might have to square somewhat with the professed purpose of law, the agencies are also allowed to make special rulings for individual clients. These are made informally, in private, on an *ad hoc* basis, which is to say, with fullest scope for caprice. As Kohlmeier points out, the agencies overwhelmingly prefer to rule on this case-by-case basis, handing down together some ninety thousand informal rulings a year over the protests of the Federal courts but not of the party oligarchs in Congress who set up the rule of caprice in the first place.

Since the regulatory agencies bring about their results—securing the monopoly system—in defiance of the express purpose of law, the link between politics and monopoly is broken. The oligarchs' determination to maintain the monopoly system is masked; the monopolists' very need of governmental protection is hidden, so much so that when corporation spokesmen bluster about government "interference," people actually take them seriously and conclude that regulation is anti–Big Business. So well does bureaucracy hide the political character of monopoly that it appears to be an economic phenomenon independent of political deeds and determinations. The monopolization of the economy truly appears to be the result of economic laws so imperative that the "efforts" of the lawmakers to curb it invariably prove unavailing. Yet it is the lawmakers who deliberately subvert their own efforts, and it is bureaucracy which now enables them to do so—regularly, secretly and with virtual impunity.

In carrying out their monopoly policy by means of bureaucracy, the party oligarchs give that policy an appearance which many economic ideologues take for reality—the seeming impotence of the political realm before the overwhelming forces of economic trends and economic power. That appearance serves the oligarchs' interests even in regard to the more noticeable failings of the regulatory agencies. Everybody knows that the agencies dispense special privilege and continually betray the public interest. Yet that betrayal is rarely laid at the door of Congress. The standard public criticism of the regulatory agencies is that they are the hapless servants of their powerful business clients (the only clients of bureaucracy deemed capable of controlling a bureaucracy) who inevitably work their will upon them in any confrontation. Yet this is taking a contrived appearance for reality. The oligarchs mask their own politics of special privilege through the rule of bureaucratic caprice and this sort of criticism deems the oligarchs to be powerless bystanders. Economic ideologues who claim to penetrate the facade of mere politics are in fact describing a politically created facade—that of the irrelevance of political power, which bureaucracy creates for its creators. The "economic" explanation of regulatory misrule is exactly the kind of explanation the oligarchs do not mind. It is the prevalence of this ideological criticism, for example, which justifies the invariable cant line about the regulatory agencies—namely that they betray the "consumers," a pretense that the "real" issue at stake is an economic conflict between hapless buyers and powerful sellers, whereas the true issue at stake is the political conflict between the citizens and corrupt political power. The very term *consumer* is a political evasion and thus the apt verbal counterpart of the regulatory bureaucracies.

It is often said, plausibly enough, that bureaucracy is the inevitable result of increased government intervention in social and economic affairs. The sharp increase in direct government intervention carried out by Roosevelt certainly brought with it a sharp increase in Federal administrative bodies, regulatory agencies, public corporations and the like. Yet the plausibility is only apparent and rests on a confusion between bureaucracy and administration. Doubtless increased government intervention has brought with it an increase in the number and variety of administrative bodies. There is nothing inevitable, however, about endowing an ostensible administrative body with scope for caprice. That is always a deliberate political act. It was not government intervention, per se, that brought about an increase in bureaucratic rule in the 1930s, but the fact that the oligarchs intervened in the economy to produce results for which they dared not be held accountable. It was in the 1930s that the oligarchs realized, as I said, that monopoly capitalism would fall apart without direct, systematic and permanent government intervention. Since they could not carry out an open monopoly policy, they had to create or adapt the giant Federal bureaucracies to do it for them. That is why bureaucracy grew under the New Deal. The chief reason for the growth of bureaucracy in our time is that the party oligarchs find it necessary to create more and more bureaucracies as the active range of their abuse of power increases.

The relation between bureaucracy and government intervention is strikingly illustrated in the case of the farm program brought into being by Roosevelt under the Agricultural Adjustment Act. This was, of course, a drastic intervention in the economics of farming, carried out for the professed purpose of solving the farm problem and rescuing the nation's farmers from their chronic plight. In fact the New Deal farm program was—and remains—nothing of the sort. The farm program was not an effort to save the nation's farmers but to get rid of them. That was the oligarchs' real purpose: to solve the farm problem by consolidating agriculture. Had they openly proposed to do this they would have needed no bureaucracy, since it could have been done in due course by quite general laws and quite straightforward administration. This, however, was more than the oligarchs dared. To expel small farmers from the land openly was beyond their political capacity. To mask the political determination of that expulsion, therefore, the oligarchs brought into being an exceedingly complex bureaucracy, one that could hand down rulings and decisions unbound by the law's declared purposes. The farm program, by now, is riddled with caprice, caprice in setting price parities, caprice in setting crop allotments, caprice in the administration of farm loans ostensibly designed to help small farmers. The essential principle of the farm program itself, to maintain farm prices by limiting production, is a weapon that can easily be used against small farmers who have the least acreage to spare.

Having established a caprice-ridden administration, the oligarchs then deliberately put the farm program into the hands of the *enemies* of small farmers—the Farm Extension Service, the agricultural colleges and, most significantly, a quasi-private body known as the Farm Bureau Federation, an outfit created by the oligarchs, patronized by the oligarchs, brought into prominence by the oligarchs (in the 1930s, just in time for the farm program) to represent the interests of the larger farmers. The epitome of the complex farm bureaucracy and the oligarchs' real farm policy is the Farm Credit Administration. Created by Congress to enable small farmers to procure loans which private banks deny them, the FCA was put in the hands of the Farm Bureau Federation. Since FCA credit procedures were at its discretion, the bureau now applies strict banking criteria to loan applications, completely subverting the professed purpose of the law and, of course, hurting small farmers. What the oligarchs did was embed their real, undisclosed farm policy in the farm bureaucracy itself, which has become, by the deliberate determination of the party oligarchs, a virtual machine for driving small farmers from the land, which it does, year in and year out with the remorselessness of a juggernaut.

By hiding the political determination of that expulsion, however, the farm bureaucracy completely masks the oligarchs' responsibility for it. The expulsion of small farmers appears to be not an expulsion but part of a long-term trend which ideologues of one sort or another attribute to industrialization, monopolization, mechanization or whatever plausible cause they can concoct. So far from being blamed for the disappearance of small farmers, the oligarchs are often lauded for their titanic, costly but futile effort to save the farmers from their preordained fate. Such perversions of reality breed yet more wretched perversions. Judging by the oligarchs' alleged efforts to save small farmers, many social commentators now write learned nonsense about "the myth of the small farmer" in America. According to their view, the farmers' mythical republican virtues have led to a sentimental cherishing of the family farm. In fact the party oligarchs have cherished the small farmers the way a tank cherishes a flower bed and precisely because the myth is not so mythic after all. Since the Civil War, at least, the most unruly, the most independent, the most republican of American citizens have been the small farmers whose fate was sealed by a law purporting to save them and by a bureaucracy set up to kill them off.

Even those who grasp that bureaucracy is the rule of caprice, however, frequently deny that bureaucracies carry out the policies of the political powers that created them. In their view, the very capriciousness of bureaucracy, the very fact that it subverts the lawmakers' intentions demonstrates the independent power of the bureaucrats. This is the fundamental view set forth in Charles Reich's *The Greening of America,* wherein the nation is described as a "corporate state" completely "out of human control." Since the notion that the American Republic is now a faceless, purposeless, bureaucratized system has gained considerable currency, it is well worth examining its root assumption, namely the alleged autonomy of bureaucracies and bureaucrats. The best place to begin is with those administrative agencies which actually enjoy formal autonomy in the sense that the political authorities officially claim to defer to their judgments, as they do, for example, in the case of the Federal Reserve Board. Since the party oligarchs justify such deference on a variety of grounds, the several justifications provide a rough catalog of the main species of independent bureaucracies.

One sort of autonomy, that of the regulatory agencies, is based on the autonomy of expert opinion: the claim that the independent discretionary power of the agencies is justified by their being "specially competent" to fulfill a legislative purpose "by reason of information, experience and careful study," to quote a 1934 Supreme Court decision. Congress, in this case, sets up the rule of the regulatory experts and then claims to defer to their technical competence. Whether they do or not, the justification for doing so is entirely spurious, for while experts are certainly necessary, their autonomy is not. If the lawmakers genuinely wished to achieve the purpose of the law establishing any regulatory agency they could eliminate the experts' autonomy almost completely. To do so they would first define the law's purpose as stringently as possible rather than defining it, as they usually do, as ambiguously as possible. Then they would restrict the agency experts to general rulings in accordance with that purpose. Wherever possible they would consult experts *before* writing the law, and having learned from them the technical means needed to achieve the law's purpose, they would make them, as far as possible, mandatory provisions of the law. Used this way the experts would be neither autonomous nor capricious. They would be the servants of law, which is precisely what the party oligarchs do not want them to be.

A second form of administrative autonomy is based on the traditional autonomy of individual professional people. A "professional" bureaucracy—public educators, highway engineers, city planning commissions, health departments and the like—is one whose autonomy arises in theory from a combination of expert knowledge and devotion to professional principle. School managers wish, presumably, to provide the best schooling, health departments the best health care, highway departments the best highways. Possessing expertise, professional bureaucracies also lay claim to unassailable motives. Their claim to autonomy is a formidable one, since their clients, by definition, are laymen, and so are accorded no more right to advise or influence them than a patient has to advise his physician. The very hallmark of a professional bureaucracy is its determined resistance to lay interference, its refusal to concede even in the face of the bitterest public opposition that such opposition has any right to be heard. In New York City, the highway authorities have been planning for three decades to build a highway across the width of Manhattan. Every time construction appears imminent, determined public opposition arises, forcing the bureaucracy to retreat. The retreat, however, has so far been tactical, since the authorities will not revoke the expressway plan. That would mean conceding that the laity had altered a "professional evaluation." As a result the expressway plan still hangs over the city like the sword of Damocles, a testament to the autonomy of professionals and a demonstration of the ultimate futility of lay interference.

A third, though only partial, form of administrative independence rests on the claim that a key element in the bureaucracy is a private body—the Farm Bureau Federation is one example of this, the state education associations another. In these mixed bureaucracies, as they might be called, the more influential the private elements are, the more independent the bureaucracy appears to be, since a private organization, by definition, originates its own notions and pursues its own policies.

A fourth sort of autonomy rests on the alleged independence of business enterprise, the autonomous administrations in this case being the so-called public corporations such as the Tennessee Valley Authority and the Federal Deposit Insurance Corporation, among dozens of others now in existence. Created by legislative enactment to carry out a public purpose, these public corporations are given the legal status of private enterprises and complete immunity from public accountability. The justification for this is that the public corporations are financially self-supporting, which proves, supposedly, that they are performing a needed public service. Here, too, the justification is entirely spurious. Since public corporations are government-created monopolies, their financial self-sufficiency may prove nothing. That a public corporation is in the black because, among its activities, it col-lects highway tolls only proves that collecting highway tolls is an easy way to make money. It scarcely proves that the corporation's other activities are being done well or are even worth doing.

Such are the major sorts of autonomous bureaucracies, those to whose judgments elected officials officially claim to defer. If I am right in saying that bureaucracy's function is to mask political deeds, then obviously there can be no such thing as an autonomous bureaucracy. Had the oligarchs created truly autonomous bureaucracies, they would be surrendering their power, not masking it. In fact the autonomy of autonomous bureaucracies is as spurious as the justifications for it. Like the god Janus, every independent bureaucracy has two faces. The face it presents to the citizenry is the face of the patron—remote, impersonal, unheeding. The face it presents to the party oligarchs is the face of the lackey.

The "independent" regulatory agencies, for example, are so completely under the thumb of the Congressional bosses—the House and Senate Commerce Committees in particular—that, as Kohlmeier notes, few men of ability want to serve as regulatory experts; being an obscure lackey is not very appealing to ambitious men. If the agencies were independent, they would of course be flouting the professed will of Congress as defined by public law. Yet the reaction of Congress to such flouting is total indifference. Since 1946 every standing committee of Congress is supposed to maintain "continuous watchfulness of the execution by the administrative agencies concerned" of laws originating in its committee. In addition, House and Senate Government Operations Committees are charged to maintain the same watchfulness over the entire executive branch, about which, we are told, they are so "jealous." As watchdogs of bureaucracy, however, Congress has been virtually asleep for a quarter of a century. As Stephen Horn notes in *Unused Power:* "the Senate Committee on Government Operations has only sporadically reviewed even part of the work of the executive branch. The standing committees with much narrower jurisdiction have done little more." What is even more remarkable about this curious laxity is that those vaunted enemies of "bureaucratic meddling," the mighty Southern Bourbons and Republican conservatives, are as lax as the liberals in Congress. That is because they are merely elements in the same bipartisan oligarchy—the right corner of its one mouth. Flouting the putative will of Congress *is* the will of the party oligarchs who control Congress. As Kohlmeier points out, the Congressional oligarchs regularly dictate agency decisions whenever an agency appears on the verge of *not* flouting the professed will of Congress.

The autonomy of public corporations is equally spurious. As just one example, the TVA, in the course of conducting its business, produces a cheap fertilizer which is highly useful to large farmers but useless to small farmers. TVA's decision to produce that fertilizer was not a commercial one. It was taken at the behest of the party oligarchs as part of their general policy of making small farmers "disappear."

Is the independence of professional bureaucracies as fake as that of the regulatory experts? To reformers of a certain stripe—those who attribute misrule in the Republic to the moral failures of the citizenry—the professionalism of professional bureaucracies is an article of faith. To such people, the indifference of professional bureaucracies to lay opinion is the cardinal virtue of professional bureaucracies, that which enables them to carry out worthy public policies without interference from a vile and purblind citizenry and the politicians who allegedly speak for them. This certainly describes enlightened opinion about the most important of all the professional bureaucracies, the so-called educational establishment, that complex amalgam of state education commissions, the Federal Office of Education, state-accredited teachers' colleges, state teacher licensing laws, private professional organizations such as the national and state education associations and, more recently, an "independent" trade union known as the American Federation of Teachers. If the educational establishment were truly autonomous, however, we would have to explain away a truly astonishing coincidence: that the educational policies of the autonomous school managers and the political interests of the party oligarchs are virtually identical, that the schools which the educators provide for America's children are precisely what the oligarchs would provide if they controlled the schools. Whatever the public schools are supposed to be in a free Republic, the schools we are given are not. This becomes quite obvious as soon as we recall what in fact they are supposed to be.

The fundamental principle of republican education, as Thomas Jefferson said, is "to enable every man to judge for himself what will secure or endanger his freedom." Republican education presupposes that schoolchildren are future citizens, no more and no less; that republican liberty is always endangered; that the ambitions of usurpers must always be resisted; that free politics is the necessary business of every free man; that the fundamentals of republican education must, in consequence, be made available to every child. The central principle of the educational establishment is to presuppose the very opposite; like the party oligarchs, the educators use the republican standard as their unfailing guide to what not to do.

It is the *sine qua non* of republican education that the public schools regard their students and the students regard each other as future self-governing citizens. It has been the constant endeavor of the school managers throughout this century to persuade American schoolchildren that they are chiefly future employees and members of industrial society. When Lyndon Johnson said in his final budget message that the main purpose of public education is to help students "expand their earning power," he summed up in his crass way sixty years of that effort and stated what republican schools can never have as their legitimate purpose. A self-governing republic cannot be equated with industrial society; an industrial society may be ruled by tyrants, and obviously so: the despotic Soviet regime rules an industrial society. There is no requirement of industrial society which bears the slightest resemblance to the requirements of liberty. This is because a citizen is not a worker and the virtues of citizens are not the virtues of employees. For the most part, their virtues are diametrically opposite—independence as opposed to conformity, equality as opposed to subordination, the habit of self-rule as opposed to the habits of obedience.

The dubious distinction of providing a "democratic" justification for teaching future citizens that they are future jobholders belongs not to Lyndon Johnson but to the notable John Dewey and the "progressive" educators in general. Democracy, said Dewey, was a "mode of associated living"; its chief attribute is intensive "social cooperation";

intensive social cooperation is also the distinguishing feature of a complex industrial society; ergo, preparing children for their cooperative part in that society is democratic education. If this sounds like a travesty of Dewey's educational philosophy, consider that the first public school system to adopt—in 1907—Dewey's educational formulas was that of Gary, Indiana, a company town founded two years before by the U.S. Steel Corporation. Economic ideologues, however, have nothing to rejoice in that. The very notion of defining a free republic by its economy follows from economic ideology, which makes its signal contribution to antirepublican education by justifying its salient principle.

Since free men cannot judge for themselves what endangers their freedom if they believe it is never in danger, it is the chief burden of the public school curriculum to persuade children that their liberty is always secure. This is accomplished easily enough. The dangers to liberty to which Jefferson referred derive from the ambition of would-be usurpers, those who would rob the citizenry of their voice in their own government. For that reason, he insisted, the study of political history—the history of men's deeds—must be the heart of republican schooling. By studying the political deeds of men, of Catiline and Cato, of Cromwell and King Charles, the future citizens of the Republic would "know ambition under all its shapes and [be] prompt to exert their natural powers to defeat its purposes." Such being the case, the school managers have virtually prevented students from studying political history. Insofar as it is taught at all, the ambitions of usurpers are omitted entirely; in the typical American history textbook, every public leader is a faithful servant of the people; only foreign rulers in the distant past had unscrupulous political aims.

Since even gutted political history still discusses the deeds of men, the school managers have tried to eliminate political history entirely. Its replacement in our time is "social studies," whose original pedagogic purpose was to imbue students with a "socialized disposition" and other virtues deemed necessary for industrial society. In elementary social studies classes, children will be taught, for example, "how milk is brought to the city" through the cooperation of numerous hands, a lesson in the complexities of "associated living" designed to impress upon the impressionable that America is mainly an intricate social mechanism in which they will one day play their part—as cogs. Recommending this sort of "education" in 1902, Jane Addams declared that when the children of factory workers learn their future place on the industrial "team," they would find the knowledge "exhilarating." In fact they find it so depressing they break the windows of their schools with rocks. At a more advanced level, social studies provides the students with pseudo-history such as studies in the "development of transportation" and the "evolution of industry." By such means American children are deliberately taught to look on history as a record of results without deeds, milkwater Marxism for children and the very antithesis of learning about "ambition under all its shapes." In high school they will probably be treated to still more social studies of "evolving institutions" (in accordance with study programs now financed by the Federal Government) and "civics" courses which teach them that a system of "checks and balances" automatically secures their liberty, a lesson with the implicit moral: stay home and mind your business. Is it any wonder that so many of America's young people return home after one year of college prattling cynically about capitalist control of the country? They have been taught to think like economic ideologues from the day they enter first grade. Is it any wonder they so often look on the American Republic as a sinister, all-pervasive system? They learned that in social studies. And considering what they do not learn about the political dangers to their liberty, is it any wonder that so many actually believe that the real enemies of liberty in this Republic are their parents?

It is also a fundamental principle of republican education that every future citizen, regardless of social background, must be given a republican education and an equal opportunity for advanced education. The very reason for free public schools, as Jefferson said, was to help ordinary citizens overcome the natural advantages of birth and wealth in the endless contention for political eminence. America's professional educators have been trying to get around this ever since it became apparent around the turn of the century that the great mass of American children would soon be receiving secondary schooling.

Preventing them from learning anything once they got to high school has been the abiding endeavor of the educators. As Woodrow Wilson himself advised: "We want one class of persons to have a liberal education and we want another class of persons, a very much larger class of necessity in every society, to forgo the privilege of a liberal education and fit themselves to perform specific, difficult manual tasks." The "much larger class" to be shunted into the then new vocational and industrial curricula were, needless to say, the less affluent. As J. E. Russell of Columbia Teachers College remarked in 1905: "How can we justify our practice in schooling the masses in precisely the same manner we do those who are to be their leaders?" Only by the republican principle of the equality of liberty which the educational establishment was bent on betraying. Hence, said Charles Eliot, president of Harvard, in 1908: "we come upon a new function for the teachers in our elementary schools and in my judgment they have no function more important. The teachers of the elementary schools ought to sort the pupils; and sort them by their evident or probable destinies," a hypocrite's way of saying their family backgrounds. Since this "new function" was a direct betrayal of republican principle, the educators eagerly seized on the Frenchman Alfred Binet's Intelligence Quotient tests, which "proved" scientifically that the masses were congenitally incapable of acquiring a liberal education in high school. The IQ tests not only gave the school managers their pretext for sorting by family background, it allowed them to blame their betrayal of future citizens on the victims themselves. "They put themselves in the scrap heap, not us," as a professor of education once put it.

To make sure that the children of the poor lack every possible educational advantage, the educators have been busy, too, denying them elementary literacy. About thirty years ago the educators virtually abandoned one method of teaching reading—by means of the alphabet and phonetics—which succeeded throughout the world and replaced it with the so-called look-say method, which was supposedly psychologically superior. Although this new method proved a failure even before it was introduced, it had for the school managers one irresistibly attractive property: it failed best among those children, generally the poorest, whose parents do not teach them the alphabet at home. Having adopted a reading method that handicaps the impoverished, the educators now blame illiteracy on their students' impoverished backgrounds, just as formerly, during the reign of the now discredited IQ tests, they blamed it on their inferior germ plasm.

Who benefits from teaching America's children that they are chiefly future employees and jobholders, that America is not a Republic of self-governing citizens but an industrial society of workers, that institutions "evolve," that political ambition is nonexistent and politics irrelevant? Who benefits from illiteracy and semiliteracy among the mass of the poor and oppressed, from ghetto schools so degraded that Harlem schoolchildren think the police make the laws? Who benefits from teaching future citizens that their liberty is never endangered from usurpers? Who benefits, quite obviously, are the prevailing political usurpers. Between present-day public education and the abiding interests of the party oligarchs the identity is virtually absolute and describes American public education even in minute details. In a country whose people supposedly worship the Founding Fathers, the writings of the Founders—the most masterful republican political analyses in political literature—are not seriously studied. In a country whose greatest man, Abraham Lincoln, said we must love our country, not merely because it is ours but because it is free, our schools teach flag worship and jingoism (flag ceremonies were approved by the National Educational Association in 1896, the year of the Populist revolt) and call that education for citizenship. "There's richness," as Dickens' Mr. Squeers observed while passing out watered milk to his students.

The point, I believe, is made. The close congruence between the educators' policies and the oligarchs' political interests is no coincidence. The educational establishment is not autonomous; its judgments are not professional judgments; it does not control the schools. Like every autonomous bureaucracy and every other professional bureaucracy, it is the two-faced lackey of the party oligarchs. It is they, not the educators, who control the nation's schools, and the public schools we have are the public schools they have given us. It was by bureaucratizing education, by wresting control of education from the suffrage of local communities through teacher-licensing laws, accreditation laws, state education commissions and the massive consolidation of school districts beginning after World War I that the oligarchs gained control of the Republic's schools. It is by means of bureaucratic caprice that the oligarchs have been able systematically to betray long-held republican principles of education, including the most fundamental one, that the public schools must be kept independent of the prevailing political powers. It is by operating the schools behind the facade of a professional bureaucracy that the oligarchs hide their control of the schools, for like every other bureaucracy, the educational establishment serves to mask the political determination of results, the results in this case being the degraded public schools of the Republic.

Because bureaucracy helps the oligarchs mask almost all their self-serving policies, it would be impossible to enumerate all the specific political functions of the rule of bureaucratic caprice. The party oligarchs use bureaucracy to subvert fundamental law, as in the maintenance of the monopoly system; they use it to hide their responsibility for unjust policies, such as the expulsion of small farmers from the land; they use it to mask the betrayal of fundamental republican principles, such as their illicit control of the schools of the Republic; they use it to carry out the unending politics of special privilege through such instruments as the regulatory agencies which corrupt with special privilege every new source of wealth that arises. In great matters and in small, the rule of caprice invariably helps the party oligarchs weaken the willingness and ability of the citizenry to act for themselves.

When the party oligarchs are forced for some reason to pass a law they do not wish to enforce, they will frequently put its administration into the hands of the established bureaucracy most capable of subverting it. If they wish to nullify a mine-safety law, for example, they put it under the Bureau of Mines, which was set up for that purpose. If they wish to renege on legislation providing easier public loans, they will, as Kohlmeier points out, put it in the care of the Treasury Department, which is sure to apply strict banking criteria. Such bureaucratic nonenforcement of beneficial law is an essential part of the oligarchs' unremitting effort to "prove" to the citizenry that politics is futile; it provides a public demonstration that even when the citizenry pries reform legislation out of Congress, it will do them no good in the end; everything will remain much the same. Before the emergence of public concern for the environment, for example, every American was supposed to believe that polluted environments were the inevitable by-product of industrial prosperity. That fiction has been smashed and the oligarchs forced to take legislative action. Having done so, they immediately bureaucratized antipollution enforcement, hoping to teach concerned citizens that public efforts to clean up the environment are futile and so re-create, by means of bureaucracy, the appearance of unavoidable pollution which previously Americans accepted on faith. The Environmental Protection Agency, a bureaucracy set up in 1970, has already taken steps in that direction. In December 1971 it issued strict rules against air polluting that will apply only to new industrial plants. By bureaucratic decree they will thus leave the air as dirty as ever, although they could if they wished give windfall bounties to corporations as an inducement to curb pollution. It is not the power of the corporate polluters which stops the oligarchs from giving them windfalls.

By disguising their deeds through the rule of caprice, the party oligarchs can also practice more effectively the perennial politics of *divide et impera,* for citizens who cannot understand why things happen as they do are easily led to blame one another for everything that goes wrong. Setting people against each other has always been a policy of those wielding corrupt power. As Alexis de Tocqueville long ago observed, a despot does not care that his subjects dislike him as long as they dislike each other, for then they cannot act together and so remain impotent. In the giant cities of the Republic where even elementary municipal services—police, sanitation, housing, transportation—enjoy enormous scope for caprice, the city bosses continually employ bureaucratized government to divide and rule the inhabitants. The municipal bureaucracies destroy mutual trust, for example, by capriciously dispensing favor and disfavor, first to one group and then to another. In one city neighborhood the streets will be kept reasonably clean, in another the sanitation bureaucracy literally strews garbage in the act of collecting it; in one neighborhood the schools will be expensively refurbished, in another they will be left to rot for decades; in one neighborhood illegally parked cars will be towed away promptly, in another abandoned cars will be left on the streets for months, disfiguring the neighborhood and demoralizing the inhabitants; one neighborhood with a playground will get a second playground; a neighborhood with none will get none. Envied and resented when they receive a capricious favor, envious and resentful when they in turn are disfavored, the subjects of bureaucratic rule are perpetually set at loggerheads. Should the municipal bureaucracies treat their clients as ethnic categories—Poles, Italians, Jews and so on—then ethnic resentments, too, will be injected into the system of mistrust, a system in which the residents of a single urban assembly district may be divided into a half-dozen warring camps, virtually incapable of talking to each other.

When it has suited the city bosses to do so, they have used bureaucracy to help them cleave a city along strict racial lines, reducing the entire citizenry to those two hapless entities, "blacks" and "whites." They will use bureaucracy to "prove" that when a few black families move into a previously white neighborhood, deterioration will automatically set in. The sanitation bureaucracy will begin to collect the neighborhood's garbage ineptly. The big banks—an arm of the political power—will cease to give mortgages and home repair loans. Housing inspectors will stop enforcing the maintenance codes governing apartment dwellings. The police will stop enforcing elementary civic ordinances (in an integrated neighborhood in New York City, a precinct captain was asked why his men never enforced the ancient rule requiring property owners to sweep their sidewalks. He replied, "Oh, we stopped enforcing that law nine years ago"). Systematically abused, the neighborhood *will* deteriorate, both physically and morally. Since bureaucratic means hide the political determination to deteriorate it, the appearance of causality is created. Black people will seem to cause neighborhoods to deteriorate, and white residents, judging by that appearance, will grow angry, resentful and frightened. This is what the oligarchs want (or they would not act as they do), but the response itself is understandable enough. Like the political scientists who think social forces are causing small farmers to disappear, the white residents, too, are the victims of bureaucratic appearance—the appearance of a fictive causality.

Ultimately, bureaucracy destroys public life itself, for the more men feel themselves gripped by impersonal forces and inevitable processes, the more difficult it becomes for them to act politically or even to think politically, so little does politics appear to matter, so difficult does it become to fix public responsibility for anything. In the giant cities, especially, the bureaucratization of government has reduced the public realm to a rump. City dwellers will wade through littered streets, ride squalid public transport untouched by a half-century's technological advance, see immense housing projects rupture the tenuous social fabric of their neighborhoods, see precious open space perpetually devoured, watch neighborhoods decay in the midst of affluence, see their public schools grow more crowded while the city population remains the same. Yet they find it nearly impossible to understand why all this should be so. Sustained by literally thousands of bureaucratic rulings, the squalor of urban life appears to just happen and to be the responsibility of no man. What there is of visible politics in the city appears to be a sort of wildly whirring gear, making all sorts of grinding noises, yet disengaged from every result. By means of bureaucratic rule, politics and the conditions of life have, to all appearances, lost their connection, and this is the ultimate political purpose of bureaucratic rule: to expropriate politics from the citizenry and alienate them from political reality.

Subject to pseudo-processes and fictive forces, free men, according to their temperament and condition, will bow their heads before the seemingly inevitable or lash out in spasmodic violence against a faceless "system," behind which stand the party oligarchs unscathed and little regarded. The cloak which bureaucracy provides for the party oligarchs is the cloak of invisibility, and they need this more than many might imagine, for their usurped power is only secure as long as it remains unregarded.

Bureaucracy and Ideology: A Postscript

I have pointed out more than once in this chapter how political ideology takes the appearances created by bureaucracy—the appearance of inevitable trends, of historical processes, of the irrelevance of political deeds—for reality itself. The truth of the matter is more general. Ideological thinking is always the intellectual complement of bureaucratic rule because what bureaucracy does in the realm of political action, ideology does in the realm of political thought. It is the essential function of bureaucratic rule to sever deeds from the results of those deeds; political ideology performs the same function. Every political ideology takes as its primary data not the deeds of men but the results of those deeds—"increasing social complexity," the "development of industrial capitalism," the "growth of bureaucracy" and so forth. Ideology then assumes as its primary axiom that these general results must be explained as the effect of some general causes. The ideology of economic power, for example, does not prove that the state is the "steering committee" of the dominant economic class; it assumes this in advance as its basic axiom and then tries to account for what happens in the light of that axiom. The kind of cause deemed to be primary, whether technological, social, economic, racial or some other, is what principally distinguishes one political ideology from another. What is common to them all is that in every case the deeds of men are assumed in advance to be irrelevant or at most a "disturbing" factor.

An axiom, however, must be self-evident; it cannot itself be explained. If it could, it would not be an axiom but a conclusion. It would be subject to the test of actuality, whereas an axiom is that to which actuality itself is subjected. The effort to explain an ideological axiom, however, arises whenever the attempt is made to show how that axiomatic cause actually affects real men engaged in real political actions. In such a case, the ideologue is no longer assuming the self-evident validity of his axiom. He is attempting to demonstrate the *source* of its causal power, as the book reviewer, previously mentioned, explained how a moneyed interest ruled over a President by noting that it hired an expensive lobbyist to speak to him, the ability to hire expensive lobbyists constituting one reason money brings political power. The reviewer's particular explanation was worthlessly circular but not uniquely so. It is not hard to show in any particular instance that a purported explanation of an ideological axiom constitutes circular reasoning; the explanation of the axiom resting on a reassertion of the axiom.

A telling example of this can be found in Baran and Sweezy's treatise, *Monopoly Capital.* The two Marxist economists take it for granted that the monopoly capitalists control the government and politics of the United States. The truth of this, they say, is too obvious to warrant explanation. They provide one, nonetheless: democratic politics costs money, the capitalists have most of the money, therefore they control democratic politics. The explanation of their central axiom takes up one short paragraph. Elsewhere, however, the two authors rightly note that the trade unions are virtually powerless. Yet the trade unions, too, provide enormous sums of money to politicians and the authors fail to detect the contradiction. If supplying money to politicians gives the monopoly capitalists control of the government, why doesn't it do the same for the trade unions? How can money be the foundation of political power in the one case and result in impotence in the other? The answer is it cannot. The statement that money does and does not bring political power is a self-contradiction and in consequence the authors' explanation of why monopoly capitalists have power is empty. On the actual impotence of trade unions all assertions about the inevitable power of money must founder. The only way out of the contradiction in the end is to say that money brings power to the monopolists because they are the dominant economic interest and does not bring power to the trade unions because trade unions are not, which is simply repeating the axiom that the dominant economic interest controls democratic politics because it always controls politics. The authors' explanation of their axiom either leads to a self-contradiction or runs around in a circle. The axiom of a political ideology cannot itself be explained.

Since the effort to explain the axiom arises whenever an ideologue tries to explain how his primary cause operates on real men, he can never actually explain how it operates on real men. The effort must fail. A political ideology, by its nature, cannot explain why political men have acted as they did. To keep from falling into absurdity, a political ideology must eliminate the consideration of deeds in offering its explanations. It cannot explain why Woodrow Wilson dragged America into World War I because that would mean explaining how its axiomatic cause operated on Woodrow Wilson. What it can attempt to explain is America's increasingly aggressive foreign policy as a general political phenomenon. Similarly it cannot explain the party oligarchs' actual efforts to create a monopoly economy because it leads to chronological absurdities, such as ascribing economic power to the recipients of corrupt privilege before privilege made them rich and consequential. What an ideology can attempt to explain is "the growth of monopoly" as a general trend or result. In a word, before a political ideology can interpret political reality in the light of its axiom, it must first recast reality into the form of general results divorced from specific deeds. This is the reason political ideology takes bureaucratic appearance for reality: it is precisely the political effect of bureaucracy to divorce results from deeds and so make them appear the product of historical processes. Since it is also the political purpose of the party oligarchs to create this very appearance, the political function of any political ideology is to provide a cover for the powers-that-be, to rationalize the political appearances they wish to create. Whether a political ideology purports to be "radical" makes no difference. It is the inherent nature of every political ideology to serve as the buttress, the rationale and the apologia for the actual wielders of self-serving power. This is why ideological thinking was foisted by the oligarchs on American education. This is the reason, too, why genuine Communist revolutionaries—Lenin, Rosa Luxemburg, Castro and others—have so often split with orthodox Marxists while they were actually trying to gain power and why they restored orthodox Marxism once they succeeded in gaining it.

"Radical" ideologues will understandably consider this a savage impugning of their motives, but I am not talking about their motives or their actual political deeds, I am speaking of ideology and its inherent role as the apologia for oligarchic power. It was not a Marxist revolutionary but the racist warmonger Woodrow Wilson who said, "The masters of the Government of the United States are the combined capitalists and manufacturers of the country." That did not stop the Democratic machine from nominating him for the Presidency. In fact it was a mark in his favor.

12.
The State of War

America's active dominion over other nations was achieved with remarkable swiftness. Latin America excepted, it was accomplished in a dozen years after the Second World War. Today, the United States has entangling alliances with more than half the nations of the world; it supports at any given moment at least a dozen different client regimes. American military bases girdle the globe and American spies and intelligence agents circulate everywhere. The American military establishment deploys a uniformed force of some three million troops and now costs the citizenry more than $80 billion a year. Whether that dominion is called an "empire" or a "Free World coalition," the most important question is how it came about at all. How could a republic which made the principle of no entangling alliances the foundation of its foreign policy become entangled in a complication of alliances unparalleled in modern history? How could a republic whose citizens only a generation ago looked on peacetime military expenditure with the deepest repugnance become saddled with the most profligate of military establishments? How could a republic whose citizens were determined as late as 1947 to disband their military forces manage to fight two distant wars in the next eighteen years?

To such questions the official answer, of course, is world Communism. According to the party oligarchs and their spokesmen, the entangling alliances, the military establishment and the active global politics of the United States were forced upon this Republic by a worldwide threat to the nation's security, the threat posed by a Communist movement to dominate the world, a threat which the United States had to resist wherever Communism, octopus-fashion, reared the tip of a tentacle. This, the oligarchs' version of the Cold War, did not evolve slowly under the pressure of the Cold War. It was unfurled full-blown to the citizenry by President Harry Truman on March 12, 1947. Applying to Congress for American aid to Greece and Turkey, Truman based his appeal not on America's marginal interests in these countries but on a capacious new definition of American overseas interests, one which claimed that "totalitarian regimes imposed on free peoples, by direct or indirect aggression, undermine the foundations of international peace and hence, the security of the United States." We were not defending Greece from a Communist takeover, we were defending the United States from a Communist takeover in Greece. This was the so-called Truman Doctrine and it has formed with little change the foundations of America's Cold War policies for a quarter of a century.

The Truman Doctrine and the policies that derived from it were based on a fundamental premise without which they would have no plausible foundation, namely that every Communist success anywhere was part of a single worldwide drive to take over the world, a conspiracy led (before Russia's split with China) by the masters of the Kremlin. In March 1947, the essential evidence for the Soviet Union's grand design for world domination was Stalin's subjugation of Poland and other states on her European border. Although Russia had been creating buffer states on her border before Karl Marx was born, that policy, the proof of the grand design, allegedly stemmed from no other source than Communist ideology.

In recent years a number of "revisionist" historians, Gabriel Kolko and William Appleman Williams among them, minutely scrutinizing the actual events preceding the promulgation of the Truman Doctrine, have exposed the soft core of mendacity at its heart. They have shown, beyond any serious doubt, that well before the Soviet subjugation of Poland, the United States Government under Truman had pursued a hostile and provocative policy toward the Soviet Union, a policy made immeasurably more menacing by the American monopoly of the atomic bomb. As part of that provocative policy, Truman reneged on various agreements reached at the Yalta Conference and announced our government's determination to keep Poland outside the Soviet sphere of influence. That Stalin would interpret this as a hostile act was certainly obvious to Truman and his advisers. From Stalin's point of view, what other interest could the United States have in Poland except an interest in weakening Soviet security at a traditionally sensitive spot? Stalin's response was swift and brutal. He marched in and crushed what little autonomy East European states still enjoyed, thereby securing on his own what the Yalta participants had previously recognized as his.

The significance of this is clear. America's rulers had deliberately menaced the Soviet Union at a vital point in defiance of previous understandings. In doing so they had been instrumental in provoking a brutal response by Stalin. Then these same rulers deceitfully declared that Stalin's reaction was not only a baseless act of aggression but something more grandiose yet—conclusive evidence of Stalin's grand design for world domination. If the revisionists are even partially correct in their analysis, the whole logical foundation for the American Government's Cold War expansion was largely concocted by the party oligarchs.

Even if the revisionists have grossly exaggerated the extent to which Truman's actions provoked Stalin's subsequent actions, the fact remains that Truman was determined to put the most menacing possible construction on Soviet aggression in Eastern Europe. If, as some "moderate" revisionists now say, early postwar relations between the United States and Russia were marked more by mutual fear and blundering than by any deliberate American provocation, neither Truman nor his successors ever admitted it. They did not say in 1947 or thereafter that Soviet aggression was *in any way* a fearful response to an inadvertent provocation. They did not say that Russia had a hundred times more reason in 1946 to be frightened of Truman's intentions than he had to be frightened of Stalin's. They did not say that Russia had long-standing interests in buffering her border with satellite states or that the United States had already recognized those interests. They absolutely denied that Soviet aggression bore any relation to traditional Russian objectives. They denied that the Soviet Union was a nation at all and insisted that it was a center of ideological force and of limitless ideological ambition and hence the reason and justification for launching the most active, most aggressive foreign policy in the history of the American Republic. As Senator William Fulbright pointed out in an essay published in *The New Yorker* in January 1972, the truly significant aspect of Truman's policies was "the eagerness with which we [i.e., he] seized upon Soviet provocations and plunged into the Cold War. If it be granted that Stalin started the Cold War, it must also be recognized that the Truman administration seemed to welcome it." In other words, even if the oligarchs' version of the Cold War were absolutely true—which it certainly is not—their eagerness to prosecute an aggressive foreign policy, to entangle the Republic in global alliances, to intervene in the affairs of distant nations, to maintain huge standing armies and to overawe the citizenry with endless alarms and crises remains a crucial element in the Cold War.

Once the oligarchs "plunged into the Cold War" in 1947 their "eagerness" never abated. Every action by the Soviet Union or indeed any speech by a Communist ruler which the oligarchs could seize on as evidence of the will to world domination they refused to interpret any other way. Whenever events cast doubt on that interpretation, they refused, nonetheless, to alter it. Instead they perpetually refurbished the menace of world Communism and brandished it anew before the citizenry. With military bases poised near Russia's borders, the party oligarchs insisted that every Russian action was baseless aggression and every American action the posture of defense. Since no other view was permitted, public men who challenged the oligarchs' view were either silenced or driven from public life. Every chance the party oligarchs had to justify an aggressive foreign policy they took; every opportunity to do otherwise they ignored. Truman's "eagerness" for the Cold War was shared by American leaders for a quarter of a century and the question is why.

Senator Fulbright himself finds this eagerness "puzzling," but there is nothing puzzling about it once we scrape away the cover of apologetics and ideology that invariably obscure plain political questions.

To begin with, the one thing the Cold War certainly was not was a "response" of democratic leaders to aggressive anti-Communist sentiment among the citizenry—the "popularity" theory of apologetics. As Truman himself admitted, *rousing* Americans to the menace of world Communism was his major domestic problem. Truman tried to do this, in part, by persuading the citizenry that world Communism was already an internal menace to the Republic. Ten days after promulgating his new Cold War doctrine, Truman instituted "loyalty" investigations for government employees, an act designed to impress upon Americans that the Communist enemy, seemingly so far from our gates, was already inside them in numbers so plentiful that no American could be trusted by his own government. The effort to win popularity was not a cause of the oligarchs' Cold War policies; sustaining popular support for those policies has been a perennial problem for the party oligarchs.

It has been said, too, that Truman, Dean Acheson and their successors "welcomed" the Cold War because of their sincere hatred of Communist despotism. That argument—the "sincerity" theory—will not wash either. The most scrupulous "friend to republican government" detests tyranny at least as sincerely as Harry Truman of the Pendergast machine ever did, yet no republican would go very far down the road to global dominion, to giant standing armies, to perpetual foreign crises and alarms, to the virtual strangling of free politics at home which Truman and his successors took at a gallop. Let one such friend to republican government speak for himself:

"Wherever the standard of freedom and independence has been unfurled, there will [America's] heart, her benedictions, and her prayers be. But she goes not abroad in search of monsters to destroy. She is the well-wisher to the freedom and independence of all. She is the champion and vindicator only of her own. . . . She well knows that, by once enlisting under other banners than her own, were they even the banners of foreign independence, she would involve herself, beyond the power of extrication, in all the wars of interest and intrigue, of individual avarice, envy and ambition, which assume the color and usurp the standard of freedom. The fundamental maxims of her policy would insensibly change from liberty to force. The frontlets upon her brows would no longer beam with the ineffable splendor of freedom and independence; but in its stead would soon be substituted an imperial diadem, flashing in false and tarnished luster the murky radiance of dominion and power. She might become the dictatress of the world; she would no longer be the ruler of her own spirit."

That was John Quincy Adams speaking on the Fourth of July, 1821. Does anyone suppose that Adams was a less sincere enemy of despotism than a machine politician like Truman and a jumped-up jack-in-office like Acheson?

It has been suggested of late that the oligarchs' Cold War was all a terrible, if honorable, mistake. In this version of the blunder theory American leaders from Truman onward have been the victims of an "obsession," which blinded them to political reality, enthralled them to their Cold War assumptions and persuaded Lyndon Johnson, for example, that a Viet Cong victory over a dictator in Saigon would bring Red China to the shores of California. Implied by the obsession theory is that America's leaders persisted in a bad policy for no rational political reason, for we call persistent behavior obsessive precisely when it serves no rational interest of the actor. How do the obsession theorists know that America's leaders were irrational in this sense? The answer is they do not know. There is no evidence that American leaders were obsessed except the fact that they persisted in a bad policy. The whole obsession theory rests on nothing more than that hoary premise of American apologetics, namely that America's elected leaders are always good men trying their best to serve the American people. Since they persisted in a bad policy they could not have done so for rational political reasons since that would make them bad men. Hence they must be the victims of a mental aberration or obsession, a spell, as the king's courtiers would have said. That the premise is a begged question is putting it mildly.

The current school of revisionists have their own conventional explanation of the Cold War, based on the ideology of economic power. As summarized by Ronald Steel in a useful essay in the *New York Review of Books,* September 1971, the revisionists as a group see U.S. diplomacy in general "as the necessary instrument of the capitalist order" and the Cold War itself as "the attempt by the United States to achieve a world order congenial to capitalist penetration." In the revisionist view the spread of Communism to new areas of the world closes down the capitalists' sources of cheap raw materials and shuts off outlets for profitable overseas investment and trade. That expansion, therefore, poses a threat to the interests of American capitalists. Since, in the revisionist view, American politics is "determined by the larger economic forces that motivate society," the oligarchs' Cold War policies represent their effort to protect the interests of their economic masters, the party oligarchs never having interests of their own.

The most interesting thing about the revisionist explanation of the Cold War is that it is virtually identical with the oligarchs' *justification* for it. Both the oligarchs and the revisionists agree that Communism is a worldwide, dynamic, expansive ideological force; both agree that it poses a direct threat to the United States. In the jargon of the oligarchs, it threatens the "American way of life"; in the jargon of the revisionists, it threatens the "social structure of advanced capitalism." Since the two phrases point to the same reality, the revisionist explanation of the Cold War is, in essence, the Truman Doctrine stated in an accusatory manner by those who think Communism ought not to be "contained."

This near-identity between oligarchic justification and ideological explanation shows up even in the details of the revisionists' economic analysis. According to several revisionists, America's leaders revealed their true economic motives as early as 1944, when Dean Acheson told a Congressional committee that America must pursue a forward postwar foreign policy in order to secure "raw materials." Why, it might be asked, do the revisionists think Acheson was explaining American foreign policy rather than attempting to justify it? Why do they believe that a Congressional hearing, that well-worn pulpit for official lying, had become, one fine day, a confessional box? The reason is purely ideological and has nothing to do with either political reality or plain common sense. Economic ideology being what it is, the ideologues invariably take an economic justification for a true explanation. According to the economic ideologues, America's rulers never tell the truth to the people except when they offer—as they often do—an economic justification for a policy and then, by a sort of political miracle, they never lie.

Even on its face, the economic explanation of the Cold War has little plausibility. If the "capitalist world order" allegedly requires the containment of Communism, then why did that same "order" require Roosevelt to wage war against Communism's deadliest enemy, Nazi Germany? (Hitler, another ideologue, asked the same question and came up with the wrong answer.) If the "spread" of Communism blocks "capitalist penetration," then why is the chief barrier to U.S. trade with Communist China the American oligarchs' ban against it? More to the point, why have the party oligarchs fought two land wars in Asia, a continent that could have fallen to the Communists in 1946 with no particular harm to American corporate interests? Why this radical disproportion between American aggression in Asia and American economic interests in Asia, a disproportion which, as will be seen, has been characteristic of American foreign policy, not since 1947 but since 1898? If economic motives truly shaped American foreign policy, such a gross and long-standing disproportion between economic interests and political actions can scarcely be explained.

In their economic analysis of the Cold War, the revisionists have simply taken over the more general Marxian explanation of imperialism first propounded by Rosa Luxemburg in 1913 and expanded three years later by Lenin. According to the former, imperialism was "the political expression of the accumulation of capital in its competitive struggle for what remains open of the non-capitalist environment." The economic key to imperialism was taken to be the capitalists' growing need to find new outlets for "surplus capital" no longer available at home. The needs of the capitalists dictating the actions of the state, the capitalist nations seized control of backward regions in order to secure commercial outlets and high profits for the wielders of surplus capital.

Two separate sets of facts have always beset the Marxian explanation of imperialism. The first is the obvious one that imperialism predates capitalism, which implies, at the very least, that if rulers had a noncapitalist motive for imperialism before capitalism emerged, they just might have a noncapitalist motive for imperialism after capitalism emerged. To an economic ideologue this is impossible. The political rulers of a country with a capitalist economy must have a capitalist motive because the state is the capitalists' steering committee. This, however, is simply repeating the ideological axiom and arguing in a circle.

The second stumbling block to the Marxian explanation is that, by strict economic reckoning, political imperialism is far from profitable. When Joseph Chamberlain tried to revive British ardor for imperialism after the Boer War, the heart of his scheme was a crusade to get British capitalists to invest in the empire, and so demonstrate the profitability of imperialism. The crusade collapsed. Then as now the great majority of capitalists prefer to invest not in their nation's colonies but in other capitalist countries. What then is the economic motive for colonies in the first place? Some investors, of course, make money but, as George Lichtheim, a leading authority on socialist thought, has pointed out, the costs of financing imperialism are levied on the great majority of capitalists to secure profits for a small minority of them. This is an odd way for the dominant economic interest to arrange things, although it is just what one would expect if the political rulers practiced imperialism for political reasons of their own. In an interesting essay in *Commentary*, Lichtheim, although himself a Marxist, actually refutes all existing economic explanations of imperialism, demonstrating that if the economic interests of the capitalists actually dictated foreign policy, these interests have not been well served and could have been better served without an imperial policy. Yet if these interests are not well served by imperialism, why believe that imperialism is the "political expression" of those interests? Why take as proof that *A* serves *B* the fact that *A* serves *B* poorly? Why believe in the economic motive of a given political policy when a different one would better satisfy that motive?*

This is the question-begging explanation of imperialism in general which the revisionists have applied somewhat dubiously to the Cold War. They ask us to believe that the American capitalist order waged two wars against Communism in Asia for the same economic reasons that prompted it to wage an even greater war on the side of Communism in Europe. What is worse, politically speaking, the revisionist explanation asks us to believe that America's self-serving party oligarchs were genuine tribunes of the Republic, for to say that they have defended America from Communism is only a failing in the eyes of a Communist.

What is truly interesting about American foreign policy is that where the economic ideologues profess to see preponderating economic interest, traditional diplomatic historians, to their chagrin, can find no preponderating interest at all. Other nations have conducted their diplomacy with relatively clear regard for their economic interests, their national security or other practical and material advantages. America has not. From the time of William McKinley to the present, the characteristic feature of American foreign policy—especially in its active phases—is the absence of any rational reason of state. During that span of time America has waged five wars and in none of them did we fight for a clear-cut national interest of the kind diplomatic historians recognize in the affairs of nation-states.

William McKinley waged a war against Spain for no national interest except America's alleged "friendship" toward the Cuban rebels and

---

*Lichtheim, perhaps, supplies a reason for belief. After refuting all existing economic explanations of imperialism, he concludes by saying that some economic explanation of imperialism must be found that will exclude "incalculable political and personal factors." To Lichtheim, apparently, the only possible explanation of a political phenomenon is an economic explanation. In his implicit view, the results of men's deeds must be explained in economic terms because to understand something is, by definition, to explain it in economic terms. The axiom of economic ideology is neither a description nor an explanation of political reality but a prescription for how to think about it.

our "traditional" anticolonialism. The only economic interest involved, namely Wall Street investors in Cuba, opposed the prospective war, since they preferred doing business with Cuba's Spanish overlords rather than with the insurgents. When McKinley started the war, however, the great "powers" of Wall Street promptly shut up and went along.

In the period of straight-out American imperialism after the Spanish-American War—imperialism begun as anti-imperialism—the whole fabric of justification was woven out of whole cloth in the manner of the Vietnam "domino theory." The oligarchs crushed the independence of a few Central American republics and turned the Caribbean Sea into an "American Lake" in order, said the party oligarchs, to protect the Panama Canal, which had to be built and controlled by the United States, according to the oligarchs, to secure passage of U.S. warships into the Pacific, which was necessitated, according to the oligarchs, by America's new need for a "two-ocean navy," which was itself necessitated, according to the oligarchs, by America's interest in China. Since our interest in China had been created out of nothing by means of an open door policy which announced America's gratuitous intention to preserve the "integrity" of Imperial China, the whole imperial enterprise rested, as far as American interests were concerned, on exactly nothing at all.

Before Wilson dragged America into the First World War, American interest in the outcome of a stalemated European conflict was virtually nil. Such being the case, Wilson had to fabricate one. The defeat of Germany, according to Wilson, would make the world "safe for democracy," and the proof of Germany's threat to democracy was that it had violated America's neutral shipping rights. These rights, however, Wilson had already sold to the British, virtually forcing Germany into a policy of unlimited submarine warfare and providing Wilson with the very pretext he wanted for going to war. Wilson's chief adviser, Colonel E. M. House, actually suggested this warmongering policy to him in January 1916 while Wilson was still trying to drum up a cause of war over the sinking of the British ship *Lusitania* in May 1915. In a cable from London, House notes that

Wilson's policy of secretly siding with the British would eventually force Germany into "transcendent sea warfare. We will then be compelled to sever relations and our position will be far better than if we do so over a nine-month-old issue and largely upon the wording of a suitable apology." Since even the violation of neutral shipping rights could not well justify a massive American war commitment, Wilson, having fabricated his pretext for war, announced that America was fighting for eternal peace and universal democracy and called for total war mobilization, a mass conscript army and the first overseas expeditionary force in our history. What these extraordinary endeavors had to do with American interests was exactly nothing. Wilson's determination to enter the European war, and enter it en masse, predated every pretext for doing so.

United States entry into the Second World War was not forced upon us by any compelling national interest either. Like Wilson before him, Roosevelt had to fabricate a *casus belli* in order to persuade Americans to fight, so little was he able to persuade the citizenry that war in the Eastern Hemisphere menaced our interests. Roosevelt's policy toward Japan was a systematic effort to back Japan against the wall and provoke her into some act of aggression against the United States that would justify a declaration of war. That effort included economic pressure upon Japan resulting in almost complete economic strangulation, diplomatic pressure which consisted chiefly of humiliating ultimatums and, in the view of some, the harboring of the entire Pacific Fleet in Hawaii, where it was militarily useless but provided a tempting target for the Japanese, a target made even more tempting by Roosevelt's never-explained failure to warn the fleet commander that a Japanese attack was imminent. Roosevelt's policy toward Germany was essentially the same. According to the official British War Cabinet minutes of the meeting between Churchill and Roosevelt in August 1941, "the President had said he would wage war but not declare it and that he would become more and more provocative. If the Germans did not like it they could attack American forces. . . . Everything was to be done to force an incident." Forcing an incident, needless to say, is not the policy of a nation directly menaced by foreign aggression, yet forcing an incident to create a cause of war was also McKinley's stratagem in 1898 when he sent the U.S.S. *Maine* to Havana; it was Wilson's strategy from mid-1915 onward; it was Johnson's policy in 1964.

The Korean War, too, required an elaborate theory of the national interest to justify America's role in it. Some months before North Korea invaded South Korea, Secretary of State Dean Acheson had publicly announced that Korea lay outside the American "defense perimeter." When the invasion took place, Truman could not readily claim that South Korea was vital to America's national security, since his Secretary of State had just said it was not. Instead he had to propound the view that the system of "collective security" was endangered by North Korean aggression. This is why he sent American forces to South Korea under cover of a United Nations "police action." Ostensibly America was not fighting for its own immediate national interests—we never are—but in the interests of a general principle and its institutional embodiment, the United Nations.

As soon as American troops drove the North Korean army out of South Korea—it took only a few months—Truman showed his eagerness for aggressive action by immediately expanding his war goals. Begun, in Acheson's words, "solely for the purpose of restoring the Republic of Korea to its status prior to the invasion from the north," the Korean War was now carried north of the 38th parallel in order to "reunite" Korea, that is to destroy the North Korean regime, a fundamental shift in policy from a defensive war in defense of no American interest to an offensive war for no American interest. (Personally for Truman the war proved a blunder when General Douglas MacArthur drew the Chinese into the battle and produced a long-drawn-out stalemate with which the American people became progressively disgusted. Truman's celebrated dismissal of MacArthur stemmed precisely from MacArthur's messing things up for him.)

There is not a single modern American war that the oligarchs could not have readily avoided had they chose. Indeed, three of America's modern wartime leaders, Wilson, Roosevelt and Johnson, were actually elected on a promise to keep the peace, a promise they each began breaking immediately upon reelection. There is not a single modern American war which was forced upon the United States by compelling interest of any kind, yet every one of America's wars since 1898 the party oligarchs gave unmistakable signs of welcoming: by fabricating incidents, by carrying out secret provocations, by concocting far-fetched theories—"dominoes" in one war, "neutral rights" in another, "collective security" in a third—to demonstrate an American interest not otherwise apparent and to hold up to the American people a foreign menace not otherwise menacing. Whenever America's party oligarchs have had the opportunity to prosecute safely a bellicose foreign policy, they have welcomed the opportunity and did so long before 1947 and before a single Communist regime existed.

The epitome of this gratuitous aggressiveness is surely the oligarchs' China policy in the years between 1898 and 1912, a policy particularly revealing because the oligarchs were forced to justify it in terms which, a few years later, became the official Marxist-Leninist explanation of such policies.

America's interest in Chinese affairs was created *ex nihilo* in 1898 when the oligarchs, for no reason of national interest, performed their first act of straight-out American imperialism, the seizure and annexation of the Philippine Islands. As Samuel Flagg Bemis noted in *A Diplomatic History of the United States,* "the acquisition of the Philippines . . . was the greatest blunder [*sic*] of American diplomacy; it led rapidly to involvement in the politics of Asia and through them of Europe." Immediately committing, in Bemis' words, a "second great blunder," the McKinley Administration proceeded to entangle the Republic still further in the affairs of China and Europe by enunciating the policy of the open door, wherein the U.S. Government committed itself to defending the "integrity" of China. At the time of its promulgation, America's economic interest in China was less than negligible. As late as 1914 American trade with China comprised 0.6 percent of our total foreign trade, which itself is a minor item in the American economy. Our capital investment in China in 1902 was a lordly $15 million. Despite this minuscule economic stake, the Roosevelt Administration by 1902 had drastically expanded its definition of "openness," in Bemis' words, "so as to include the territorial and administrative integrity and the independence of China." The American policy of the open door had "now rapidly floriated into the preservation of all China in full sovereignty against foreign encroachments" from Japan, Russia, Germany, France and England. By virtue of this wholly gratuitous expansion, "the Government of the United States was drawn further and further into the diplomatic entanglements of the Far East." Since Far Eastern entanglements meant entanglements in the affairs of the European powers, the oligarchs had succeeded in entering, by the Chinese back door, the hitherto forbidden domain of European politics. This was one of the chief reasons for the open door policy, yet not a single national interest was being served. As Bemis put it: "If the expansionists . . . had even taken the pains to study a few statistics of trade and investment demonstrative of the small stake which the United States had in the Far East compared with other parts of the world, or the problems of strategy involved, we are constrained to believe they would not have embarked so precipitously upon the conspicuous but unprofitable and foolhardy venture into the world politics of Asia, so alien to American continental traditions and interests, so dangerous to the welfare of the United States."

Passing over Professor Bemis' mental constraints, the fact was the oligarchs' effort to inaugurate an aggressive foreign policy in and through Asia was severely handicapped by America's lack of an economic stake in such a policy. By the time William Howard Taft took office in 1909, the oligarchs' first effort at an imperial foreign policy was dying of inanition. To pump new life into imperialism, Taft decided to create an American economic stake abroad. Officially termed "Dollar Diplomacy," the new policy was described by Taft in 1910 as "active intervention to secure for our merchandise and our capitalists opportunity for profitable investment." Once having created such an economic stake, the U.S. Government could then forcibly intervene to "secure the loans" or "protect the property" of American capitalists abroad. This, as Taft himself said, was a necessary concomitant of Dollar Diplomacy and in fact the point of the exercise.

The problem, however, was that China and Central America were the only feasible objects of an American imperial policy (the oligarchs could not readily intervene in Europe), and American capitalists had little interest in either. Since America's "surplus capital" would not flow into China, the Taft Administration had to pump it into China. After securing an American loan to the Chinese government, Taft then turned around and pressed a reluctant J. P. Morgan, the Republican party's banker, to underwrite it, thus creating by political action an American economic interest in a country which the oligarchs wished to plunge into anyway. In short, three years before Rosa Luxemburg defined imperialism as the "political expression" of advanced capitalism, Taft was demonstrating that the very reverse was true, that the export of American capital to China was the economic expression of, and the hoped-for economic justification for, the imperial policies of the party oligarchs. "Capitalist penetration" of China was no more than the reluctant tool of the oligarchs' aggressive foreign policy. When Wilson publicly denounced Dollar Diplomacy in 1913 (Wilson grasped that making economic interests the sole pretext for imperialism would hinder, not promote, an aggressive American foreign policy), J. P. Morgan immediately withdrew his capital from China. So much for "surplus capital" leading the "state" into imperial ventures. So much, too, for the "economic motives" shaping American foreign policy. Seven decades after Wall Street investors vainly opposed the Spanish-American War, a half-century after J. P. Morgan sent his money in and out of China at the oligarchs' bidding, Lyndon Johnson called in the corporation managers and told them bluntly to support his Vietnam intervention in the teeth of imminent inflation, of risks to their profit margins, of dangers to their overseas competitive position and of economic instability in general. Does anyone suppose that the Vietnam War or any other aspect of American foreign policy was dictated by the "economic forces motivating society"? Anyone who can believe that can believe anything.

In prosecuting an aggressive foreign policy, the party oligarchs have been driven by no cause or interest external to themselves: by no fundamental economic interest, by no genuine threat to the security of the Republic, by no irresistible popular demand. Except in the post–World War I period, when the American people, out of universal disgust with Wilson's war, were determined to renew the republican policy of no entangling alliances and the world at large gave the party oligarchs no opportunity to overcome that determination,* American foreign policy has been gratuitously aggressive since 1898, a policy carried out for no compelling reason except the oligarchs' wish to prosecute an aggressive foreign policy. Their reason for wanting such a policy, however, is scarcely mysterious and certainly not irrational. An aggressive foreign policy safeguards the power of the power wielders and strengthens their control over those whom they rule. This is a political commonplace applied by historic rulers a thousand different times, and Americans understood it clearly enough when they opposed entangling alliances.

The political advantages of an aggressive foreign policy are both obvious and manifold. It distracts the citizenry from domestic interests and concerns. It makes national strength, national unity, national security and national resolve the paramount standards by which all else is judged. Under an aggressive foreign policy the common good ceases to be the good of the individual citizens and becomes instead the good of the nation. Under an aggressive foreign policy a republic of self-governing citizens becomes a corporate entity, a mere nation-state, one whose highest purpose is preserving the status quo. An aggressive foreign policy enables the oligarchs to stifle reform on the grounds that reform would be "divisive," or would cost the "confidence of business," or would be a "luxury" in a time of peril and sacrifice. It enables the party oligarchs to silence independent voices and crush political insurgents on the grounds that they weaken national unity and give comfort to the nation's enemies. In the crises and

---

*A fairly rare element of partisanship was also involved. After World War I, the bosses of the splintered Republican party realized that only an "isolationist" policy could bring Western, antiwar Republicans safely back into party ranks. Needing a safe common ground, the Republican bosses found it in popular dislike for Wilson and his war, and gave vent to it retroactively by defeating Wilson's League of Nations proposal.

alarms of an aggressive foreign policy, collusion between the two parties scarcely requires a mask; it can parade itself as virtuous bipartisanship in the service of national survival. Under cover of an aggressive foreign policy the party oligarchs can serve their interests with an ease impossible in a peaceful republic. In the name of national defense they can dispense grotesque windfall privileges such as the oil import quotas and the "national defense" highway fund. In the name of national security they can shroud government in the mantle of secrecy and infringe on the liberty of the citizens. Under an aggressive foreign policy the republican standard itself is gradually inverted. The government, to borrow Madison's phrase, becomes the Censor of the people rather than the people being the Censor of their government. It is the citizenry who must now prove their "loyalty," while the government taps their telephones, monitors their private mail and organizes "patriots" to root out neighborhood traitors. Submission replaces independence; fear replaces hope; the citizenry acquires the habit of obedience and loses the habit of self-rule; the turbulent sea of liberty becomes frozen in the false peace of national unity. If there are risks inherent in an aggressive foreign policy—and there are—they are greatly outweighed by the political advantages it brings to those who wield usurped power.

There is nothing puzzling, therefore, about America's gratuitously aggressive foreign policy or about the oligarchs' successful efforts to drag the Republic into five wars. What an aggressive foreign policy accomplishes by slow degrees, a state of war accomplishes in a trice. Overnight it kills reform, overnight it transforms insurgents into traitors and the Republic into an imperiled realm. Overnight it strangles free politics, distracts and overawes the citizenry. Overnight it blasts public hope. The risks of war are very great—as Johnson learned to his sorrow—and the party oligarchs have not launched wars for lighthearted reasons. They have done so because war seemed to them the only way to protect their power in a moment of particular peril. The proof of this is obvious on inspection, for the immediate domestic background to every modern American war—the Korean War partly excepted—was a clear and present danger to party control of politics. Johnson's war was not unique.

The immediate background to the Spanish-American War was the great Populist revolt against the party oligarchy, defeated nationally in the 1896 elections but still a potent insurgent force in several Southern and Western states. As Samuel Bemis observes, America's leaders, after 1896, were eager for a war of some kind "to swallow up American civil dissension" and to "lance the boil" of Populism, as one warmongering Senator suggested to McKinley. Two-party collusion was operating as usual. William Jennings Bryan, whom the Democratic bosses had nominated to split the Populist party, made clear his approval of a war against Spain and of the imperialist policies that followed. When the annexation of the Philippines came up for a controversial vote in the Senate in 1899, the "Great Commoner" went to Washington to urge Democratic Senators to vote for it, and it passed by one vote. Only when imperialism was safely launched did the Democrats consent to oppose it.

The immediate background to the First World War was the rise of the Western Republican insurgents and the immensely widespread demand for radical republican reform, a demand which eventually had to be met and diverted by President Wilson, who had already praised imperialism as "an affair of strong government" and who considered the tight party oligarchies of Imperial Britain the highest form of politics. After funneling a few notably fake reforms through the Democratic machine in Congress—an antitrust act which the Republican insurgent George Norris rightly called "the greatest victory of a legislative nature that has been won by the trusts and combinations," a Federal Reserve Act which Senator La Follette rightly denounced as an act "legalizing the money power" it was supposed to destroy—Wilson announced in October 1914 that "my programme is practically complete." The era of reform was over—by Wilson's personal decree. A mere Presidential fiat, however, could not freeze political action in a self-governing Republic and Wilson searched around for some potent means to block further reform. Pouring patronage into the city machines helped, but could not suffice; a vicious effort to wage war in Mexico (in the name of Mexican "self-determination") helped but could not suffice. It was Wilson's extraordinary daring to see in the stalemated European war—a war which every American wished to stay clear of—an opportunity to strangle free politics and set oligarchic rule on secure foundations after almost twenty-five years of perilous insurgency. As Wilson himself said early in 1917 in one of the most extraordinary self-fulfilling prophecies ever made: "Once lead this people into war and they will forget there was ever such a thing as tolerance. [In December 1915, Wilson had set the standard for tolerance by publicly denouncing "hyphenated Americans" for "disloyalty."] . . . The spirit of ruthless brutality will enter into the very fiber of our national life, infecting Congress, the courts, the policeman on the beat. . . . The Constitution would not survive it; free speech and the right of assembly would go."

It would be tedious to describe Wilson's efforts, amounting to conspiracy, to drag America into war against Germany while professing to remain "neutral in fact as well as name." Acquiescing in every gross British violation of American neutrality, including Britain's illegal blockade of Germany, Wilson continually denounced every German countermeasure with the most farfetched and bellicose assertions of neutral right, such as the right of Americans to sail on foreign ships carrying munitions to Britain. Cherishing every American life lost at sea as a potential *casus belli*, he defeated every sensible measure to avoid loss of life. When a popular resolution forbidding American travelers to sail in the war zone was submitted to Congress in February 1916, Wilson and the Democratic machine defeated it. According to Wilson, if America made one such concession to Germany, "the whole fine fabric of international law must crumble." This, while Britain was seizing American cargoes and flying American flags on her supply ships. Once again collusion was operating perfectly. In the 1916 elections, the Republican hierarchy conveniently attacked Wilson, not for his secret warmongering, but for his excessive neutrality, which helped Wilson win reelection as the man "who kept us out of war." (The Republican bosses had no wish to win the Presidency in 1916; given the powerful insurgents in their ranks, it would have been impossible for them to go to war. Characteristically they let the Democrats do it.) Once in the European conflict, Wilson made sure that the "spirit of ruthless brutality" entered American life. His Administration enacted laws making it a crime to speak against the government or its policies; it organized a massive effort to crush, to silence and to jail dissenters as "hirelings of the Kaiser"; it created state "committees of public safety"; inspired vigilante organizations and unleashed a reign of political repression unparalleled in American history. The war to make the world safe for democracy Wilson launched for no other reason than to make oligarchy safe from democracy at home. Then he paraded himself as a visionary idealist until the American people exacted their just revenge.

The immediate background to America's entry into the Second World War was Roosevelt's determination to bury the New Deal and crush yet another popular movement for reform. Such a movement cannot be defeated by merely doing nothing. It requires, as Wilson understood, a countervailing movement of equivalent strength. For this reason, Roosevelt, a few months after the court-packing defeat, suddenly spied on the far horizon a clear threat to the security of the United States: the Japanese attack on Peking in July 1937. In the teeth of overwhelming antiwar sentiment (which would last virtually until Pearl Harbor), Roosevelt immediately began drumming up "preparedness" propaganda and laying the foundations for another capacious redefinition of America's overseas interests. In October 1937, in one of his most unpopular speeches, Roosevelt warned the nation that if an aggressor succeeded anywhere in the world "let no one imagine that America will escape." To "prove" how deeply aggression in China endangered the United States, Roosevelt made national defense the chief theme of his January 1938 message to Congress and the paramount concern of his Administration that year. To help rid American diplomacy of that perennial drag on a forward foreign policy, namely our negligible economic interests abroad, Secretary of State Cordell Hull advised the nation in January 1938 that America's foreign interests "are not measured by the number of American concerns residing in a particular country at a particular moment nor by the amount of investment of American citizens there, nor by the volume of trade. There is a broader and more fundamental interest—which is that orderly processes in international relations must be maintained." In short, from the first opportunity that Japan provided in July 1937, Roosevelt devoted himself to smoothing the way for a profound American involvement in the wars of the Eastern Hemisphere. When a Japanese pilot sank the U.S. gunboat *Panay* in China in December 1937, Roosevelt, just one year after winning the greatest mandate for reform in American history, tried vainly to drum up war fever.

It can be argued that Roosevelt was morally right to bring America into the Second World War, but that will not explain why he did so or why he began preparing for intervention so early. A moral justification for acting is not the same as a political reason for acting. If it were, then every ruler in history was governed by high moral principle, since every ruler ascribes righteous motives to himself. In the case of Roosevelt, are we to believe that he launched America on a war course in 1937 just because he thought it morally right to do so? He had done nothing "right" for the five preceding years of his Presidency; he had betrayed the people and his trust from the day he entered office; he had done more to saddle this Republic with antirepublican institutions than any single American President. Can we seriously believe that suddenly, one fine day in 1937, he decided to act in accordance with the highest principles of morality and justice? Can we seriously believe that moral principles set him on a course of action that would kill reform when he had already tried to kill reform without benefit of moral principles? Why should we believe of any leader that he did something for good reasons when he had already done the same thing for bad reasons? For five years Roosevelt had looked on evil and injustice in this Republic and turned his back. Can anyone seriously believe that in 1937 he looked on evil in China and Central Europe and decided then and there, in a fit of idealism, to root out the distant infamy? To refer to Lincoln's speech once again, it is impossible to know absolutely, but we find it impossible not to believe that Roosevelt took the Republic down the path to war not because the war was morally justified but because it was politically expedient.

It might be asked, does it matter what motives Roosevelt had for acting as he did? The answer is it matters greatly if we wish to understand why Truman was eager for the Cold War, why Johnson launched the Vietnam War; if we wish to understand who rules us and what they have done in our name to safeguard the power they have usurped from us.

There is nothing "puzzling" about Truman's "welcoming" the Cold War, nothing puzzling about his provocative policy toward the Soviet Union before 1947, nothing puzzling about his insistence on a Russian grand design for world domination. There is nothing puzzling either about how Truman communicated his "eagerness" to every party politician for a quarter of a century. If the present-day oligarchs have been able to prosecute a forward foreign policy beyond the wildest dreams of the "expansionists of 1898," they have done so for reasons which their predecessors shared. American foreign policy may seem a patchwork of blunders and inconsistencies to the diplomatic historian, but this is because they omit the one consistent feature in American foreign policy, the power and interests of the oligarchs who frame it.

What allowed the party oligarchs to carry out their Cold War policies so successfully is beyond the scope of this book, although certain elements in that success are obvious. The great triad of oligarchic institutions, monopoly, bureaucracy and trade unions, had already strengthened party power considerably; to have millions of American citizens inside warmongering trade unions makes no small contribution to the success of any aggressive American foreign policy. That the Second World War appeared a just war was also an important factor, for if Wilson's war renewed the citizens' determination to stay clear of foreign entanglements, the defeat of Hitler did not. In 1946 Americans overwhelmingly looked forward to peace and disarmament, but crusades against overseas tyrants had a credibility they never before enjoyed in our history. Describing the various factors, both domestic and foreign, that enabled the oligarchs to carry out their Cold War policies is the task of the political historian. It is sufficient to have shown here that the oligarchs made and seized their opportunity because it served their abiding political interests to do so. The truth is, it enabled them to lay a foundation under their usurped power that stood them in good stead for a generation.

It is no coincidence that between 1938 and the 1960s—the period coterminous with a successfully aggressive American foreign policy— free politics in America was more dead, political hope more thoroughly blasted, the prospects for reform more dim than in any other equal span of time in our history. During the period of the Cold War, the party oligarchs were able to savage troublesome politicians for being "soft on Communism" and do this so readily that party ranks were virtually stripped down to their essential core of bosses and henchmen. During those years of political degradation, the "liberal" Democratic party could, with impunity, make a Senator from the Texas ruling clique the leader of its Senate contingent and let a handful of men in the House Rules Committee control the legislative destinies of the nation. During that same period of political degradation, the isolationist wing of the Republican hierarchy could, with equal impunity, underwrite the Truman Doctrine of aggressive internationalism by accusing the Democrats of being insufficiently anti-Communist. During that same period false issues flourished and real issues were readily falsified. Public medical care for the aged, the simple and logical extension of the Social Security Act, could be proposed by Tammany-liberals as a visionary reform and successfully attacked by Republicans as "creeping socialism," as if Republicans had not criticized Roosevelt in 1934 for failing to submit a social security measure. It was a period so politically degraded that when the Congressional oligarchs wanted to get rid of an honest regulatory commissioner they quoted his early writings against trusts as proof of Communist leanings, as if the Sherman Act had been the work of fellow travelers. It was a period so politically degraded that a Democratic nominee for the Presidency could be described as a fresh political voice for demanding an end to a nonexistent missile gap and for criticizing a Republican administration's inability to fight "brush-fire wars." During the Cold War period virtually all public issues were foreign issues, which is to say, no issues at all. While every kind of inequity flourished at home, the oligarchs could rivet people's attention to the islands of Quemoy and Matsu. During the Cold War period a citizen would have sought in vain from one coast to the other for five eminent elected officials who spoke with an independent voice. During that period the oligarchs' control over American politics was more complete than it had ever been before, more so even than the 1920s. The Cold War has served the party oligarchs well.

Yet complete party control of politics cannot be secured permanently in this Republic because the liberty of the citizens cannot be destroyed nor political hope permanently blasted. Legitimized by a Supreme Court decision, a grass-roots civil-rights movement made the first great breach in the party monopoly of political action. Blighted in 1937 and again after 1948, political hope rose steadily like the water level in a reservoir, despite every foreign alarm and distraction. It crystallized around the memory of an assassinated President who had done his best, ironically, to blight it. It gave his successor an overwhelming electoral victory and a great Congressional majority. At that point, the newly elected President, whose political career spanned the entire era of political degradation, whose years of fame coincided with the years of the Cold War, acted on the blind assumption that the oligarchs could by now get away with anything and dragged the nation into Vietnam as if war had become as routine as stuffing a ballot box. It has been left to the party oligarchs, faced with a resurgence of free politics, to repair the damage wrought by Lyndon Johnson. It has fallen to his Republican successor to shore up the crumbling foundations of the Cold War system and make it look credible again.

13.
The Principle of Waste

The most obvious consequence of the Cold War is America's present-day military establishment with its three million fighting men, its more than one million civilian employees, its twenty-two thousand prime arms contractors and its more than two million dependent defense workers. If the oligarchs' determination to prosecute an aggressive foreign policy predates by half a century America's contemporary military machine, the political advantages of the military machine have greatly strengthened their determination. It has enabled the party oligarchs to solve what for them is a grave political problem—how to waste scores of billions of dollars a year.

The problem arises from a fundamental condition created by monopoly capitalism. That system, as Baran and Sweezy and others have demonstrated, cannot generate demand for its products and outlets for investment large enough to absorb the surplus wealth it generates. Since surplus wealth which can be neither invested nor consumed will not be produced, "the normal state of the monopoly capitalist economy is stagnation." Without the government's help, "monopoly capitalism," according to Baran and Sweezy, "would sink deeper and deeper into a bog of chronic depression." If the country is to avoid a depression and another collapse of the monopoly system, the government must stimulate demand by means of enormous annual public expenditures.

That the government must pour billions of dollars into the economy each year does not, to conventional political understanding, seem like much of a problem. It would seem to be an unparalleled opportunity for improving the general lot of the citizenry. Virtually every city, town and hamlet in America is in dire need of public revenues. What could be more immediately beneficial to all Americans than the allocation of a much-needed $30 billion a year out of Federal revenues to restore, improve and revive local communities? Almost everybody suffers to some degree from polluted air, polluted waterways and a despoiled and deteriorating environment. To accomplish real and sweeping environmental improvement (not just keeping things from getting worse) would cost scores of billions of dollars. What could be simpler than spending every cent required, since the money must be spent anyway? Poverty in America could be virtually eradicated with the stroke of a legislative pen and would, in addition, open vast new markets for the merchandise of the monopoly industries. Again, since the money must be spent, what could be more reasonable than eliminating poverty once and for all?

Yet the oligarchs' efforts in these and other areas have been notoriously grudging. Only the most intense public pressure gets anything done at all. (It was the bludgeon force of several Congressional election defeats at the hands of "environmentalists" that finally forced Congress in 1972 to act against municipal water pollution. In 1966, without such organized pressure, the oligarchs characteristically passed a water-pollution law expressly designed not to work. Recent revenue-sharing legislation, a long-overdue step in the right direction, will, at its present $5 billion level, serve chiefly to keep things from getting worse, i.e., relieve the public pressure. In *The New York Times,* Daniel P. Moynihan revealingly hailed the legislation as a "major event" because it proved that the "political system can respond." That the party oligarchs actually did anything to meet a grave public need Moynihan quite correctly considers an abnormal occurrence.) On the other hand, under no public pressure whatever, the same oligarchs lavish almost half the annual Federal revenues on military and space programs without the slightest regard for economy, or even, as will be seen, for their own estimate of the needs of national defense. Given a golden opportunity to spend large sums of money on programs beneficial to all, the party oligarchs demonstrably prefer to spend them as wastefully as possible, and the question, as always, is why.

Baran and Sweezy are candid enough to raise the question but being Marxist ideologues they cannot answer it. Since monopoly capitalism, per se, only requires that the money be spent, the reason politicians do not spend it beneficially, according to the authors, is because particular economic interests hurt by some particular beneficial expenditure use their particular economic power to block that expenditure. Since some special interest is always hurt by some particular beneficial expenditure, the net result is that the politicians cannot spend much money beneficially and so are forced to spend it on the military machine.

To explain why local communities have deteriorating public services, the two authors note that such communities depend principally on the property tax for revenue, a tax which is particularly onerous to wealthy residents because it cannot be shifted to consumers the way income and corporation taxes can. Such being the case, the politically powerful rentiers resist efforts to raise the property tax and, in consequence, public services decay. Only an economic ideologue would call this an explanation. If small-town rentiers were really so powerful, why have they consented to burden themselves with a property tax in the first place? Why don't they use their alleged power to make the Federal Government share out $30 billion a year in shiftable income and corporation tax revenues? In that way they could live in far pleasanter surroundings at far less personal cost. All the two authors have shown, in fact, is that the small-town rich have so little political power they cannot get their streets cleaned at somebody else's expense.

In like manner, the authors attribute the lack of adequate medical care in the nation to the powerful opposition of the American Medical Association, and attribute the lack of adequate public housing in the cities to the powerful opposition of real-estate speculators, so that in three successive explanations the corporate rulers of America are epitomized in turn by small-town rentiers, a professional guild and a bunch of urban hustlers. None of these interest groups has any economic control over the giant corporations, or much to do with monopoly capitalism, yet they allegedly share in the political power of the great corporations. The reason they do is quite inexplicable. If the monopoly capitalists have all the power, as the authors believe, why should the AMA, a real-estate speculator and a coupon-clipper have any?

The truth is, the two Marxist economists, in their attempt to account for particular political misdeeds, have had to abandon the notion of corporation power and fall back on the more vulgar form of economic ideology which holds that any particular political act is dictated by the particular special interest which profits by it. The absurdity of this view is exposed, as I have already said, by the elementary political fact that if a beneficial political act hurts one special interest it will also benefit some other special interest. If inadequate medical care benefits the AMA, for example, better medical care would benefit the life insurance companies, which profit greatly by an increasing life expectancy, since they set rates on the shorter and pay out on the longer expectancy. If inadequate urban housing benefits real-estate speculators, adequate public housing greatly benefits building contractors, construction unions, local banks and other economic interests, including many real-estate speculators. If lifting the oil import quotas would hurt the oil interests, it would benefit the petrochemical interests. What is more, any large beneficial expenditure of funds can be made to provide (and usually is made to provide) windfall bounties to some private interest or other, as Johnson made his rent subsidy law into a windfall for small banks. For every private interest using its alleged power to block a beneficial expenditure, there are always other private interests which should be using their power to support it. If we ascribe the politicians' failure to enact beneficial reforms to the resistance of particular interests, we are left with a truly noteworthy coincidence—that particular economic interests enjoy power to block beneficial deeds yet have no power to support beneficial deeds.

Du Pont is a great power except when its interest is the common interest in removing oil import quotas. The life insurance companies are great powers except when their interest in better health care for all is the common interest of all. The construction unions are powers in city politics except when their interest in fat building contracts would improve the lot of city dwellers. Just when a particular economic interest should be more powerful than ever—when it is temporarily identical with the common interest—it turns out to lack any power. When it has the majority of citizens on its side, elected officials ignore it; when it has nobody on its side, elected officials become its slave. This is a remarkable sort of power indeed. Yet save for the fact that the party oligarchs refuse to enact reforms, there is no evidence whatever that it exists. It is only manifest when the oligarchs refuse to enact reform. It is then conjured up as a particular *external* force to explain each particular refusal. In other words, on the blind assumption that the party oligarchs have no interest of their own in not enacting reform, we are asked to believe in the existence of a totally self-contradictory, utterly implausible power whose sole function is to prevent them from enacting reforms, and in the case at hand, to prevent them from spending public money beneficially. The doctrine of special interests and their power rests on nothing but the central premise of political apologetics—that America's politicians would serve the electorate faithfully if nonpolitical forces greater than they did not forever stand in their way.

Pressed to spend scores of billions of dollars each year to maintain the monopoly system, the party oligarchs have a compelling reason of their own for spending it on a profligate military establishment, and, since it is the basic principle of action of those who wield party power, it bears repeating. The usurped power of the party oligarchs, perpetually threatened by political liberty, can only be maintained through a ceaseless effort to discourage the exercise of that liberty. The party oligarchs must perpetually try to demonstrate anew that politics is futile, that politicians are powerless, that public hope is public folly, that whatever is must be, that whatever happens is inevitable, that every citizen's real enemy is the citizen next door. That is why the opportunity to spend billions of dollars yearly on improvements of benefit to all is not an opportunity but a peril to the oligarchs. The existence of a profligate military establishment constitutes, therefore, a compelling confirmation of all that I have been trying to demonstrate about power in the American Republic today.

To carry out by government action some large, generous and clear-cut improvement in the life of the citizenry would undo all that the oligarchs strive perpetually to achieve: it would reveal the power of politicians, the reach of political action and the noninevitability of many conditions of life. To the exact degree that it was beneficial, it would encourage citizens to act in their own behalf, and their very gratitude to the party which enacted the reforms would endanger the leaders of that party. It would encourage activists, civic improvers and ambitious men of all kinds to enter every political club of that party in every town and district and neighborhood, threatening organization control of local party politics. Neither party organization can afford to be a genuine party of reform. This is the reason, as I have said, why both American parties have a "reform" wing and an "obstructionist" wing: the one to promise, the other to betray. There is no need to conjure up obstructive special interests to explain the oligarchs' refusal to spend public money beneficially.

To the general peril of beneficial reforms, particular broad reforms add their own particular perils. The allocation, without bureaucratic control, of $30 billion a year to local communities in the country would revive local hope and local political activity, for men become interested in local politics in proportion as their local government has the power to accomplish things. Yet the existence of lively and open politics in every self-governing community is itself a grave danger to party control of politics: it opens up opportunities for independent men to win local office and local renown without prior approval of the party organizations. By continually bringing new men into public life, it provides the permanent condition for breaking up every local party monopoly of politics. It therefore threatens local party collusion and the whole system of statewide collusion. This is the reason the party bosses in most states have persistently starved local communities of revenues and forced them to make shift with the property tax, the alleged power of small-town rentiers notwithstanding. The less revenue a local government has, the less it can do and the more moribund and controllable local politics becomes. In addition, the more financially hard-pressed a local government is, the easier it becomes for the state party bosses to strip it of local powers it can no longer finance, a process of state centralization which the oligarchs have been carrying out in most states for generations. Strengthening and augmenting local self-government is the very opposite of what the party oligarchs try to accomplish.

There is a similar reason for the oligarchs' reluctance to spend money eradicating poverty, a reluctance dramatically underscored when Johnson averted a promised war against poverty with a real war in Asia. (Lest anyone attribute this to popular sentiment, it is worth recalling that Johnson won a great election victory after promising the former and was driven out of office for undertaking the latter.) Since the eradication of poverty, by opening new markets, would be far more equitably beneficial to the giant corporations than the arbitrary, lopsided awarding of military contracts, the only interest served by the persistence of poverty is that of the party oligarchs: the poor are relatively easy to control. Mired in daily economic anxieties, distracted from public concerns, grateful for mean favors, inured to insult, to futility, to the arrogance of bureaucrats, they have served as the bulwark of machine politics for many generations. There is a backhanded recognition of this truth in the views of certain left-wing elitists— Tammany-socialists, so to speak—when they argue that local self-government or local control of schools is a "middle-class value" of no concern to the poor as such. What they mean is that the poor are less likely to defend, or exercise, their liberty than citizens free of the treadmill of penury. This is exactly true, and that is what makes them an asset to oligarchy. America is perhaps unique in this regard, that material plenty and economic security do not render the American citizenry politically docile. It makes them more active and more demanding. It is no coincidence that the movement for civil rights, the growing demand for general reforms, for participation in government, for greater "control over one's life" swelled to a climax during a period of unparalleled economic boom.

The oligarchs' interest in maintaining poverty (or poverty ameliorated by welfare bureaucracies which also keep the poor under control) puts them in something of a dilemma. They must maintain a fairly prosperous level of demand for the sake of the economy while simultaneously maintaining pockets of poverty, a task which requires the capacity to distribute wealth in such a way that the hard-core poor remain poor. For accomplishing this, as will be seen, the annual military budget is uniquely well adapted.

The political role of the military budget is therefore an obvious one. Given the huge sums involved, it is the only practical way to waste public money which the oligarchs would otherwise have to spend in ways perilous to their power. Obviously, the Cold War has been the oligarchs' indispensable pretext for doing this. The military needs created by the Cold War cannot account for the size of the annual military budget, because even by the oligarchs' own estimate of the Soviet military menace, most of the money spent on national defense is wasted money. What governs the annual military budget is no recognizable military purpose, not even an ominously aggressive one, no definable estimate of the needs of national security, not even one based on the alleged Kremlin drive to dominate the world. What chiefly governs the military budget is the need to spend enormous sums of money in a useless way. The allegedly powerful Pentagon is simply a receptacle for wasteful expenditure, just as a city dump is the receptacle for the refuse of a city.

There is scarcely a significant item in the military budget which does not reveal this principle of waste. Take the Democrats' "partisan" issue of 1959–1960, the missile gap, which was modeled on an earlier, equally fictitious bomber gap. When Kennedy entered the White House, he certainly knew there was no such gap in America's missile defenses. Eisenhower had said as much on January 12, 1961, in his final message to Congress. General Maxwell Taylor, Kennedy's own military adviser, had said as much, since in his view America's existing two hundred intercontinental missiles were sufficient to deter any Russian attack. Kennedy's Secretary of Defense, Robert McNamara, publicly denied—until Kennedy silenced him—the existence of a missile gap shortly after taking office. Nonetheless, a few weeks after Eisenhower had publicly derided the missile gap, Kennedy informed Congress with brazen impudence that America was passing through "an hour of national peril" due to inadequate military defenses and initiated the construction of eight hundred more missiles. Not only was this a deliberate waste of money, it conveniently paved the way for a still further waste of money. As soon as the Russians began building missiles to catch up, the oligarchs ordered a second round of weapons building to counter the new Russian threat, thus getting two spasms of expenditure where, by any merely military estimate, none would have sufficed. When military estimates are inconveniently frugal, they are invariably ignored.

Such double buildups are characteristic of the oligarchs' budgetary strategy of wastefulness. First the oligarchs order construction of useless bombers, sitting-duck aircraft carriers and the like, on the grounds that the Russians are allegedly contemplating some menacing military buildup. Then they order a second buildup on the grounds that the Russians are actually building, usually in response to our initial buildup. Thus the oligarchs get one spurt of waste for the thought and another for the deed. Known as the arms race, it is actually a one-contestant chariot race with the American horse dragging the Russian chariot along, with the result that even those present-day military items which appear to be based on existing Soviet weapons have their origin in deliberate waste, since the Russians would not have built many of those weapons had the party oligarchs not built first and faster.

Incapable of rationalizing this race even by their own elastic standards, some Pentagon strategists argue that the real strategic value of the arms race is not military but economic. Allegedly it will impoverish the Soviet Union and bring harm to its rulers, although it does no harm to America's rulers. The fact that the party oligarchs can always find Pentagon generals to justify waste is often taken as evidence of the power of the generals, whereas it simply proves that the politicians can always find generals to shill for them. If the illustrious General Taylor was dismayed by Kennedy's missile gap lies, as he should have been, given his public views, his dismay is not on record. The general who seriously embarrasses the party oligarchs will soon find himself on the road to oblivion. He might even lose his retirement sinecure in an arms corporation, since these allegedly sinister ties between the Pentagon and the arms contractors are, for the most part, patronage jobs dispensed to compliant generals by the party oligarchs and provided by equally compliant arms corporations. A "political" general in America is not a military man seeking political power but a garden-variety careerist trying his best to serve it. Civilian control of the military, that bogeyman of the liberal press, is not, and never has been, a problem in America. The problem is civilian control of the civilians in power.

Another graphic example of the principle of waste is the so-called ABM or antiballistic missile defense system. This was first officially proposed by the House Armed Services Committee in 1966 and ordered into existence by Johnson in 1967, over the opposition of Defense Secretary McNamara. McNamara's opposition was understandable enough. By 1967, the oligarchs had already wasted some $20 billion on missile defense systems which had proved either unworkable or obsolete before deployment. (Building weapons in full knowledge that they will be obsolete before they can be used is a common practice of the oligarchs and perfectly epitomizes the principle of waste.) Moreover, the $20 billion ABM Sentinel was devoid of any justification strong enough to deceive a ten-year-old. According to the Johnson Administration, the Sentinel was supposed to shield American cities from a Chinese missile attack, a menace allegedly confronting the Republic in the mid-1970s, when the Chinese would possess a few intercontinental missiles. Since the Soviet Union, with many times that number of missiles already in hand, was deterred by America's huge retaliatory force, the sole justification for an anti-Chinese missile shield was that the Chinese were insane and would accept total incineration for the short-lived joy of destroying a few American cities. The real reason the oligarchs wanted to build a $20 billion ABM system was simply that they wanted to waste $20 billion. That an ABM system, once installed, could easily be doubled or tripled in scope and so made to devour perhaps $100 billion was the particular appeal the ABM had for the oligarchs.

For a variety of reasons—disgust with the Vietnam War, mistrust of the Pentagon, the sharp resistance of suburban communities to having Sentinels in their backyard—the Sentinel ABM came under the public spotlight in the winter of 1968–1969. Since the mad-Chinese justification for it was totally incapable of withstanding public scrutiny, Nixon was forced to abandon it. He did not, however, abandon the ABM, which, like most military expenditures, is an expense in search of a reason. Citing evidence of an entirely new Russian threat to American security (which the Johnson Administration, committed as it was to a Chinese menace, had not detected a mere two weeks before Nixon took office), the new President proposed an entirely new justification for the ABM. It would be taken out of the inhospitable suburbs and used to defend American missile launching sites against the possibility of a Russian "first-strike" aimed at America's retaliatory weapons. Less absurd than the mad-Chinese argument, the Nixon pretext for Safeguard, as it was now called, was equally empty, since the possibility of Russia actually destroying American retaliatory capacity in a first-strike was nil. Even if a Russian attack destroyed every land-based American missile launcher—which it could not do—America has an entirely separate submarine attack system which can destroy the Soviet Union many times over and a third separate bomber attack system which purportedly could do the same. All that is required to destroy the Soviet Union is some fifty delivered warheads, and by 1969 America had well over four thousand to deliver, thanks to the original missile gap lies. Nevertheless the ABM Safeguard was narrowly approved by a hard-pressed Congress. Having lost one justification for wasting $20 billion, the oligarchs successfully shifted to another.

This, however, was not the end of the story. One of the many arguments against the ABM was that an ABM defense would be useless, since, for every expensive antiballistic missile America built, the Russians could easily build a far cheaper attack missile to counter it. Thus, in Defense Secretary McNamara's words, there would be "no gain in real security" but merely a colossal waste of money. For the purpose of approving Safeguard this simple argument was ignored, but not forgotten. In February 1970, the Department of Defense began developing a "new," cheaper ABM to replace the "old" one. "The need for such a system, weapons specialists say," according to a

New York Times account, "is based on the impression that the Soviet Union can develop additional warheads for each SS-9 intercontinental missile more cheaply than the United States can respond by adding Safeguard defense missiles." In other words, the argument which should have been used against building the first ABM system was being used a year later to justify building a second ABM system. Anyone who looks for a rational military or strategic purpose in this curious procedure looks in vain. The only purpose involved is deliberate waste, for if the oligarchs actually took seriously their own estimate of our national defense needs, they would not have spent a penny on an ABM.

Another example of the principle of waste is the oligarchs' response to the circumstance that the Army, in order to justify missile building, habitually overestimates the number of Soviet missiles, while the Navy, in order to justify more aircraft carriers, missile frigates or other nautical boondoggles, habitually downgrades the estimated number of Soviet missiles. Obviously, if the party oligarchs were actually concerned with the needs of national defense, they would have to choose between the two contrasting estimates. Operating under the principle of waste, however, they accept both estimates and build missiles for the Army, ships for the Navy and useless strategic bombers for the Air Force, the perennial appeal of bombers being that they are particularly costly items since they have to be built in fleets. The latest generation of such bombers will eventually cost $75 billion for a fleet of 250 which, say many experts, will be obsolete by the time it is ready.

Examples of the principle of waste can be multiplied indefinitely. It is in accordance with the principle of waste, for example, that no military project is abandoned merely because some other weapons system makes it redundant. It is in accordance with the same principle that the oligarchs approved construction of seventeen hundred fighter planes of a new and complex design before a single prototype of that plane had ever flown, which proved some $8 billion later to be virtually useless. It is in accordance with the principle of waste, too, that the oligarchs build giant aircraft carriers which would be useless in a nuclear war and proceed to equip them with equally useless fleets of antibomber defense planes. It is the perfect reflection of the policy of waste that the government in the past decade has paid out $20 billion to arms contractors in excess of the original contracts and that between 1955 and 1968, according to the Budget Bureau, some 60 percent of all electronic components purchased by the Federal government were defective, the ineptitude, inefficiency and boodling of the weapons-makers reflecting their quite accurate understanding that the chief purpose of the military budget is to waste public money. It is in accordance with the principle of waste, too, that the government in the 1960s spent $50 billion to land a man on the moon, since the space race serves the same basic purpose as the military one. With the moon landing achieved, the oligarchs are now developing a useless $10 billion space shuttle in order to reopen the cosmos as a dumping ground for public funds.

The final demonstration of the principle of waste, however, is the fact that the military budget perpetually increases. The reason for that increase has little to do with expanding needs of national defense, for those needs have hardly grown. The number of missiles needed to destroy the Soviet Union has not increased appreciably since the 1950s; the threat of a Soviet attack on Western Europe has not increased over the years; the defensiveness of China has been demonstrated under fairly intense provocation. The reason the oligarchs keep increasing the military budget as far as they can has nothing to do with military needs. The truth is, as America's productive capacity increases, the amount of public expenditure needed to maintain effective consumer demand also increases. As a result the oligarchs must constantly contrive new ways to increase military spending. This is the reason Johnson added $4.1 billion to his last non-Vietnam military budget to counterbalance a $3.5 billion cut in his Vietnam budget. This is the reason the oligarchs give the Pentagon hundreds of millions of dollars each year in research funds to concoct and keep moving down the budgetary pipeline new and more outlandishly costly weapons. This is why, in any given year, the annual military budget contains seed money for space shuttles, new ABM systems, advanced bombers and the like, thereby providing the oligarchs with a budgetary backlog they can later expand at will. This is why the Nixon Administration has vehemently insisted that an arms limitation treaty with Russia makes it necessary to increase military expenditures. This is why the oligarchs have been telling the public for years that the termination of a war costing $20 billion a year will not produce a "peace dividend" for domestic concerns; a peace dividend is the last thing the oligarchs want.

Averting a grave threat to party power is, I believe, the oligarchs' chief reason for creating and sustaining the bloated military establishment. It is not, however, the only one. The annual military budget also brings the oligarchs certain positive political advantages. By dispensing billions of dollars each year to twenty-two thousand arms contractors, the party oligarchs have created a network of economic dependents more sharply subservient, more directly subject to their caprice, than the ordinary monopoly corporations are—the categories of arms contractors and monopolists, of course, overlap. In this sense, the military budget is simply an enormous pork barrel of special privilege, the privileges taking the form of windfall profits, of no-risk profits and, most importantly, of enormous outlays of capital supplied by the Pentagon to arms contractors in the guise of "progress" payments. The Lockheed Georgia Division, for example, received 90 percent of its outlays for a transport plane from the Pentagon itself and diverted $181 million of it for its own private use, that single item of boodle being larger than the Federal Government's total annual expenditure on urban transportation. As the recipients of special privilege, the arms contractors have become a ready source of huge sums of political money and other services to the oligarchs. As the sole customer of such great corporations as Lockheed, the oligarchs have created for themselves virtual corporate fiefdoms whose profits they plunder, whose executive board seats, legal fees and other perquisites are patronage plums in their giving. The ways in which the oligarchs shake down their arms clients are, of course, varied, but one method is particularly revealing. The principal shareholder in the now defunct General Dynamics Corporation was a man called Henry Crown, who also happened to be the chief financier, or "fat cat," of the Cook

County, Illinois, machine. The oligarchs awarded huge contracts to their hopelessly inefficient General Dynamics fiefdom and siphoned off part of the profits into the Chicago machine with Crown serving as the main conduit.

What is more, the military pork barrel spreads special privilege far beyond the confines of the arms contractors; it directly creates at least two million industrial jobs, every holder of which is all too dependent for his well-being on the well-being of the party oligarchs and the success of their corrupt policies. By virtue of the military budget, a large number of ordinary citizens have been given a direct stake in corrupt power.

By means of the military pork barrel, the oligarchs have also carried the routine politics of special privilege one quantum leap forward. In the routine of privilege-dispensing, the wielders of corrupt power bestow privileges on new sources of wealth wherever and whenever they arise. Military boodle, however, is privileged wealth which the government itself creates. The oligarchs can dispense it wherever they want, whenever they want, to whomever it suits them to favor, like a rich man distributing gratuities. By a legislative stroke authorizing a new weapons system, the oligarchs can create out of nothing an entirely new source of wealth, just as by their annual reenactment of the military establishment they annually re-create the old ones. By decisions made in the bowels of the Pentagon, they can distribute boodle as they choose, since 90 percent of all military contracts are awarded without competitive bidding, which is to say, capriciously. Formally, the Department of Defense awards contracts, but all important decisions are made by the party oligarchs, the Pentagon being a servile bureaucracy like all the others. Because the oligarchs wanted Lockheed-Georgia to get the C-5A transport contract, they had their "top Pentagon officials" overrule the Pentagon's own Source Selection Board, which had recommended Boeing on technical grounds. Because Kennedy wanted to give the TFX fighter contract to General Dynamics in Texas, he saw to it that the Pentagon's selection unit was again overruled, again disfavoring "powerful" Boeing when it had equity on its side. To achieve this, Kennedy named a General

Dynamics lawyer, Roswell Gilpatric, as his Deputy Secretary of Defense and a Fort Worth lawyer, Fred Korth, as his Secretary of the Navy shortly before the Pentagon made its "decision."

The fact that the party oligarchs can distribute military boodle wherever and whenever they choose allows them, for example, to pour military boodle—contracts and jobs—into those states where party power appears to be in danger and to do so whenever such danger arises. During the Kennedy-Johnson years, Texas went from eleventh to second among states in the amount of defense outlays it receives. This is usually attributed to the influence of Johnson, but this is only partly true, if true at all. The more important reason is that in the early 1960s, as I said, the ruling clique of the Texas Democratic party was in serious danger of losing control of the party. By pouring billions of dollars of defense boodle and boodle jobs into Texas, the party oligarchs were trying to help the Texas gang retain their power, a matter of great importance since the outbreak of free politics in Texas would have political repercussions throughout the South.

A similar political reason explains why California far surpasses other states in the amount of arms money it receives—almost three times as much as New York State. California's sunny climate has nothing to do with its attractiveness. The fact is, California, alone among the large states, has been chronically difficult for party bosses to control. It is still far from being a tight oligarchic state, but in the mid-1950s California politics was much more open than it is today. The $10 billion in defense outlays which California now receives every year has certainly played a part in this.

Lastly, the fact that the party oligarchs can dispense and withdraw military boodle at will has also helped them strengthen their control over Congress, for it is the bastions of the oligarchs, the Armed Services and Appropriations Committees, which control the military pork barrel in Congress. A compliant Congressman troubled by unemployment in his district can have it promptly diminished by the suitable bestowal of a military contract; a Congressman tempted to take an independent line can have unemployment inflicted on his constituents if he steps too far out of line. Through their control of the military boodle, the oligarchs can make a hack Congressman appear a genuine power in the House and an unruly Congressman appear inept and useless in the eyes of his constituents. Party politics is a system of political rewards and punishments controlled as far as possible by the party leaders, and the annual military budget, through its unparalleled size, its geographical extent and its flexibility, has added greatly to the tools at the oligarchs' disposal.

Little more, I think, needs be said. The party oligarchs have every reason of their own to feed the military-industrial complex and no reason of their own to stop. That is why the American Republic today is saddled with the most profligate military establishment in history, twenty-five years after the American people, following a victorious war, were looking forward to peace and disarmament. Without the fictions and fabrications of the oligarchs' Cold War policies, without its perpetual crises and alarms, such a military establishment would have been politically impossible, indeed virtually unthinkable. The oligarchs' interest in sustaining the Cold War is, therefore, a very great one. It combines all the profound and perennial advantages of an aggressive, entangling foreign policy with an unequaled opportunity to use the wealth of the citizenry against them. The Cold War has become, understandably enough, one of the chief pillars of oligarchic power.

That pillar, however, is now crumbling. Johnson's war has badly undermined the credibility of the Cold War. Even timid political voices are now willing to term it an obsession, a remark which a few years back would have cost them their political lives. The days when the party oligarchy could alarm the entire nation over the fate of Quemoy and Matsu are temporarily over. How the oligarchs will repair the public damage to their Cold War system I do not know and will not venture to predict. In the meantime, the spontaneous resurgence of republican skepticism about America's global role, a skepticism which President Nixon regularly denounces as "neo-isolationism," constitutes one of the many grounds of hope for the republican commonwealth today.

14.

The Restoration of Self-Government

The near-monopoly of American politics by two collusive party syndicates is not one problem among many. It is the first and fundamental one as well as the wellspring of most of the others. As long as the present oligarchy rules, we will not have a restrained and peaceable foreign policy; we will not see racism languish and mutual respect grow among the citizenry. We will not see special interests curbed, economic dependence diminished nor special privilege stripped from the overprivileged. We will not see bureaucratic caprice curtailed nor our schools made fit for the children of free men. We will not see the public wealth beneficially spent. The government will continue to turn into a Circumlocution Office when called upon to remedy a common grievance or correct a glaring abuse.

The party oligarchs do not act as they do out of a random and gratuitous malevolence. The party oligarchs are neither malevolent nor benevolent; they are self-interested. What they have done they have done, first, to usurp the citizens' power and then to secure that usurpation. To expect them to carry out voluntarily, in a fit of political altruism, reforms that endanger their power is a sad and fatal delusion. To expect reformers acceptable to the bosses to do so is a vain and forlorn hope, hope in the service of the enemies of hope and so one more falsehood in the system of public lies that now darken our public life.

For the free men of this Republic there is only one way to make a new beginning. We must, in Lincoln's words, "meet and overthrow the present ruling dynasty." We the citizens of the Republic must find the means to break up party control of politics and strip the usurpers of their corrupt and corrupting power. This cannot be done, however, by a national mass movement, because no mass movement ever overthrew an oligarchy without setting up another in its place. What perpetually and radically imperils the ruling oligarchy in this Republic is the political liberty of the citizen and its vigilant exercise, a liberty which the oligarchs can impair but not destroy, the exercise of which they can discourage but not forbid. The only certain means to overthrow the present ruling dynasty without setting up another is to augment political liberty itself; to increase the capacity and willingness of the citizens to act in their own behalf, to make it easier for free men to enter public life, to bring issues that interest them into the public arena, to bring forward for elective office independent men who have won their trust, to make it easier for independent men to win their trust and so by a vigorous exercise of liberty to hold elected officials accountable while regularly punishing those who prove themselves perfidious.

I say augment political liberty because we already enjoy in this Republic the constitution and framework of liberty, a form of government and a system of rights expressly established by the Founders to supply and to ensure—as far as constitutions alone can ensure—the capacity of every citizen to act freely in public matters. That intent—a truly revolutionary intent—appears most obviously in the great constitutional immunities that safeguard freedom of speech, freedom of assembly, the freedom of the press, freedom from double jeopardy, from arbitrary searches and seizures and the like. These fundamental rights and immunities are not, as professors and pedagogues so often tell us, mere safeguards for private men against an encroaching government. They were set down to protect the citizens' capacity for public and political action. The Founders did not fear that a would-be usurper would abuse private men in their private concerns. What does a tyrant care what a man says only to his wife? As long as their subjects remain private men, tyrants have rarely done them political harm. It is only men in their public capacity as citizens who require constitutional immunities, for it is the free, lawful political activity of free men that endangers the power of usurpers. The major provisions of the Bill of Rights are protections of public rights, and it is only because the Republic was founded to secure the citizens' capacity to act politically that we have such a Bill of Rights. Without that large and secure capacity for acting, a capacity extended equally to all citizens under the Constitution, voting of itself would be meaningless and majority rule would merely ratify the reign of a tyrant. As Thomas Jefferson said in 1781, "It was not for an elective despotism that we fought." It was for equal political liberty, a system of government in which there is no permanent division between rulers and ruled, between those who act and those who are acted upon.

The Founders also provided—indeed invented—an even more profound principle of free government, the great "Federal principle," in James Madison's phrase, of geographically separated powers. Under the federal principle, the aggregate concerns of the Republic are placed entirely in the hands of the general government, which is completely autonomous in its proper sphere. More local concerns are placed in the hands of the several state governments, each of which is autonomous in its proper sphere. By the Federal principle of separated and autonomous powers, the Republic does not form a pyramid or hierarchy, atop which one elective despot might rule over all. The Federal Government derives no authority from the states, the state governments derive no powers from the Federal Government. Should a usurping faction gain control of the general government—which itself is divided—the liberty and equality of the citizens would still remain secure in the several states, and by their continued capacity for free political action, the citizenry in due course would peacefully topple would-be usurpers of the general government, as they toppled the Hamilton faction in the early days of the Republic.

By means of the Federal principle, would-be usurpers of the people's liberty were set a truly difficult task. To secure their corrupt power in the central government, they would have to gain control of the majority of state legislatures as well. In order to gain such supreme and comprehensive power, they would have to forge a national political coalition whose members came from a diversity of organized and independent political communities representing a diversity of interests, factions and sentiments. Such a variegated coalition, as Madison pointed out, could not be readily united by a narrow and dangerous interest, but only by one so broad that it could not differ markedly from the common interest. Under the Federal principle the very coalition an elective despot needs to gain supreme power would defeat his own designs. Madison was quite right, for whatever else has been done to republican liberty, we have never suffered the reign of an elective despot, an extraordinary achievement in itself, given the history of other republics.

It might be said, however, that the Constitution has "failed" since the present-day party oligarchs have surmounted the great constitutional obstacles set in the path of usurpers. Yet this would be looking at matters through the wrong end of the telescope. It is precisely because the Founders constituted the Republic for liberty—and how many revolutions have accomplished that since?—that party power still remains precarious despite its great magnitude. It is because of our republican foundations that those same parties can never be turned into exclusive clubs, for the number of new men who rise constantly into public life is too great under the constitution of liberty for the party managers to practice a rigorous exclusion. It is because the Founders constituted the Republic so that there would be no permanent division between those who act and those who are acted upon that American politics even today is more open, the independent political activity of the citizenry more decisive, than in any other extensive nation. It was the independent, unsuppressible political activity of free Americans which a few years ago brought down a hated President during wartime and forced the ruling parties to reverse their war policy, something that could happen in no other country without a change in the system of government or a constitutional crisis. It is because we were constituted not for "good government" nor "responsible party government" but self-government that America's citizens even today enjoy greater access to information about their government than the average European street agitator even imagines any government would provide. Yet the party oligarchs, through a long and arduous effort, covering many decades, many perils and many reversals (the record of that effort is the as yet unwritten history of the post–Civil War Republic), have prevailed in large measure over the constitutional handicaps placed in the path of their ambition. That is why the foundations of liberty must today be augmented.

The augmentation of political liberty, I must also add, is the principle and goal of neither the official Left, the official Right nor the official Center of the so-called political spectrum. What is truly remarkable about that spectrum is that all its official voices—I say "official" to distinguish them from the opinions of ordinary citizens— agree in denying that the abridgment of political liberty is the central issue of our time and the perpetuation of usurped power the major source of our ills. The dogmatic, ideological Left thinks the augmentation of liberty futile, or even a conservative trick, since in their view real power lies with the manufacturers of toasters and toothpaste. On the other hand, the conservatives and the liberals, so far from fearing the abridgment of liberty, tend to deplore the excess of popular government in America, an excess which, in the conservative view, has led to government shackling of "free" corporate enterprise in order to appease the masses; an excess which, in the liberal view, has led to the perpetual frustration of beneficial reforms by a stubbornly conservative electorate, the same electorate which the conservatives consider the ready dupes of liberals. Indeed it is often said nowadays that America suffers from an excessive dispersal of power, that the Constitution, outmoded by social change, now stands in the way of basic reforms. In this view self-government is blamed for what its enemies have done against it. The truth is, the political spectrum lies at a perfect tangent to political reality, for its official voices are united in telling the citizenry that what the party oligarchs never cease thinking about, namely political liberty, the citizens should not think about at all.

It is the mark of how unchanging the essential requirements of liberty are, amid so much else that changes, that the two fundamental means to restore self-government today were proposed by Thomas Jefferson 160 years ago as "the two great measures . . . without which no republic can maintain itself in strength." The first is the extension of local self-government to every citizen of the Republic, or, in Jefferson's words, "to divide every county into wards and to impart to those wards those powers of self-government for which they are best qualified. . . . In short to make them little republics." The second is the establishment of republican education in the public schools of the ward republics, education whose principle and purpose, again in Jefferson's words, are "to enable every man to judge for himself what secures or endangers his freedom." These two fundamental measures—local self-government and republican education for all—are not a panacea for our ills; they are the *sine qua non* for curing them. They will not usher in the millennium, they promise only a new beginning, "the dawn of the salvation of the Republic," to once again quote Jefferson. Without them self-government will never be restored nor the evils of usurpation abated.

When Jefferson made his proposals for the augmentation of liberty, ward republics already existed within the Republic and indeed predated it. "Called townships in New England [they] are vital principles of their government," Jefferson noted in a letter to John Adams in 1813, "and have proved themselves the wisest inventions ever devised by the wit of man for the perfect exercise of self-government. Each ward would be a small republic in itself and every man in the state would thus become an active member of the common government." It was the vitality of the existing townships, "units of the Republic" in Emerson's phrase, which struck Alexis de Tocqueville as the true security of democracy in America. "I heard a thousand different causes assigned for the evils of the state but the local system was never mentioned among them. I heard citizens attribute the power and prosperity of the country to a multitude of reasons but they all placed the advantages of local institutions in the foremost rank. . . . Only those censure [local self-government] who do not know it." For Tocqueville as for Jefferson, "local assemblies of citizens constitute the strength of free nations. Town meetings are to liberty what primary schools are to science; they bring it within the people's reach; they teach men how to use it and how to enjoy it."

What Jefferson proposed as the great measure for securing self-government in the young Republic was no political novelty then nor is it a political novelty today. What he called for was the extension of local self-rule to all those citizens who did not then enjoy it, principally the inhabitants of the Southern states, where the county was—and remains—the smallest local unit of government. As long as great numbers of citizens were not enfranchised in "small republics," had no voice in "local assemblies" and little share in the active exercise of power, Jefferson feared—indeed dreaded—that usurpation would succeed despite every constitutional safeguard. Tocqueville agreed: "A nation may have a system of free government but without the spirit of municipal institutions it cannot have the spirit of liberty."

Events have not proven Jefferson and Tocqueville wrong, but eminently correct. Today, a comprehensive party oligarchy has in great measure usurped the liberty of the citizen, monopolized the sphere of political action and gained control of the very officials whom the citizens elect to represent them. The historic core of that oligarchy is the Democratic party machine which not only predates the Republican party but which, by collusion, made a boss-controlled Republican party syndicate possible. And what have been the bastions of the Democratic party? The Southern states and the cities, which differ in every way except in this: the citizens of neither enjoy local self-government. In the South, where the counties were never "divided into wards," there a political oligarchy has ruled for generations. In the cities, where the citizenry forms an undifferentiated mass without local institutions, without local assemblies, without the smallest share in local power, there machine politics long ago sprang up to spread corruption and usurpation, by collusion, throughout the body politic. If the extension of local self-government throughout the commonwealth is the primary means to augment the foundations of liberty, the establishment of local self-government within the cities strikes at the jugular of oligarchic power.

At present the political structure of most states exhibits a radically unrepublican condition: the existence of two legally unequal classes of citizens. One class, usually comprising roughly half a state's population and taking up most of its geographical extent, enjoys the franchise of local self-government. Although their township governments have been drastically reduced in power and autonomy by the party oligarchs and deadened politically by the prevalence of collusion, these citizens still have a share in power and an opportunity to exercise political liberty. The second class of citizens, comprising the rest of the state's population, lives on the other side of a boundary line—the "city limits"—within which no unit of the Republic exists, where almost nobody can exercise political liberty, where so far from sharing in public power, the inhabitants can scarcely locate it, so bureaucratized and invisible has power become within the monolithic city political units which rule them. If a citizen lies just outside that boundary line, he is deemed fit to elect local school boards and to have a voice in the direction of local concerns. If he lives just within it, he is deemed totally unfit for local self-rule. A citizen who commutes daily to downtown Manhattan from the nearby suburb of Scarsdale is a member of a unit of the Republic. A citizen who commutes to downtown Manhattan from Brooklyn is a member of an impotent mass. It all depends on which side of the line he lives whether he enjoys local liberty or whether it is virtually impossible for him to act politically except as a toady in a party machine.

Yet that line, which makes all the difference, is not a natural boundary. It is drawn by a state legislature, which decrees, in the act of drawing it, that a monolithic municipal corporation will rule everyone falling within it. The arbitrariness of this procedure goes almost totally unregarded. It is commonly assumed, more or less implicitly, that people are ruled by a municipal government because they are city dwellers and live in an urban center. This is not strictly true. A man may belong to what is indubitably an urban center yet not be a city dweller in the political sense. If his house is two inches past the city line, politically speaking, he is not a city dweller. On the other hand, a man may live in a rural village yet wake up one morning to find himself living as a city dweller under a municipal government. It all depends on how the state legislature draws the boundary line. When the New York legislature annexed the rural county of Queens to the City of New York in 1866, thousands of farmers became New Yorkers overnight and subject to the rule of Tammany Hall. When the Pennsylvania legislature in 1854 decided that the Philadelphia city government, hitherto ruling over a two-square-mile area, would henceforth rule an area 129 square miles wide, the citizens of some twenty-nine self-governing communities overnight became Philadelphians under the central rule of a municipal government. However the social agglomerates known as urban areas may have grown, the political unit known as the city does not "grow." It is a deliberate political creation which only "grows" when a state legislature destroys adjacent units of the Republic and annexes them to a municipal corporation. A city dweller, in short, is often a townsman on whom the ax of annexation has fallen. He still lives in a local community—does anyone live nonlocally?—but his community, by legislative decree, has no local power.

There is nothing arbitrary, therefore, about the creation of local governments within the existing city monoliths. What is arbitrary was the destruction of local governments through their political absorption into the municipal corporations. Doubtless the twenty-nine districts surrounding little Philadelphia had come to require by 1854 the central management of many of their concerns—sewerage disposal, water supply, road-building and the like. To that extent—and only to that extent—centralization was justified. It does not follow, however (multiboroughed London is proof of this), that because a local community can no longer manage certain governmental functions it must be stripped of all of them. Because a township surrenders control of its local sewers does not mean it must surrender control of its local schools, or its local police or its local licensing and taxing powers. Yet the destruction of all local power is what state legislatures have done almost invariably when they annexed self-governing suburban villages to the municipal corporations. Usually "administrative efficiency" was the pretext, but this was never the reason for expanding the municipal monoliths; people today do not speak of the blight of cities because giant municipal governments are efficient. The real reason state legislatures destroyed local self-government in the communities they annexed to the municipal corporations is the very reason local self-government must be established in the cities: because "local assemblies of citizens constitute the strength of free nations," because ward republics for all is that "without which no republic can maintain itself in strength," because a mass of citizens with no direct share in power, no local assemblies, no local political arenas, is easy for political usurpers to control. The establishment of ward government within the cities is only in part an innovation. It is in equal part a restoration of what has been deliberately destroyed.

To draw up an exact blueprint for urban township government would be unnecessary and premature, since men will learn what is best through many trials and errors. A few salient principles, however, are worth emphasizing.

The first is that the urban township should encompass, as far as possible, populations no larger than those of the townships—not villages—existing outside the city limits. In this way the government of a state would be divided into roughly similar units of the Republic and every citizen of that state, whether urban, suburban or rural, would be on an equal footing, whereas today, with the division of states into township dwellers and urban masses, the two classes of citizens are readily persuaded to look on each other as grotesque, alien and dangerous.

The second, and most important, point is that the urban townships or wards cannot be mere decentralized arms of the municipal government, administering its policies and subject to its commands. Administrative decentralization—which is already being discussed in many quarters—is not local self-government but a travesty of it. If the locally elected ward government is the mere local arm of the city government, then there is no point in electing it, and if it is the elected representation of the ward's electorate, it has no business representing the central city government. Whatever powers are assigned to the townships, the townships must be autonomous within their proper sphere, deciding as well as implementing local public policies. The extension of local self-government to the cities is the extension of the Federal structure itself, the constitutional structure of powers geographically divided and autonomous within their own proper spheres.

The general principle for determining the proper sphere of the urban township is, obviously, that no township government can enjoy the power to decide matters affecting other townships, for that would be a usurpation. Each local township can only enjoy power over that which is genuinely local. Certainly they must control their own local schools through autonomous, separately elected school boards. The townships can also exert direct control over local public housing, manage local sanitation, control the licensing and inspection of local enterprises, draw up and enforce their own housing-maintenance, safety and building codes, manage and build local parks, and provide for general recreation. The urban township can also bear primary responsibility for the maintenance of law and order, either through direct local control of the city's foot police (the detective and other special squads remaining a municipal prerogative) or through a supplementary local force of its own. To draw up a definitive list of township functions, however, would be presumptuous without general debate and critical discussion. To insist that every local function be assigned at once to the local townships would be imprudent. The scope of local power should be gradually increased as the townships prove their capabilities.

The creation of urban townships or ward governments in the cities does not mean the dissolution of the municipal government. What properly belongs to the city government must remain in its hands— the great urban housekeeping functions such as sewerage and garbage disposal, mass transit, highways, water and power supplies, the maintenance of downtown areas, supervision of the public museums, central parks and the like. Nor does the creation of township governments mean the creation of independent regimes totally divorced from the rest of the Republic. A local urban township would have no more right to annul general laws and abridge the citizens' constitutional rights than a rural township does. Ward governments are not little city-states, they are units of the Republic and link citizens to the greater Republic. It is the present islands of urban impotence which are cut off from the commonwealth.

The question of financing is intimately bound up with the whole intricate modern question of financing local government. Whatever combination of local taxes, if any, and direct state appropriations is adopted, the chief concern must be to safeguard the independence and integrity of the ward governments. As far as state appropriations are concerned, therefore, they should be allocated strictly on a per capita basis, alike for all the state's urban townships. This would prevent state legislatures from showing favoritism to particular ward governments and setting all of them at loggerheads. There would be some practical inequities in this method of per capita financing, but since the ward governments are carrying out elementary governmental functions, not economic development plans, these practical inequities would not be as great as some might suppose. The practical advantage of preventing state legislatures from dispensing capricious favors to particular ward governments far outweighs the disadvantages of equal financing. To the question, where will the money come from, the answer is, where do the municipal bureaucracies get their money? If America is rich enough to pour money down the ratholes of corrupt bureaucracies, it is surely rich enough to finance local liberty.

As for the form of ward government, opinions may justly vary, and here, too, experience and trial will doubtless prove a better guide than purely a priori considerations. It would seem to serve the interests of self-government best, however, if the ward governments were directed by locally elected councils of small size and administered by men appointed by and responsible to the council. In this way politics and policy would be kept separate from day-to-day administration while administration would remain directly accountable. Since it is the fundamental purpose of ward government to create a public space in which men may freely exercise the liberty of political action, it seems advisable that each member of the local council be elected by the voters of electoral subdivisions of the ward. By establishing small electorates for each council position, such subdivisions would give men a chance to canvass the voters and gain local office without the support of large organizations or the need for personal wealth. Access to public office would not be foreclosed to anyone interested in playing an active part.

The ward republic is the primary public space of the greater Republic, the one political arena which citizens may enter freely without toadying to a ruling dynasty, where even if they are not ambitious of public life, their opinions are the direct concern of the local council, where their personal support must be perpetually sought, where they cease to be exclusively private men for whom politics is the mere play of flickering shadows. Ward government would, first and foremost, make politics and power visible again and so restore to city dwellers a grasp of political reality, a grasp now so weak that they cannot even identify the foot on their necks. With the curtailment of bureaucratic caprice, public squalor, public neglect and public inequities in the city would cease to appear in their present disguise as the responsibility of no man. Should things go wrong in the ward governments, the citizenry would know whom to blame and what could be done to rectify matters. Each ward government would thus be a permanent local wellspring of hope. By its very existence, ward government would help the urban mass shed that profound apathy and cynicism which the city oligarchs constantly endeavor to instill.

By making politics visible again, the urban masses would come to understand it better. They would learn about the shapes of political ambition, about political courage and political poltroonery, public fidelity and public betrayal, for they would see these for themselves on the public stage of their local political arena. This is what Tocqueville meant when he said that local liberty alone "sheds a light enabling all to see and appraise men's vices and virtues as they truly are." Each ward government would be a portion of political reality that could not be expropriated.

Because there would be local forums for the expression of opinions, because men would regularly hear the opinions of others, the members of the urban mass would no longer be compelled to nurse their grievances in private where, unchecked by others, they inevitably become magnified, distorted and ripe for exploitation by mob rulers and demagogues. It is the impotent mass, incapable of identifying its betrayers, foreclosed from peaceful political activity, which breeds the licentious mob. As Tocqueville observed: "Those who dread the license of the mob and those who fear absolute power ought alike to desire the gradual development of provincial liberties." On the other hand, only the citizens enfranchised in self-governing communities can truly begin to understand the requirements of liberty, the need to tolerate the opinions of others, to respect the right of all to speak, to assemble, to criticize and oppose. This is what Tocqueville meant when he said that "town meetings are to liberty what primary schools are to science; they bring it within the people's reach; they teach men how to use it and how to enjoy it." A mass of exclusively private men does not even understand why people require public rights in the first place.

It is local self-government, too, said Tocqueville, which alone "can deliver the members of a community from the isolation which is the lot of individuals left to their own devices, and, compelling them to get together with each other, promote a sense of active fellowship. In a community of free citizens every man is daily reminded of the need of meeting his fellow men, of hearing what they have to say, of exchanging ideas and coming to agreements as to the conduct of their common interests." No longer a faceless mass but fellow citizens in the several ward governments, city dwellers would cease looking on each other as mere ethnic and racial specimens or simply as half-ominous strangers who just happen to use the same streets. The division of political power within the cities would thus help to heal the ethnic and racial divisions within cities which it has profited the city bosses to perpetuate and to deepen.

Racism in the cities would languish because, under the ward system, it would be difficult to incite it and keep it alive. Men who can identify their political betrayers do not readily blame their troubles on the skin color of their fellow citizens. Men who are not treated as racial categories by designing politicians and bureaucrats do not think of people as mere racial categories. Few men would pride themselves on merely being "white," unless other citizens were officially being treated as merely "black." That was the essential logic of the Jim Crow system in the South. It was chiefly because local self-government discourages racist politics that the Southern oligarchs never divided their counties into wards. They knew full well that when men act together as citizens and share in common concerns they see each other not as racial specimens but as fellow citizens and equals, for we are equal only as citizens.

There is no question whatever that ward government would bring more honest, more responsible and more beneficial government to the cities. I say this in full awareness that local councils can become corrupted, that local cabals may perpetuate their power. The truth is, the ward system would provide improved government because, at the absolute minimum, it could not possibly provide worse government than most cities have suffered for the past hundred years. Even if they wished, ward governments could not waste as much money as the municipal bureaucracies swallow up each year; they could not possibly build public housing more brutish and dispiriting than those the bureaucracies now build; they could not take more bribes than grafting city officials now take or treat city dwellers with more contempt than the municipal powers now treat them. Most importantly, they could not possibly govern under the basic principle of municipal government: to do nothing whatever to improve the lot of city dwellers until sheer public outrage boils over into the streets.

The ward system would also begin to restore genuine law and order to the crime-haunted cities. Under the local system, there would no longer be submerged classes and races perpetually abused by bureaucrats and treated by the city police as inhabitants of a conquered terrain. Under the local system, too, tacit sympathy for the lawbreaker, one of the roots of high crime in urban ghettos, would begin to wane, for the criminal is only a hero among people brutally misruled. When the criminal defies not "them" but the citizens of a self-governing community, when he flouts not the capricious will of insolent authorities but the lawful represented will of ordinary citizens, the criminal becomes just a criminal again and the common enemy of all. Instead of patrolling conquered territory and feeling themselves the enemy of its inhabitants, the police would once again become the lawful servants of a self-possessed citizenry, whereas today the urban police operate in a public vacuum, which demoralizes and eventually corrupts them. By simultaneously restoring respect for law among all city dwellers and respect for city dwellers among the law enforcement agencies, local self-government in the cities would begin to lift the pall of criminality and fear which now envelops our poisoned urban life.

The virtues of ward government, however, cannot be discussed in isolation because the ward system would not exist in isolation. Its beneficial effects would spread far beyond the confines of cities and bring common benefits to all. By opening public arenas for the exercise of liberty, the urban townships would mean the continuous entry into public life of numerous independent men, the continuous winning of public office and public renown by men supported only by the local electorate and the good opinion of their neighbors. It means a citizenry alerted to its interests, politically engaged and hopeful; a citizenry with opinions and the chance to form common opinions; a citizenry organized for common action and represented by their own spokesmen. This the city oligarchs have never before had to face and the city oligarchies could not survive it. The division of the urban mass into dozens of self-governing ward republics means the destruction, or near-destruction, of city machines, those ultimate garrisons of the national party oligarchy, its historic, indispensable and permanent base camps.

At present the city bosses have little trouble, for example, fending off insurgents within the basic units of the party system, namely the state legislative districts. Such insurgents, for the most part, are obscure people who have never before held elective office, there being no local elective office to hold. Only by dint of the most heartbreaking labors can they even make their names known to the urban mass and even then they cannot win the city dweller's trust, for they have no opportunity to do so. The insurgents who succeed are so few in number and can do so little once elected that they are easily eliminated or co-opted by the party organizations. Under township government, however, the situation is drastically altered. Not only is the electorate more alert, engaged and hopeful than the urban mass ever is, not only are there far more independent men entering public life, but independent aspirants to legislative seats—perhaps former members of the local councils—would have active supporters, local fame, the earned trust of their local communities. They could not be turned aside so readily by the district political clubs.

Losing control of the avenues to public renown and of legislative nominations would not be the only perils facing the city oligarchs. Attacked from below, so to speak, by the constant incursions of strong independent challengers, they would also be attacked from above by elected officials, for the ability of the party oligarchs to bend legislators to their will would be sharply threatened by the very existence of ward governments in the city. Party hacks in the state legislature would no longer be betraying a supine mass, but a citizenry with its own local officials to speak in their behalf and a strong interest in doing so. As Jefferson pointed out, should higher officials "become corrupt and perverted, the division into wards constituting the people in their wards a regularly organized power, enables them, by that organization, to crush regularly and peacefully the usurpations of their unfaithful agents." Given the choice between losing the organization's favor and losing their legislative seats, even the most servile party hack would choose to retain his seat. One by one, the whole arsenal of party rewards and punishments would be wrested from the city oligarchs. To maintain anything like their present power, the city bosses would have to gain control of the majority of seats in the majority of local councils in the city. It is not excessive optimism to believe that they could not manage this, and even if they did for a time, the open politics of the wards would, in due course, topple them once more. It is not excessive optimism because even today, with only a disenfranchised urban mass to manage, with the constant collusion of a fake opposition, with giant bureaucracies to hide their abuse of power, the city oligarchs are not secure. Doubtless local ward machines would contrive means to survive in various pockets of the cities, but whereas today independent political actors form the beleaguered minority in cities, under the ward system it is the remnants of the city oligarchies which would form the beleaguered minorities.

This in itself would be an accomplishment of the first magnitude. The breakup of the city bastions would mean, among other things, the city oligarchs' loss of control over the state parties as a whole.

They would no longer be able to ensure defeat in their "losing" districts under the system of mutual noncompetition which forms the *sine qua non* of party power. Wherever city machines were broken up, genuine electoral competition would begin to appear throughout the districts of a state. Though the two-party system would doubtless remain (the citizens' demand for a clear-cut election decision on the Presidency virtually ensures a two-party system in America), the two state parties in a reformed state would begin to become what the oligarchs perpetually try to prevent them from becoming—coalitions of active, independent local citizens trying to win elections on one or another party label. Thus the establishment of ward government in the cities and the destruction of the city bastions would mean the beginning of the end of collusive politics and usurped party power in every urbanized state and so in the national parties as well. It would mean the beginning of the restoration of self-government, free politics and responsible power throughout the Republic. It would mean the beginning of the end of the hegemony of the Southern Bourbons, those native headmen kept in power for so long by the Northern city machines. By a sweet historical irony, the liberation of Northern cities through Jeffersonian democracy would be the beginning of the liberation of the South, the beginning of the end of its semicolonial status and the final laying of the ghost of the Civil War.

At this point it may well be asked what is to prevent the genuine representatives of the citizenry from carrying out policies even worse than those of the party usurpers? Doubtless this is the fear of a minority but it is certainly a genuine fear. To say in reply that the citizenry will prove themselves wise, vigilant and liberty-loving would, of course, be fatuous. Yet some major grounds for fearing and mistrusting the citizenry can be eliminated without making empty pronouncements about the virtues of "the people."

The first baseless ground is the fear of the American citizenry as a mass, politically manipulated as a mass. The American people, under the Federal principle, do not form a national mass, and the establishment of ward government in the cities would break up the only real

312

masses that exist. Americans are not only citizens of the Republic, they are also citizens of autonomous states, of cities, counties and self-governing townships. That profound and complex dispersion of power almost inevitably breaks up mass movements, which is what it was intended to do. The moment a mass movement aspires to power, it must touch down in most of the five thousand assembly districts, tens of thousands of self-governing communities and fifty autonomous states. The more independent politics is in each of these political communities, the more representative its public life is, the more readily will the citizenry convert local members of any mass movement into representatives of its local interests and concerns. The movement would cease at once to be a mass movement. When the Ku Klux Klan emerged in the early 1920s, for example, the movement was swiftly transformed into a loose federation of state Klans each tinctured by the prevailing politics of the state in which it acted—extremely vicious in the vicious political climate of Texas; virtually benign in the free politics of Oregon. Only if genuine local liberty were completely submerged by a national oligarchy could a national mass movement succeed in gaining power. The more free local politics is, the less likely are mass movements to arise. It was Wilson's brutal wartime suppression of free politics and his savage blasting of honest hopes which bred the Klan movement in the first place. With whom does blame for the Klan rest? With the American people and genuine self-government or with Wilson and the party oligarchy?

The second baseless ground of fear derives from the notion that Americans today "get what they want" and what they want is vile—the myth of the nonexistent oligarchy. In this view, Americans love to elect Presidents who promise peace for the sheer pleasure of being dragged into war; they delight in dreaming up tax loopholes for millionaires and regressive taxes for themselves; they rejoice in seeing special privilege dispensed to the overprivileged; they enjoy nothing better than foul air and poisoned waterways; they delight in having bureaucrats treat them with contempt; they relish electing fake reformers to blast their reviving hopes so they can sit home and blame their troubles on other people's skin color. They take deep pride in a political life in which campaign pledges are open jokes, a political life filled with windbaggery and lies, a political life in which when they grew fed up with an unwanted war they were forced to choose between a Presidential candidate who praised the war's goals and a man from the hated administration that started it. To understand who now has power in America and what they have done to keep it does not prove that the American people are "good," but it does lift much of the odium laid upon them by those who attribute to representative government what the usurpers of representative government have done. The citizenry will hurt their own interests by occasional blunders and follies, but the usurpers of their power infringe their liberty and betray their interests through deliberate and necessary policy. As Jefferson said, "The evils flowing from the duperies of the people are less injurious than those from the egotism of their agents." For this reason, he said, "our liberties can never be secure but in the hands of the citizens themselves," for "no other depository has ever yet been found" to safeguard it for them.

Yet if the people of this Republic are the only "safe depository" for freedom and equality, this does not mean that they form a perfect depository. That is why the second fundamental measure for securing self-government was for Jefferson, and remains today, the establishment of republican education for all. By teaching every person how to judge for himself what will secure or endanger his freedom, republican education would try to ensure, as far as it is humanly possible, that the citizens themselves become the firm and enlightened partisans of the Republic, which is nothing more or less than the constitution of their liberty. It means a citizenry which tries to apply to every important public measure and policy the fundamental republican standard—does it augment or abridge the exercise of liberty? Does it weaken or strengthen corrupt, irresponsible power? It means a citizenry which understands that the struggle to maintain a genuine republic is itself a never-ending struggle, that equal liberty, in Lincoln's words, "must be constantly labored for, and even though never perfectly attained, constantly approximated."

Since people cannot even begin to understand the requirements of their liberty without a grasp of political reality, the heart of republican education, the very core and spine of its curriculum, must be the study of political history, that vast and wonderful stage of public action, which reveals what is most noble and most vile in men, which discloses the scope of man's power over forces and processes, which displays ambition under all its shapes, which tells stories of the death of kings and of republics. Such stories, in truth, would be far more interesting to the young, just as they would be far more instructive, than the prancing of Dick and Jane, the "evolution of transportation" and the whole farrago of "social studies" which is now obliterating the very idea of political history from the minds of the young in accordance with the oligarchs' fundamental pedagogical commandment: thou shalt not be taught what free men must know. I have no doubt that America's educators will prove as ingenious and imaginative in forging the curriculum of liberty as they have been in framing the curriculum of oligarchy. What they need is a change of employers.

The only way to secure republican education is through genuine local control of the schools by the citizens of the nation's self-governing communities. This means, most obviously, the abolition of all central school bureaucracies such as those now existing in many cities. It also means the dismantling of the entire educational establishment—the teacher licensing laws, accreditation laws, state educational commissions, the Federal Office of Education and every other instrument by which the common schools of the citizenry have been wrested from their hands even where local control formally exists. Let the local citizens elect their own school boards and let the boards staff them as they choose, accountable to no one except the community itself. This is the absolutely necessary condition for republican education, that without which we shall never enjoy it. Only the citizens have an abiding interest in providing republican education for their children. It is therefore safe in no other hands. Doubtless local communities will blunder, doubtless pedagogical windbags and school board demagogues will temporarily win over one community or another. As with liberty itself, however, the evils which flow from the ignorance of free men are far less injurious than the miseducation carried out by general and deliberate policy. The educational establishment has managed the public schools for most of this century and it has deliberately degraded them for as long as it has managed them. It was not the American people who called for "vocational education"; it was the educators who invented it and the party oligarchs who promoted and financed it. It was not the American people who conceived the notion that ordinary children were congenitally incapable of learning anything but an obsolete trade, or the even more insane notion that a child might be too poor to learn how to read when he is not too poor to learn how to speak. It was not the American people who wanted their children sorted out by their "evident or probable destiny." Americans, at the very least, want to be proud of their children. They invest their fondest hopes in their children. In thousands of communities in America the public schools are housed in the town's finest public buildings and set on the town's best land. No people on earth have shown themselves more generously devoted to the education of their children than Americans. Behind a smoke screen of pedagogical cant, the school managers have betrayed our generosity in abject service to the ruling powers. Judging our schools by the standard of liberty, the citizenry could not possibly provide worse schools for their children than the school managers have given them.

If genuine local control of the schools is the necessary condition of republican education, it is not in itself a sufficient condition. Republican education will not spring up automatically with the dismantling of the educational bureaucracy. All that can be said with fair certainty is that the better the citizenry understands the requirements of liberty, the more sharply will they feel the need for republican education, the more clearly will they perceive its outlines, the more readily will educators come forward to win their approval with suitable curricular plans. That improved understanding of liberty—an understanding which Americans have not lost even now—will come about partly through its exercise in the ward republics of the greater Republic, established where today they do not exist and invigorated where today they are but half-empty forms. That improved understanding will come, too, with the gradual weakening of the party oligarchy and the consequent reemergence into public life of men who speak to free men of their freedom and uphold the republican standard in public affairs. The general augmentation of liberty will help bring about, doubtless by fits and starts, the gradual establishment of republican education. Thus the two great measures which form the *sine qua non* for the restoration of self-government would borrow strength from each other and make of both a genuine new beginning for the Republic.

Those who would propose great public measures are responsible, at the very least, for supplying grounds for hoping that they can be achieved. Such grounds for hope certainly exist in the American Republic. Some of them are general and permanent, some are particular and temporary. Party power, which is always precarious, is somewhat more precarious today than it has been in some time. The enfranchisement of black people in the South poses, for the moment, a considerable peril to the present party arrangements. So, too, does the growing disenchantment with the Cold War. There are other encouraging signs. After more than three decades the chief elements in what might be called the New Deal system are beginning to show hopeful cracks. A whole generation of young Americans has grown up in rebellion against bureaucracy and now demands a greater voice in the conduct of affairs. Faith in trade unionism is sharply declining; in some industrial unions the younger workers are openly contemptuous of their leaders and the hollow farce of collective bargaining. The temporary conjunction of inflation and unemployment has led to a reexamination of the economy and the revival of interest in an antitrust policy, that ancient republican weapon. In short, holes are beginning to show for the moment in the system of lies that now blankets public reality. Lyndon Johnson's betrayal of the electorate in 1965 has made Americans question once more the state of representative institutions and the fidelity of their elected representatives. The voters' faith in the party leaders, never very great, is at its lowest ebb in many decades. It was not for nothing that the Democratic party bosses in 1972 were compelled to make an elaborate show of party reform and declare an end to the era of boss rule. Any day is a good day to fight for liberty, but this day is more propitious than most.

To these particular and essentially temporary grounds for hope there is another, imperishable ground: the political legitimacy of the cause of self-government in a Republic constituted for liberty and self-government. Beneath the feet of every citizen lies the foundations of the Republic. Beneath the party oligarchy lies nothing but unexposed mendacity and successful fraud. It is this which accounts for the peculiar condition of American politics, at once so puzzling and so infuriating to foreign observers; the existence of a public life polluted with lies yet virtually untainted by public cynicism. The true voice of political corruption has not yet been heard in this Republic—the voice of the usurper who openly claims that his might is his right, that power belongs to whoever can grasp it. The party oligarchs make self-government a sham, but they dare not call self-government a sham. They wield great power but they claim no right to such power; they are forced to deny its very existence.

Hypocrisy, it is said, is the respect vice pays to virtue, and so it is with the incredible hypocrisy of public life in America. It is impossible for party politicians to be candid about anything, for what they would soon have to admit in candor is that they stand opposed to self-government and the constitution of liberty. That they dare not do. That corrupted the Republic is not. The authority of a free constitution lived under for nearly two centuries has a weight and force in public life which is beyond human ken to measure and beyond the oligarchs' power to defy. It is the force and weight of that authority—and Americans recognize no other authority—which stands behind the cause of liberty and of every citizen who elects to fight for it. The party oligarchs wield innumerable weapons but one mighty weapon is denied them in any struggle to oppose the augmentation of liberty. They cannot tell American citizens that they are unfit for self-rule. By an apparent paradox it is the adherents of liberty in this Republic who are free to speak and who speak with authority. It is the ruling dynasty which is gagged.

Those who would speak for ward government in the cities will not be addressing the deaf. The urban mass is no longer predominantly a herd of grateful, impoverished immigrants. Less grateful and far more prosperous, city dwellers are beginning to feel keenly their political impotence, their remoteness from government, their deep estrangement from one another. Under the ambiguous heading of decentralization, the issue of local power is already being discussed in some cities and in the columns of the urban press. The city dweller's desire to act together with his neighbors, to do something, however small, about the conditions of his life, has already given rise to local tenants' and block associations to discuss and carry out limited projects of local improvement. It is the city dweller's wish to speak and act in public concerns, to gain a measure of control over his public fortunes, which the adherents of local liberty can speak to and embody. As the first step toward winning ward government in the cities, local citizens can form their own local assemblies and councils in the wards, legislative districts, planning districts or other existing territorial divisions of the cities in which they live. These local assemblies would be the exponents as well as the proponents of local self-government. In these assemblies local citizens would come together and act together and by that very act of association they would at once wield a modicum of local political power. They could begin to hold local elected officials accountable to them, call on local bureaucrats and police captains to explain themselves, see that local ordinances are properly enforced, try to effect local improvements on their own. By their existence and example they would remind people in the district what it is like for once not to be treated with utter contempt and hence what fully constituted ward government holds out for them. By this means the spirit of local liberty would be infused in the future self-governing districts of the cities and begin to permeate the whole.

The cause of local liberty can—and will—win allies and adherents, for the augmentation of liberty does not divide men, it unites them. It is not a political program or an ideology. It is not even, strictly speaking, an opinion. It promises only the prospect of having opinions that matter, whatever those opinions happen to be. It is not a white cause nor a black cause, not a poor people's cause nor a middle-class cause, for it takes nothing from anyone and gives something equally to all. The cause of local liberty is neither conservative nor liberal nor radical, though in the genuine meaning of those terms it is all three combined. It is truly radical because it strikes at the roots of the present ruling dynasty; it is truly conservative because it stands on the venerable foundations of the Republic; it is liberal because it liberates. Doubtless cynics will say that Americans are not interested in governing themselves and do not want the cares of liberty. The party oligarchs, however, are wiser than the cynics. That is why they are never cynical in public. It is not because Americans are indifferent to liberty that the oligarchs keep "friends to republican government" from holding public office. It is not because self-government is the rarefied ideal of the enlightened few that the oligarchs try to keep republican issues out of the public arena. They know that liberty and self-government form a standard to which Americans will repair. That is what the ruling dynasty knows and fears, and their fears, as always, are identical with our hopes.

INDEX

324

Tennessee
  Democratic party, 16, 29, 101
  Republican party, 11, 16, 29, 46, 101
Tennessee Valley Authority, 123, 235-237
Test Ban Treaty of 1963, 117
Texas
  Democratic party, 21
  Republican party, 100
Thurmond, Strom, 55, 67-68, 99, 100
Tocqueville, Alexis de, 244, 300-301, 307-308
Townsend, Francis, 26-27, 93, 130
Township government, *see* Ward government
Trade unions, 78, 131, 177, 195, 202-203, 215, 317
  collective bargaining, 197-223, 207, 317
  Democratic party and, 197-201, 213, 220-222
  education, view of, 214
  individual rights, 210-211
  strikes, 209
  Taft-Hartley Act, 158, 202-203, 209, 221-222
  wage leadership, 204-205
  welfare legislation, 216
Truman, Harry S., 55, 68, 89, 144, 145, 221
  foreign policy, 145, 252-257, 263, 273
Truman Doctrine, 252-253, 257, 274
Trusts, 85, 124, 174

Udall, Morris, 58, 199, 201
United Automobile Workers, 205
United States Steel Corporation, 124, 181, 192, 239
Unused Power: The Work of the Senate Committee on Appropriations (Horn), 56, 236

Vermont, Democratic party, 11, 13, 23, 29, 72
Vietnam War, 27, 108, 143-160, 200, 219, 266, 275
Virginia
  Democratic party, 44-47
  Republican party, 44-47, 99-100
Voting Rights Act of 1869, 103
Voting Rights Act of 1965, 65

Wagner, Robert, 26
Wagner Act, *see* National Labor Relations Act
Wallace, George, 65, 100, 215
Ward government, 215, 300, 302-312
Warren, Earl, 228
Wealth Tax Act, 131
White, Theodore, 18, 73-74, 87, 88
Wicker, Tom, 54, 66, 112-114, 141, 157, 159,
Willkie, Wendell, 89
Wilson, Woodrow, 82, 144, 157, 187, 215, 241, 250, 263, 313
  domestic policy, 64, 220
  foreign policy, 89, 249, 261, 266, 269-271
Wisconsin
  Democratic party, 11, 14, 18, 24, 30, 69, 70
  Republican party, 24
Working Men's Party, 214
Works Progress Administration (WPA), 128
World War I, 188, 198, 215, 243, 249, 261, 267, 269
World War II, 195, 252, 262, 271-272

Yarborough, Ralph, 56, 100